Music in American
Combat Films

Music in American Combat Films

A Critical Study

WESLEY J. O'BRIEN

McFarland & Company, Inc., Publishers
Jefferson, North Carolina, and London

For Deb
who knows better than anyone
that Nick was right.

Soldier on.

LIBRARY OF CONGRESS CATALOGUING-IN-PUBLICATION DATA

O'Brien, Wesley J.
    Music in American combat films : a critical study / Wesley J. O'Brien.
        p.   cm.
    Includes bibliographical references and index.

    ISBN 978-0-7864-6343-5
    softcover : acid free paper ∞

    1. Motion picture music — United States — History and criticism. 2. War films — United States — History and criticism. I. Title.
ML2075.O37 2012
781.5'420973 — dc23
                                              2012021131

BRITISH LIBRARY CATALOGUING DATA ARE AVAILABLE

© 2012 Wesley J. O'Brien. All rights reserved

No part of this book may be reproduced or transmitted in any form or by any means, electronic or mechanical, including photocopying or recording, or by any information storage and retrieval system, without permission in writing from the publisher.

On the cover: *The Green Berets* (1968) (Warner Bros./Photofest); background image © 2012 Shutterstock

Manufactured in the United States of America

McFarland & Company, Inc., Publishers
  Box 611, Jefferson, North Carolina 28640
    www.mcfarlandpub.com

Table of Contents

Preface 1

Introduction: Film Scoring Practice and the American Combat Film 3

I. Scoring the Classical Combat Film and Conventions of the War Film Protagonist: *The Story of G.I. Joe* 19

II. The Vietnam Conflict Scored as a Conventional War Film: John Wayne Plays John Wayne in *The Green Berets* 42

III. The Ambivalent Hero: Major Heroic Malfunction in *Full Metal Jacket* 72

IV. Vietnam Redux: Scoring the Conflicted (Post–9/11) Hero in *We Were Soldiers* 97

V. Heroes Without a Cause: Scoring Practice and the Devolution of Combat Film Heroism in the Wake of Vietnam 116

VI. Re-Presenting "The Good War" 134

VII. Comparing Classical and Current Scoring Practices 158

Notes 177

Works Cited 180

Index 186

Preface

Music in American Combat Films is an exploration of how a number of filmmakers have used the visual and, in particular, the musical mechanisms of film to facilitate various representations of men as they confront various representations of war. My central purpose is to interrogate the film score as a somewhat leaky system of meaningful signs. Leaky, because although meanings associated with musical signs are often conventional, they are by no means fixed, and there are no clearly delineated rules for musical signification in the same sense as there are for the signs of verbal language. I explore the function of these mechanisms within the context of their filmic stew to determine how they work to generate meaning and whether or not, or to what extent, their function or their characteristics have changed over time, as have the representations of the men and the situations that they facilitate. Along the way, it is impossible not to make ancillary observations regarding who these men are, whether they are or are not "heroic" and the always-shifting cultural or ideological implications suggested by whether or not we are attracted to, repulsed by or ambivalent towards them.

With regard to those observations, I think it is important to note that I do not write with an agenda. I am not trying to prove anything with regard to war, masculinities or heroism. Although it is true that when changes occur within the patterns of film genres those changes become significant with regard to what they suggest about the changes in cultural attitudes that precipitate them, it is also true that the process of change is neither unified nor linear. Indeed, it is slow and often messy; and for every observable example of change in narrative, thematic, visual or musical pattern there are usually other examples to suggest consistency. Thus, without meaning to equivocate, the observations I make are about possibilities rather than certainties, and while I believe that such observations are made thoughtfully and within the context of firm theoretical ground, this is not to say that other conclusions are necessarily inaccurate.

I would also like to point out that I am investigating representations, and although the conclusions I draw from them often reflect popular attitudes, they do not necessarily reflect all realities. It is a point that I often work to hammer home to my students — that if, for example, I demonstrate the self-serving or destructive nature of some current representations of heroism and posit what such representations suggest about the devolution of, say, truth, justice, and the American way, it does not mean necessarily that there *is* such a devolution — at least not for everyone — only that we are witnessing a projection (ahem) of possibilities.

Nonetheless, I would suggest that our identification with the representations explored as positive or negative and our reading of their relevance within the cultural milieu at the time of their creation, as well as at the time of our experience with them, can reveal much about our individual and shared attitudes regarding gender, the practice of war, those who practice it, and cultural expectations in general. If such is the case, then this information contributes to the knowledge we have about ourselves.

Introduction: Film Scoring Practice and the American Combat Film

Music with Purpose

The meaning an audience creates out of the experience of a musical encounter depends as much on context and a perceiver's previous experience as it does on style and structure (Meyer 262). Where a piece of music is experienced, under what intellectual, physical or emotional circumstance, and in tandem with what other stimuli contribute as much to its message as do the realms of composition, arrangement and performance. This context-dependent meaning-making is particularly prevalent now that the majority of the music we hear is recorded electronically — disembodied, so to speak, from its origins.

Recording technology has not only changed the *how* of musical experience; it has changed the *why*. As Walter Benjamin observes, "[...] technical reproduction can put the copy of the original into situations which would be out of reach of the original itself" (733). The result is, that with varying degrees of attentiveness, we listen to music in our homes (while doing other things), in our cars, in the supermarket, in our workplaces, and so on. Some of us select specific genres or even artists to complement our activities — we prefer one genre for driving, another for working and still another for romance. In advertising, music is an aid to the overall persuasive intent of the medium — a mnemonic device, an attention-getter, an audience indicator. In the workplace, music functions as a distracter, a mood enhancer, an inducer of fantasy to make the time pass easily and thereby increase production (Gorbman 57). For better or worse, because of music's portability effected by mechanical reproduction, musical experience is no longer strictly aesthetic, no longer relegated to the concert hall, no longer the prerogative of a privileged elite.

Integrated with other activities or media, either accidentally or by design, musical experience is imbued with extra-musical function. In practice, the meaning of music is not, as, for example, Eduard Hanslick or Igor Stravinsky would prefer, that of a self-contained system with its own non-associative relationships and values. (Susanne Langer, for one, has called this view an "evasion" and "a silly fiction" [237].) Aided by electronic reproduction, we no longer just listen to music, we *use* it; and in so doing, we invite it to influence our activities and experiences in ways that had been previously impossible. Nowhere is this functional aspect more ubiquitous than in film, where music is an integral part of filmic meaning-making conventions. Among other things, film music convinces us of the emotional content of a scene, indicates historical context, creates identifications with characters, indicates the passage of time, and provides continuity (Gorbman 73).

Since December 28, 1895, when a pianist sat down in a Parisian café to accompany a premier of early film works by the Lumière Brothers (Prendergast 5), music has become an integral part of the ecological system of image, sound and dialogue that is film. Music's conventional inclusion in not-so-silent silent film is explained by various scholars in various ways. Some suggest that it was meant to neutralize the sound of noisy projection equipment. Others say its presence counteracted the unease an audience experienced at seeing ghostlike images move silently across the screen. Some have explained the inclusion as a natural extension of theatrical tradition, arising not only from melodrama, but from a tradition rooted in the ancient Greek chorus. Still others suggest that the rhythmic characteristics integral to both music and moving image demand the symbiotic relationship because audiences are not "accustomed to apprehend movement as an artistic form without sound" (Prendergast 4).

Yet whatever reason or combination of reasons led to its original inclusion, and whatever role technology has played to enable greater control over the integration of sound and image, music has become an integral and indispensable part of the filmic code, an essential ingredient in the audience's ability to make meaning out of the film experience. Claudia Gorbman writes: "Whatever music is applied to a film segment will *do something*, will have an effect — just as two words one puts together will have a meaning different from that of each word separately, because the reader/spectator automatically imposes meaning on such combinations" (15–16).

The possibilities for these combinations are many, as are their meanings. In addition to the functions mentioned above, film music adds dimension to characters and provides various mechanisms by which audiences identify with them. Through coded musical conventions and cultural-ideological associations with music and musical genres, film music enables greater dimension in the depictions of settings and situations; it clarifies a character's response to such situations, informs the viewers' own responses to the character, and facilitates viewers' perception of a third dimension through increase or decrease in volume. In the case of composed scores that follow traditional Hollywood scoring practice, "Narrative film music 'anchors' the image in meaning. It expresses moods and connotations, which, in conjunction with the images and other sounds, aid in interpreting narrative events and indicating moral/class/ethnic values of characters" (Gorbman 84). In the case of scores compiled from pre-existing music, previously formed associations with specific songs or genres create a mechanism that facilitates viewers' "paths of identification" (Kassabian 2) with conventional and non-conventional characters.

There have, of course, been many studies of film representations, particularly as related to gender. But comparatively few (and this is also true of film studies in general) include music as part of the filmic stew that contributes to the viewer's negotiation of meaning. Of those studies that do foreground music's place within the filmic text (e.g., Gorbman, Kalinak, Kassabian, Otter), the lion's share have focused on music's role in informing feminine representations. Gorbman, Kalinak and Otter have written primarily about classical Hollywood scoring practice, i.e., musical conventions that were codified during Hollywood's so-called Golden Age in the 1930s and 1940s; and Kassabian's *Hearing Film* interrogates the current widespread use of compiled scores to represent non-traditional feminine roles — roles that depart from those typical of Hollywood's Golden Age. Another tendency among these and other writers seems to be toward choosing melodrama over other genres as the preferred vehicle for analysis. Certainly, this is understandable considering that the stuff of melodrama is the representation of overblown emotion (Kolker 233) and that virtually all writers on the subject agree that music's most durable contribution to film is its capacity to represent emotion (in various ways, depending on the writer). Even its name, which identifies the genre as the combination of melody and drama, suggests that it is a natural choice for such analysis. But just as certainly, music's role in the overall narrative meaning-making process is vital to other genres as well.

I have discussed the *what* of musical purpose — what it does to represent setting, character and theme, what it does for the viewer-listener's understanding, and so on — but it is also necessary to introduce something about *how* music manages its various roles within the mise-en-scène. Much has been written about musical meaning in general — literature that approaches musical meaning from aesthetic, cognitive, philosophical, psychological and physiological perspectives, and many components of these perspectives are represented in the chapters that follow. Primarily, though, the film score is considered here as a set of conventions — a system of codes:

> [T]he implicit rules by which meanings get put into social practice and can therefore be read by their users. Codes involve a systematic organization of signs. [...] Semiotics shows that language and representational media, such as cinema and television, are structured according to specific codes. Cinematic codes include lighting, camera movement and editing. [...] The term "code" has also been used by Stuart Hall to describe how cultural texts [...] can be encoded with meaning by producers, and are then decoded by viewers [Sturken and Cartwright 351].

Claudia Gorbman identifies at least three categories of musical codes that function in film. She suggests that music has its own "purely *musical* signification, creating tension and resolution through highly coded structure and syntax" (2). She also identifies purely cinematic musical codes, which are encoded as such when certain musical characteristics repeatedly accompany certain kinds of narrative situations. Such signs come to be associated with the narrative material that they traditionally accompany. In cases where the score includes music that preexists the film, associations can also preexist the specific filmic text — a third category Gorbman identifies as cultural musical codes. Other, more general examples of cultural coding involve viewer-listeners' associations with particular instruments, rhythms, styles, etc.— what David Elliot refers to as the "interpretation of a musical design" (199) or what Leonard Meyer calls "compositional strategies" (20). Additionally, because of its ubiquitous place in film scoring practice, no discussion of musical codes would be compete without particular attention paid to the leitmotif — a specialized category of musical code, usually coded (or "baptized") within the mise-en-scène and thus made specific to a particular film. Richard Wagner is generally associated with the technique, which is a fundamental component of his opera style. Hollywood scoring practice employs a simplified version, "a musical phrase, either as complex as a melody or as simple as a few notes, which, through repetition, becomes identified with a character, situation or idea" (Kalinak 63). During the classical Hollywood period, the leitmotif became a scoring convention that dominated nine out of ten film scores (Chion 51) and remains key to many contemporary scores as well.

How Does This Study Differ?

Among the body of literature analyzing film music, Claudia Gorbman's *Unheard Melodies: Narrative Film Music* is arguably one of the most influential in providing a practical model of musical function based upon classical Hollywood scoring practice encoded in the "Golden Age" of the thirties and forties. But even now, over two decades after its publication, most works on film music concentrate primarily on classical Hollywood scoring practices, and even when contemporary filmic texts are analyzed, that analysis draws heavily on models like Gorbman's, which are rooted in those practices codified during Hollywood's Golden Age. That this is so testifies to the enduring function of Hollywood's musical codes as identified by Gorbman; and it will become clear that this present study owes much to her work. Her model is used freely throughout as a benchmark for comparing current practice with that of classical Hollywood. However, even Gorbman suggests that because of emergent scoring practices, new approaches to analyzing musical scores — particularly those that use popular music — are necessary (163).

Anahid Kassabian's *Hearing Film: Tracking Identifications in Contemporary Hollywood Film Music* examines such new approaches and posits changing gendered representations of women as one significant reason for them. To clarify, a brief discussion of such gendered representations and their relationship to musical codes is warranted. "Traditionally," according to Laura Mulvey, "the woman displayed has functioned on two levels: as erotic object for the characters within the screen story, and as erotic object for the spectator within the auditorium [...]" (838). Katherine Kalinak has identified two broad categories of feminine objectification on screen: "The Virtuous Wife" and "The Fallen Woman," and both she and Claudia Gorbman have connected similar categories to traditional scoring options:

> A film of the forties is airing on television. Even though you're in the next room, you are likely to find that a certain kind of music will cue you in correctly to the presence of Woman on screen. It is as if the emotional excess of this presence must find its outlet in the euphony of a string orchestra. I refer here to Woman as romantic Good Object, and not to old women, or humorous or chatty women, or femmes fatales (who possess their own musical conventions — jazz, brass, woodwinds...) [Gorbman 80].

In response, a central thesis in Kassabian's work is that because these semiotic codes of Hollywood scoring practice were created to represent female characters confined to two sexualities, The Fallen Woman and the Virtuous Wife (Kassabian 69), and because such constraints no longer apply in many current representations of women, identification is facilitated by other kinds of musical codes. In other words, conventional musical codes lose their usefulness when the representations they facilitate are not conventional. For Kassabian, compiled scores (scores created from pre-existing, often popular, music) offer a significant solution to the limitations imposed by traditional scoring practices because of such scores' "wider range of possibilities for female characters" (Kassabian 71). In various ways, perceivers' previously formed associations with songs, recording artists and genres inform their responses to a film's narrative elements, and in particular, create "paths of entry for identifications" (73) with female "narrative agents."

It is important here to underscore that traditional scoring practice is not inadequate simply because the characters Kassabian discusses are women, but because they are *different kinds of women* than music had, by-and-large, been called upon to represent when film music's representational function was initially codified. Kassabian's own example of *Thelma and Louise* illustrates this point. Film audiences of the 1930s and 1940s would not have been asked to empathize with the plight of two women fleeing traditional, culturally prescribed domestic roles because they had shot someone dead in the parking lot of a saloon. It is a changed cultural climate, then, and changing attitudes toward women's roles within that cultural climate, that precipitates the existence of "nontraditional" female roles, and so, necessitates nontraditional musical representations of those roles.

While *Hearing Film* focuses on musical representations of female roles, there is a dearth of material available exploring musical codes for males. Steve Neale, for example, points to possibilities for masculine displays similar to those discussed by Mulvey (Neale 18–19); however, unlike Kalanak, Kassabian and others, his discussion does not consider musical elements. Does musical scoring practice differ in relation to differing male representations as writers like Kassabian indicate it does for women? Is (and if so to what extent) Gorbman's model of scoring practice altered by different depictions other than those for women? Does, for example, a postmodern protagonist such as Joker (Matthew Modine) in *Full Metal Jacket* or an "academic pussy" such as Hal Moore (Mel Gibson) in *We Were Soldiers* require different musical codes to create identification because traditional scoring techniques are not suited in the same ways that they are for representing "traditional" heroes portrayed by, say, Robert Mitchum in *The Story of G. I. Joe* or John Wayne in—well, nearly every film he made?

This study expands upon inquiries such as Kassabian's and Kalanak's by examining the other side of the same coin. My focus will be music's function as an element in the representation of one specific kind of male representation — that of the soldier in war films. I examine ways male protagonists are represented musically by composed and compiled scores containing traditional and nontraditional codes of Hollywood scoring practice and attempt to show a relationship between different approaches to scoring practice and different representations of male protagonists in combat films. In so doing I will be examining a specific aspect of how film music represents our worlds and the culturally constructed, gendered representations that inhabit them.

Why War Films?

I have mentioned a number of excellent studies exploring scoring practice in melodrama to facilitate representations of femininity. This study investigates similar questions, but with specific focus on masculinities. Questions include: How do scores function with regard to masculinity? Do scoring practices for differently constructed masculinities depart from those conventions encoded during Hollywood's Golden Age? To what extent are such departures driven by characteristically different masculine representations — representations that have changed over time to accommodate popular attitudes?

My focus on male protagonists in selected combat films departs significantly from what has already been done for melodrama, and to the extent that this is a study of mediated heterosexual masculinities (a distinction made necessary by the recently abolished policy of don't ask don't tell), the combat film is an appropriate genre because its narrative core continues to emerge, by an large, from representations of masculinities.

In "Masculinity and Machismo in Hollywood's War Films," Ralph Donald writes: "Jeffords (1989), Leed (1989), and others maintain that war itself is a gendering activity, one of the few remaining true male experiences in our society. Even the increasingly androgynous American armed forces' most recent liberalizing of regulations regarding sexual equality stops short of parity in combat assignments" (126). Nonetheless, within the last decade there have been some notable changes with regard to women in the military. In the *Army Times* David Wood writes that although women are still technically "excluded from 'direct-combat' roles in the military" (1), the lines separating combat and non-combat roles are becoming increasingly blurred. But the pertinent question here is whether such change has affected the still predominantly *represented* versions of heterosexual and homosocial masculinity in war films; and, more importantly, whether or not such changes have in any way altered the war genre so that it is no longer a predominantly male arena.

While there are indeed recent films that place women in combat roles, e.g., the *Alien* franchise (1979, 1986, 1992, 1997), the *Tomb Raider* series (2001, 2003), and *Avatar* (2009), the fact that these are fantasies speaks volumes about persistent cultural attitudes regarding women's place in combat. So too do confections like *Private Benjamin* (1980) and *Private Valentine* (2008) featuring tag lines such as (respectively) "the army was no laughing matter until Judy Benjamin joined it" and "the few, the proud, the blonde." While two relatively recent films, *Courage Under Fire* (1996) and *G.I. Jane* (1997), seem intent on more authentic representations of women in combat, in one way or another, the focus remains on masculinity, regardless of the sex of the characters. In *G.I. Jane,* for example, the success of Lt. Jordan O'Neil (Demi Moore) is predicated upon her ability to "take it like a man," and she "validates phallic power by telling her abusive commanding officer to 'suck my dick' […]" (Linville 103). Further, despite the suggestion that new technologies allow greater integration of the sexes by leveling the playing field in combat situations where mechanized muscle replaces masculine muscle, these technologies tend to reaffirm rather than abrogate the male as primary combatant. Susan E. Linville observes:

> As a result of "smart bombs" and contemporaneous developments in the weaponry and culture of the U.S. military, the Gulf War was the first to call into serious question the distinction that had limited women to non-combat assignments. […] Yet if combat technologies have worked in part as equalizers, iconographically, most weaponry has remained rigidly aligned with masculinist ideas of power. The ironic result, argues Robyn Wiegman, is that female integration into the military creates the very context in which "the exteriorization of the masculine body as technology most effectively functions […]. Simply put, phallic technology served to neutralize the threat that the presence of female combatants posed to the reborn masculinity of the Gulf war — and to war in general as a privileged arena of masculine display" [104].

Linville further suggests that *Courage Under Fire*'s narrative structure, i.e., its use of interviews and flashbacks, foregrounds the male soldiers' experience thus marginalizing that of Karen Walden (Meg Ryan): "[T]he film generates considerably more concern about the potential damage to young men in the gender-integrated military than about how women such as Walden — or her young daughter — might survive and succeed in that world" (106). Significant, too, is that Walden's gender is made ambiguous by paradoxical narrative components. On one hand, she is masculinized by one of her men, who refers to her as "butch," as well as by her harsh, throaty vocal style as she barks commands; conversely, she is denied masculine characteristics by her need to explain the tears she sheds as "just tension" and by the response of a mutinying soldier when she demands his weapon. "There's no way you're taking away my weapon, cunt," he says — a response that makes salient the Freudian implications of the weapon itself — Linville's "phallic technology" — as well as the fact that Walden does not (and would like to) have it.

But the point here is not to indict the combat genre for its shabby treatment of women. That's another book. The point is to show that these representations exemplify ways in which the mechanisms of film still tend to subvert the possibility of femininity in combat situations, thereby maintaining the genre's predominant focus on masculinities, and thus confirming the combat film's appropriateness for this study of masculinities viewed through a musical lens. It should also be noted that I am not arguing here that an investigation of the male experience within the context of war encompasses male experience everywhere, or that heterosexual masculinities offer the only kind of gendered representations worth exploring within the context of combat films. Such a claim would be indefensible. Beyond the need for authentic representations of female soldiers, the demise of don't ask don't tell clearly offers filmmakers new and significant narrative possibilities with regard to gays in the military. Nonetheless, just as melodrama has provided an appropriate venue for exploration of music's representation of some kinds of femininities, the American combat film currently offers a fertile arena within which to explore how music facilitates representations of some kinds of heterosexual masculinities.

Because they are often structured as ensemble pieces in which the narrative objectives are seldom achieved without the efforts of more than one character, films in the combat genre allow comparison of a number of different masculine roles at once. While this study concentrates on the most salient of these roles, usually the officer in charge, there is often opportunity for comparison with other masculinities represented within the mise-en-scène. Worth mentioning because of their prevalence here is the role of war correspondent. Such narrative agents can inform our reading of the principal character in significant ways. They are often the leader's confidant; their capacity as reporters charge them with interpreting actions and events and providing ideological commentary. The war correspondent can sometimes be seen as bridge to the civilian (or spectator's) world, thereby informing our responses to the principal character and his soldierly responsibility. Thus, many of the films analyzed here include representations of the war correspondent.

Things Change

Regarding the question of nature vs. nurture within genre studies discourse, perhaps one of the most compelling arguments for the latter is that expectations and beliefs about what it means to be a man or a woman are demonstrably historical — that "masculinities come into existence at particular times and places, and are always subject to change" (Connell 185). That this is so works against the belief that gendered behavior is a hard-wired inevitability, and suggests, at least to some extent, that these roles are socially constructed. Reflected by representations in popular culture, such change is itself a primary reason that genre study offers insight into cultural attitudes — what Siegfried Kracauer identified as the "collective dispositions or tendencies as prevail within a nation at a certain stage of its development" or the "psychological pattern of a people at a particular time" (8). A bedrock of genre study is that when changes occur within the generally static narrative, thematic and visual patterns which differentiate one film genre from another, such change is significant — notable because it records, confirms or portends changes in the attitudes of the culture at large.

The pertinence of all of this to the present study is that any sign system — in this case film scoring practice — will also reflect such representational change inasmuch as it is part of that representation. Thus, a comprehensive approach to analyzing film music's function within a particular genre ought to consider that function during different historical periods, particularly those in which representational change is anticipated or demonstrable. These considerations have figured largely in the periods represented here, as well as in the specific films I have chosen to analyze. Two components considered here are: one, how to establish a benchmark— conventions of scoring practice to provide a basis for comparison — and two; how to ensure film selections containing representations significantly different in character so that the contrasting characteristics of the representations provide insight into the scoring techniques that facilitate them. Because, as already suggested, ideologies shift over time, and because representation is dictated by ideology, choosing representative films that fall into widely separated time periods will ensure different representations. Robert Kolker writes:

All Hollywood genres [...] articulate the ideological norms of the culture, which are always, simultaneously, shifting and remaining the same. [...] Ideology is [...] like the culture that adopts and acts upon [it], always under negotiation and undergoing change or accommodation. It is a complex, shifting array of representations and is given form, expressed in the culture's dominant fictions [182].

Regarding war films in particular, Stanley Solomon agrees:

Because the war film, by tradition and possibly by nature, is so susceptible to propagandistic uses, it becomes extremely difficult for a filmmaker to shape its thematic import: the film tends to take its theme ready-made from the prevailing public view of war at the time of its production [246].

The point is made: Just as ideologies shift over time, so too do representations. The films considered here fall into time periods beginning approximately 10–20 years apart. Within each time period, I provide an in-depth analysis of a number of sequences in at least one film while at the same time more briefly addressing material from other releases to demonstrate the larger context. The temporal distance between representations is an intentional strategy to clear room for the shifting ideologies suggested above. In other words, because my intent is to explore different approaches to scoring practice in response to different kinds of representations, the distance between films allows for the necessary changes to occur.

Classical Period

I begin with films released during the so called Golden Age of Hollywood. Most film scholars, including André Bazin (30), suggest that this period begins roughly around 1930 (with the coming of sound and panchromatic film) and continues well into the mid to late 1940s. It is a good place to start, not only because a raft of World War II films were released in robust support of America's war effort, but particularly to establish a benchmark from which to examine the processes of cinematic representation. The period is significant for having ushered in the classic, conventional mechanisms of narrative film — that amalgam of filmic codes, including lighting, editing, sound, shooting techniques, scoring practice, and so on, generally referred to as classical Hollywood style. These filmic codes became entrenched and were thus repeated from film to film, and in many ways still inform filmic narrative structure. Among these codes, key to this study are those of classical scoring practice, perhaps most succinctly identified and categorized by Claudia Gorbman (73). But Gorbman, as previously indicated, demonstrates these principles primarily as they apply to melodrama, thus specific application to combat film provides a crucial context within which subsequent practices can be compared to establish similarity or difference.

The film of focus selected for the classical period is *The Story of G.I. Joe* (1945)—"the ultimate example of World War II combat films. [...] The film has a maturity and relentless realism that was possible only as the war neared its end" (Koppes and Black 304). The protagonist is a war correspondent. The film contains a combination score—a score that contains both preexisting popular music as well as original music composed for the film. The combination score allows exploration of the two most common approaches to scoring, i.e. the use of music created specifically for the film and music with more flexible, culturally inscribed associations that preexist the film.

Vietnam Period

Films about the Vietnam War present a significant departure from the generally supportive combat cinema of classical Hollywood. Indeed, while the 1940s saw hundreds of films extolling "the good war," only one narrative film specifically about Vietnam, *The Green Berets* (1968), was released during the war. Probably, this is because Vietnam had become the most unpopular and divisive war in U.S. history, and popular audiences were uninterested in, and unmoved by, messages of support. At the same time, producers were unwilling to cash in on popular, negative sentiment by releasing movies critical of the war while it was still being waged. This raises an important point, which will be revisited a number of times in this study: a significant factor influencing the nature of soldierly representation is the proximity of the war film to the conflict it depicts. "The motion picture industry recognizes a certain moral duty in an era of national emergency, and is, so to speak, drafted into the war effort. [...] Thus it is no wonder that many films made during a national conflict take on an aura of intolerable one-sidedness later" (Solomon 246). Although we will see in subsequent chapters that this is no longer necessarily the case with regard to representations of Middle Eastern conflicts, representations of protagonists in films made during the depicted war will generally be supportive of that war, while post-war depictions will accommodate varied representations. To provide for differences in representations, then, it is important to choose films made during the depicted conflict as well as those made at various periods after it. For the period during which the war was waged, the choice of *The Green Berets* is self evident as it is the only choice that exists. Like *The Story of G.I. Joe* the film uses a combination score and has a news correspondent in a prominent role.

Post-Vietnam Period

I have suggested that the Vietnam War's unpopularity precipitated a turning point in representations of combat heroism — that following the war, American audiences were less inclined to find resonant the same sort of flag-waving, chest-thumping God-and-country patriotism that informed a lion's share of soldierly representations that preceded it (O'Brien 59). This is not meant to suggest that there were not negative representations of fighting men before Vietnam, or that Vietnam single-handedly spawned the anti-war genre. Nonetheless, the war did create an atmosphere that precipitated the release of a disproportionate number of particularly virulent attacks on the American military and the ideology behind its campaigns. By the late 1970s (by 1970, if we include *MASH,* Robert Altman's thinly camouflaged response to Vietnam), representation of soldiers embody abrupt departures from conventional representations of the classical period. In "Dialectical Disorientation in Vietnam War Films: Subversion of the Mythology of War" Karen Rasmussen and Sharon Downey identify radical departures from previous representations and attribute them to the "sociopolitical controversy surrounding Vietnam" (176). Films from this period "offer a disturbing vision of war as destructive, of its rituals as hollow, and of human actions in war as morally ambiguous" (177). This is a marked departure from war film's traditional "melodramatic portrayals of men performing virile, courageous deeds designed to protect helpless civilians from some sort of aggressor" (Donald 125). Perhaps significantly, this is also the period that, according to Kassabian, saw a marked departure from traditional Hollywood scoring practices: "During the 1980s, the number of films scored with popular music soundtracks rose dramatically. Films from a wide range of genres appeared with pop soundtracks of various kinds" (61). Given the simultaneous convergence of these two documented departures from convention, this period provides rich opportunity for the investigation of changes in soldierly representation.

With regard to consistency, *Full Metal Jacket* (1987) is an appropriate choice for focus. It contains a combination score, a combat correspondent and a narrative that revolves around the military unit. While other excellent films from this period contain combination scores (e.g., Coppola's *Apocalypse Now*); and others center around the military unit (e.g., Stone's *Platoon*) none contains or makes as extensive use of these elements in combination as does *Full Metal Jacket*. *Apocalypse Now*, for example, takes the stuff of its narrative not from the military unit but from the psychological struggle between two men and does not contain a central combat sequence within which the protagonist takes an integral part. *Platoon* contains only one sequence employing popular music. Hence, it is the combination of an appropriate score and appropriate narrative structure that makes *Full Metal Jacket* a particularly apposite choice.

Vietnam — The Sequel

By the years leading up to and just beyond the turn of the century, in contrast to the period discussed above that seemed to embody an intentional destruction of the American soldierly myth, there emerged a number of films that, at least on the surface, worked to get it back (e.g., *Courage Under Fire* (1996), *Saving Private Ryan* (1997), *Black Hawk Down* (2001)). Among these, Randall Wallace's *We Were Soldiers* (2002) is unique, because it works to reposition popular sentiment about Vietnam, seeking dignity and empathy from its audience, not for the war effort itself, but for the men who fought it. Here, perhaps, are initial rumblings of the currently popular (though arguably schizophrenic) concept of supporting the troops but not the war that their efforts facilitate. The film's protagonists provide a marked departure from both of the previous versions of Vietnam wartime masculinities — the hard-bodied John Wayne version (played by John Wayne) and the disengaged, ambiguous, traumatized, or psychotic versions represented in most of the Vietnam films that came after. They are an extension of the changed soldierly representations that pivot on popular American sentiment about the Vietnam War, and as such, are a crucial part of the changing face of the myth of the American soldier.

The filmic components of *We Were Soldiers* are appropriately consistent with regard to the other films I have focused on so far — much of the narrative revolves around the military unit, the film contains a prominent character who is a war correspondent, it contains a protagonist intimately involved in the central combat sequence and employs (at least to some extent) a combination score.

Middle Eastern Conflicts

I have suggested more than once that when change comes to the patterns that constitute film genre it does not necessarily follow a predictable trajectory. If some of the combat films of the late nineties and early noughties seemed to veer from the generally negative representations present in many post–Vietnam combat films by positing a kinder, gentler attitude toward American soldierly representations (e.g., *Saving Private Ryan* and *We Were Soldiers*), that attitude did not extend to representations about the wars in the Persian Gulf. Beyond a return to the suspicion and in some cases open hostility with which popular culture viewed the Vietnam War, many of the representations of Middle Eastern conflicts beginning with the first war in the Persian Gulf in 1991 depart from convention in other significant ways, not least of which is a willingness to cast a negative light on a war that is currently being waged. While I discuss a number of films from this period, I focus on *The Hurt Locker*, primarily because I find its combination score functions in particularly compelling ways in its representation of what I have called the devolution of American heroism.

Re-Presenting World War II

Because this study set up a point of departure by exploring classical Hollywood scoring practice in the World War II combat film of the 1940s, it became clear as I wrote that an examination of relatively recent films about the same war would provide a valuable (and perhaps necessary) way to reflect upon changes in that practice over time and to address questions that emerged from my examination of other conflicts. As I indicate in the "Re-Presenting 'The Good War'" chapter, the question arises as to whether the post–Vietnam War heroic devolution that is evident in films such as *The Deer Hunter, Full Metal Jacket* and *Apocalypse Now* (to name just three) and in nearly all of the films depicting the wars in the Middle East is a symptom of the public unease with particular wars or whether it is based upon a broader disillusionment with the American soldierly myth in general. But what seemed at first like a relatively uncomplicated question proved elusive, made so by the substantial variation in soldierly representations and narrative agendas embodied in these films. This variation suggested a somewhat different structure in approaching these films.

In chapters up to this point I chose to include a focused analysis of sequences from one selected film with the knowledge that the representations and thematic material in it were at least broadly representative of other films made during the period from which it emerged. But because I became less comfortable about selecting a representative film of focus from the pool of post–1990s World War II films that limned their protagonists and the war itself with such widely discrepant representations, I chose to survey the period rather than focus specifically on a single "representative" film. Although in doing so I run the risk of providing the reader with a little about a lot and a lot about nothing, I am nonetheless comfortable that the result benefits by being more inclusive overall, if not focused specifically.

I

Scoring the Classical Combat Film and Conventions of the War Film Protagonist: *The Story of G.I. Joe*

This chapter applies the functions of traditional models of Hollywood scoring practice to representations of masculinities the 1940s combat film. There are a number of good reasons to start with this period. It allows us to set a benchmark by examining represented masculinities that emerged during what we have established as that period when musical function in the classical Hollywood film was initially encoded — when the system became conventional. These representations can then be compared (in subsequent chapters) to those masculinities that came later as the passage of time ushered in changes in social attitudes about the myth of American soldiers and as the patterns of the genre responded to those changes. It allows us to establish that classical scoring practices are pertinent to the mechanisms of a genre other than melodrama. It prepares the way to answer questions as to whether or not different kinds of representations of masculinity are signified differently — by differing musical mechanisms — by a film score (the overarching question driving this study), and if so, then how and from what do the scores differ.

As indicated, Claudia Gorbman has identified seven scoring principles belonging to classical Hollywood film[1]: invisibility, inaudibility, signifier of emotion, narrative cueing, continuity, unity and a principle allowing for the violation of the previous six (73). Once again, in demonstrating these principles, Gorbman concentrates her in-depth examples of musical representation primarily on female roles. Other writers, too, who reference Gorbman's work with regard to the classical Hollywood film score, including Katherine Kalinak and Anahid Kassabian, are primarily interested in its relationship to feminine roles. What we are left with, then, is some basis for comparing contemporary musical representations of femininity with classical (or conventional) representations of femininity, but no such basis for comparisons of masculine representations. Thus, the purpose here is to show how classical principles function within the context of a combat film that foregrounds masculinity.

Before moving the discussion to individual scores or musical cues, it is necessary make some observations about the position or general characteristics of protagonists to establish a basis for correlating those characteristics to the music that helps represent them. In some respects, the protagonists in combat films are positioned differently than are protagonists in other genres, and this difference necessarily affects the way they are represented musically.

Characteristics of the Roles Within the Narrative

William Wellman's *The Story of G.I. Joe* (1945) follows the popular World War II war correspondent Ernie Pyle (Burgess Meredith) as he travels with, and reports on, the missions of the common foot soldier in Europe. As in all combat films, there are major battle sequences, but just as important to the narrative are depictions of the soldiers' work-a-day worlds and the personal and collective response they exhibit — pining for home and for loved ones, responding to the deaths of fallen comrades, dealing with poor food, poor shelter and profound weariness. While Pyle and Lt. Bill Walker (Robert Mitchum) are the principal protagonists, much of the narrative is structured as a string of vignettes involving many individuals — small dramatic threads that collectively provide an overall sense of the conditions endured by the troops. Other key characters include Sgt. Steve Warnicki (Freddie Steele) who is consumed by his desire to get home to see his wife and newborn son, and Pvt. Dondaro (Wally Cassell) who considers himself a great lover and is obsessed with dreams of women. It is probably worth noting here that both of these character-types had by now become conventional to the combat unit in combat films, undoubtedly to alibi the heterosexuality of the soldiers within the nearly exclusively male world of the combat unit.

It is not unusual for war films to include a journalist as one of the protagonists (e.g., *Objective Burma* [1945], *The Story of G.I. Joe* [1945], *The Green Berets* [1968], *Full Metal Jacket* [1987], *Three Kings* [1999], *We Were Soldiers* [2001]). He often befriends the officer commanding the combat unit around which the narrative revolves. But while the sequences involving the journalist Pyle and the officer Walker provide key narrative material, the ways in which Pyle relates to and comments about the other soldiers are also vital to the film's overall narrative structure. It should be noted that combat films sometimes dedicate as much (sometimes more) screen time to those under the leader's command as they do to the leader himself, despite the fact that the leader receives top billing. Note, for example, that we learn more about the home life of Sgt. Steve Warnicki (Freddie Steele) in *G.I. Joe* than we do about that of Lt. Bill Walker (Robert Mitchum); and Pvt. Aloysius K. "Smacksie" Randall (William Bendix) is far more memorable for his anti-authoritarian antics in *Wake Island* (1942) than is his commanding officer Maj. Geoffrey Caton (Brian Donlevy). The point is that combat films foreground different characters at different times, a distribution of narrative focus less pronounced in the narrative patterns of other genres. Because this formal distribution of focus — this tendency to dig more deeply into secondary characters than is customary in other genres — provides an important explanation for certain scoring characteristics, it is appropriate to explore it at some length.

Stanley Solomon says the following:

> [I]n comparison with other main character types of the other major genres [...] the character most readily identifiable with the war genre, the military figure, is less central to the war film than the Western hero is to the Western, the star performer to the musical, the figure of terror to the nightmare world, the criminal to the crime film, or the investigator to the detection film. Obviously, war as a broad topic is not so immediately referable to an individual as are the topics of other genres [244].

Solomon's point is that the subject of war in film often includes war's impact on people and ideas not immediately involved in battle situations, e.g., ideological issues that inform the depicted struggle and, of course, the "folks back home": lovers, mothers, children and society in general. This explains why the journalist — or some equivalent confidant — is often prominently included in the narrative for his function of providing information about the war to those at home, as well as his function of commenting on the ideology that informs the conflict. Solomon is also alluding to the fact that singular focus on one character is deemphasized because of the nature of battle, which is never carried out by an individual (except for in action-adventure pabulum such as the *Rambo* series and its ilk). Rather, it is often the group of individuals who act together as a single narrative agency in accomplishing an objective or a series of objectives: planning, training, implementing, and, ultimately, either winning or losing.

The characteristics discussed above posit a possible explanation as to why the conventional combat film made within the tradition of classical Hollywood scoring practice often does not assign specific musical material to specific characters. Despite the ubiquitous use of the leitmotif during this period, which came to "dominate nine out of ten film scores" (Chion 51) as a kind of filmic shorthand for encoding specifics about "a character, situation or idea" (Kalinak 63)," the leitmotif functioning in combat films to represent a specific male character is often notable for its absence. It is true that when a woman finds her way into the combat narrative, usually as the "girl back home" or in the role of company nurse, a leitmotif will be baptized to identify her as a particular soldier's romantic interest; thus, the use of the leitmotif for "Woman as romantic Good Object" (Gorbman 80) is not itself uncommon in American combat films, e.g., *The Flying Tigers* (1942), *Immortal Sergeant* (1943), *Sands of Iwo Jima* (1945). However, in those sequences that depict or relate to the war itself, the score works to illustrate the setting, atmosphere and overall tone of the mise-en-scène within which the "generalized opposition to the spiritual force represented by the enemy" (Solomon 244) takes place. It is far less likely to represent a particular soldier. While three of the themes in *G.I. Joe* do indeed function as leitmotifs, they do so in a general capacity, as we shall see. At least one reason, then, that specific musical signification is not assigned to specific characters is the distribution of narrative focus among characters. Because the narrative patterns of the combat film often position the audience to view the narrative agency as the unit rather than the individual (even though the unit is comprised of individuals), the musical signification reflects this pattern in its more generalized function.

But despite the fact that music is called upon to illustrate the general mise-en-scène rather than to illustrate the characters individually, its illustrative function can indeed tell us a great deal about the characters because it tells us a great deal about the situations to which we see them respond. If, for example, a piece of music contributes to our understanding that a situation is fraught with danger, then the actions of a character within that setting informs our reading of him. Thus, in setting a benchmark for comparing representations of war film protagonists, it is sometimes necessary to examine the overall function of the music in given sequences, and then explore how that function relates to the characters themselves. Similarly, it is also appropriate to examine the general characteristics of the fighting unit and then examine the protagonist's response to, function within, and responsibility for that unit.

Main Title: An Overview of the Narrative

Like Westerns, combat films often use a song with lyrics rather than an instrumental piece as the main title (*Sands of Iwo Jima, A Walk in the Sun, Gung Ho, The Green Berets, Apocalypse Now, Full Metal Jacket*, to name a few). This approach not only performs the conventional function of identifying the genre and setting the atmosphere and mood of the film (Gorbman 82, Kalinak 98) through the formal properties of the music, but the lyrics can contain explicit comment on what is to come: the film's ideological bent or the stuff of its thematic material regarding other elements such as characterization.

The Story of G.I. Joe is interesting in that an orchestral fanfare is juxtaposed with an excerpt of a plaintive traditional song performed by a male vocal ensemble. It begins with a tympani roll followed by a sprightly fanfare. These musical elements accompany the visual of a large, white military star insignia followed by the film's name and thus immediately signify the military theme. This lasts for about fifteen seconds after which the orchestration disappears, segueing into the much slower, harmonized vocal section (without instrumental accompaniment). The vocal section lasts for about thirty seconds before the orchestral theme returns. The abrupt change in character from orchestral fanfare to a slow male chorus then back to full bombastic orchestral material indicates by its contrast that there are two simultaneous components to this narrative: one, the military aspect, and two, the "the attitude of characters confronted with the situation of war" (Solomon 244). That the plaintive vocal enters at precisely the same time we see the acting credits is further indication that it represents the attitude of the characters themselves. That the music that signifies this attitude is surrounded by the military theme indicates that the represented attitude is a response to the military surroundings.

As suggested previously, the lyrics, written in the first-person, make this attitude explicit. The singer explains that although he has left home, he will nonetheless return regardless of what obstacles might stand in his way. Thus, the attitude itself is represented by the plaintive quality of the melody, and the lyrics indicate precisely what it is that the men are plaintive about.

This marvelous piece of musical shorthand indicates in a matter of minutes precisely what the narrative is based on: a group of men who want nothing more than to do what they must so that they can return to the lives they left behind.

Walker's Men: Before the First Battle

The yearning for home is individualized via musically informed close-ups of the soldiers in an early sequence during which they make their first camp while traveling to the front. This collage sequence shows the soldiers in their tents preparing for sleep, either individually or in pairs, as they exchange banter. The shots are connected by related musical cues, each of which function to indicate the men's thoughts of home. It begins with a radio operator's excitement when he tunes in a Berlin broadcast of Artie Shaw's "Summit Ridge Drive," an American medium tempo blues tune performed by a small swing ensemble. "Hey fellas," he shouts, "get a load of this: Artie Shaw!" Music in this style could have been heard in any number of dance venues around America in the '40s, and its function here is to recall such scenes to the homesick, weary and anxious men. This purpose is cemented by the voice of Axis Sally (Shelly Cullen), the American-born propagandist whose Radio Berlin broadcasts were heard nightly and were intended to demoralize Allied soldiers by, among other things, reminding them of their loved ones back home. As we see a montage of the soldiers in their bed rolls, Sally taunts them about their wives and girlfriends, planting fears of indiscretion, as a mellifluous string orchestra arrangement emerges behind her. Of such music, Claudia Gorbman has this to say:

> A film of the '40s is airing on television. Even though you're in the next room, you are likely to find that a certain kind of music will cue you in correctly to the presence of Woman on screen. It is as if the emotional excess of this presence must find its outlet in the euphony of a string orchestra. I refer here to Woman as romantic Good Object [...] [80].

Here, of course, "Woman as romantic Good Object" is not on the screen, but in the minds of the men staring silently out of their tents at the stars. She has been put there by the musical convention of a lush string arrangement accompanied by Sally, who speaks in a sultry voice of the girls back home, of German girls who know how to "entertain" American soldiers and of the invincibility of the unbeaten German army. Sally paints a picture of apple-pie America (a picture that includes the dance venues represented by the music) that is clearly understood by the film audience and thus creates identification with the soldiers. She suggests that the American soldiers do not have a chance for success against the superior German army (which meets with a scattered chorus of loud reprisals from various parts of the camp). Finally, she introduces the song whose melody has been playing behind her: "I'll now sing Germany's latest hit with lyrics written especially for my American friends." The song is Ann Ronell's Academy Award-nominated "Linda," a slow love ballad performed, as indicated above, with a lush string arrangement. The lyrics tell of a small café where two lovers met and frequented. The café is now empty, and he song poses the question as to whether or not the man's lover is still waiting for him, or if she has forgotten him in favor of another. When Sally ends her song, and the radio is silenced, one of the soldiers holds his guitar as he sits in the door of his tent. "It was Nazi music," he says. "Now it's mine. Our first German prisoner." He plays "Linda" on his guitar as we see the men continue to settle in.

Thus, the music in this sequence recalls scenes of home for the soldiers via the American swing music, and facilitates the soldiers' imaginations regarding the romantic scenarios that might follow such scenes via the love ballad. Through their own extra-diegetic associations with dance music, and through the conventional coding of the lush string orchestral music, the audience identifies with the associations that the soldiers experience. The musical cues create a narrative through which the soldiers' imaginations travel, and as the soldiers' thoughts are revealed to the viewing-listening subject via the film grammar of the close-up paired with the mechanism of music as an indicator of the soldiers' points of view (Gorbman 83–84), the representation of their thoughts, fears, and desires is facilitated. By framing the soldiers separately, the sequence individualizes their desires, while, at the same time, demonstrating their commonality via the suturing mechanism of the musical cues. Finally, we are reminded of the troops' consciousness of the war's impending danger and the hope for victory when the soldier plays the tune on his guitar, figuratively taking the German music hostage. This abrogates the enemy's threat, both domestic and military, with which Sally has sought to code the music. The music has been "Americanized," thus annexing it's associations so that they work for rather than against the troops.

Walker and Pyle: Before the First Battle

Both Lt. Bill Walker and Ernie Pyle are among those framed during the sequence discussed above; however, there are notable differences in both the visual and the musical signification. Significantly, Walker is shot in very much the same way as are the rest of the men. Through the visual connection created by the musically-sutured shots (a principle Gorbman terms "continuity" (73), aligned with classical Hollywood's style of minimizing the viewers awareness of cuts) we understand that in many ways Walker has much in common with the men he leads: a history (of which we learn more later) that allows him to empathize with them. This commonality, for example, explains why we have seen him turn a blind eye to regulations and allow the men to keep a stray dog; it explains his own pain at the nervous breakdown of one of his men because he has been away from his family for so long (we learn later that Walker's wife left him because of his military service), and why he half-seriously threatens a supply lieutenant with his life if his troops do not receive a turkey dinner for Christmas. We understand that his responses are informed by this similarity between his background and thiers, a commonality that is initially demonstrated largely by the score in this early sequence.

Yet Walker's relationship to his men is also something of paradox. On the one hand, as we have seen, his concerns are not far removed from theirs; thus, he can identify with them. On the other hand, he is duty-bound to circumvent their individual concerns and desires and turn them into a single, cohesive outfit (we will see later that the orchestral theme from the main title generally functions to signify this cohesion, which facilitates the successful accomplishment of Walker's objective). Further, his understanding has limits when fairness to the company as a whole is concerned, or where their security could be threatened. Note, for example, that he does not hesitate to punish Pvt. Dondaro (Wally Cassell) for being AWOL when he is caught returning from a love tryst with a local Italian woman.

Ernie Pyle is not framed during the camp sequence in the same way that Walker and the other soldiers are. While Sally sings her love song and we see the full-frame faces of Walker and the other men staring skyward longingly, we see a full-body shot of Pyle, his back to us, on his knees adjusting his bedroll. Visually, the separation from the other men is clear. He is alone, the only man who is not sharing a tent, and the only one whose face is not shown in close-up while Sally sings. Although we do eventually see his face framed in close-up after the singing has stopped, he is not staring at the sky sighing in response to Sally's sultry-voiced love song. He is looking for his hat. While this functions on the surface as a joke about his age and baldness (his head is cold), the more pertinent point is that he is to be understood apart from the other men. While the others are moved by the music, he is unaffected. Thus his difference is not only marked visually, but musically as well. This difference is not just age-related — it is also a difference in motivation. He is not here to fight, but to record. Not to *be* one of the men, but to comment *about* them, to preserve their struggle and bridge the information gap between the war and the country that is fighting it. If the men, and so, Walker, are to be seen as heroes, then they must first be seen. "In all tales and histories of honor, in peace as well as in war, from the heroic period to the present, the presence of some spectator is crucial, to validate the behavior of the combatants and to carry their story both to those not present and to future generations" (Braudy 57). Hence it is the journalist's function to make the men visible to those who are not immediately present to see them.

Pyle's Relationship to Walker and His Men

A sequence that characterizes Pyle in this capacity is a collage of shots in which we see him in various situations, usually at his typewriter. The sequence provides a temporal bridge between Pyle's initial experiences with Walker's outfit and his reunion with them a year later, after they have been seasoned by battle experience. The montage is not only visual, but verbal and musical as well. Ernie's own voiceover contains the words that he is putting on paper; we also hear soldier's voices (from inside his mind) containing the snatches of interviews and comments from men he has encountered along the way — men who provide the stuff of his columns. The musical element contains connecting material which allows smooth transition among the shots, voices and ideas. Too, it quotes from previous themes. We hear bits of the main orchestral theme, and the vocal theme first introduced in the main title. Also included is the melody of "Linda." These materials have been previously coded by various situations: The vocal piece from the main title is coded by association with its lyrics. It indicates the resolve of the men to perform their task and then to return home. The orchestral material first heard in the main title (referred to in this chapter as the main military theme) has generally accompanied the men throughout the narrative as they are performing their work-a-day soldierly duties: on the move, heading into battle, digging in, etc. The "Linda" melody, as already discussed, is associated with romance, the "Woman as Good Object" (Gorbman 80) so to speak, which stands for girlfriend or wife, either real or imagined. It is generally heard during down-time sequences when the men have the chance to rest and, of course, to think.

It would be incorrect to suggest that these musically-created associations are meant to represent Pyle himself. Instead, they refer to the men he is writing about. The associations are part his memory of the men recalled for his columns. Thus his function as a recorder of the fighting men's hopes, fears, dreams etc., is signified by the music that accompanies the image of him writing; and while the voice-over points explicitly to a soldier's background, the music provides an affective dimension to that background. Further, just as Pyle is shown writing about many different men from many walks of life, so too does the music move quickly from one melodic idea to another — a collage of melodic ideas to signify a collage of different characters.

The design of this performance[2] differs from previous statements of the melodies it contains, and this, too, contributes to the signifying process. Overall, the performance is lighter, both in orchestration and volume (e.g., the full brassy timbre of the main military theme's melody is here stated by a single trumpet; the male vocal group is replaced by a soft string arrangement; the Linda theme is altered rhythmically and temporally). These changes in musical design suggest that the associations are removed from the diegetic "present"— that they are Pyle's recollections, his internal monologue. Similarly, the change in musical character (in tandem with the verbal indicators) keeps us from applying the associations to Ernie Pyle himself: we understand that he is not the one with the recollections of romance, he is not the one seasoned by battle. Thus this cue signifies Pyle as the eyes and ears of the men he writes about. He is the mediating filter through which their stories, and the war effort in general, are made known to others.

Capt. Walker and the Main Military Theme

Those who *are* seasoned by battle, the soldiers about whom Ernie writes, are often represented as a group by the main military theme (the orchestral section of the main title). While the representation is a general one, i.e., while it usually accompanies long shots of the soldiers working together in various situations, it is also an indicator of the protagonist Walker's abilities — his success in accomplishing his purpose of turning the individual soldiers into a cohesive outfit. Early in the film, when Pyle first joins Walker's troops, he says to Walker, "That's a pretty good lookin' outfit you got." Walker replies, "They're not an outfit yet. Maybe by this time tomorrow we will be." Pyle puts the question to Walker again a year later when they are reunited (following the Pyle montage discussed above). As the troops file past the two men, Ernie says, "Well, you got an outfit now?"

"You bet your life we got an outfit," Walker replies. "They're killers. They better be." What follows is a long violent sequence in which the troops liberate San Vittorio. When they march into the town amidst celebratory images of the townspeople, the long shot of the victorious Americans is accompanied by the main theme, an orchestral melody scored heavily for the brass section. As indicated below, its moderate tempo, instrumentation, and the accent placed upon the strong first and third beats of each measure associates it stylistically (and appropriately) with a military march.

Although this musical cue, once again, does not specifically signify Walker as would a theme of his own, the fact that it accompanies and is therefore associated with the success of those under his command indicates his ability to bring that success about. Stylistically, the theme's formal elements characterize it in a number of ways as military marching music: "Music originally designed to promote orderly marching of a large group, especially of soldiers.[...] generally in simple, strongly marked rhythm and regular phrases" (Harvard Dictionary of Music 504). The melody is performed in unison by brass (as is a lower contrapuntal line) with steady rhythmic underpinnings of a snare drum. The steady unwavering pulse suggests 2/4 time, which is sometimes referred to as march time and is, of course, aligned with its military function. Indeed, it has already been baptized with military associations by its part in the main title (heard initially as we see the military star insignia). Hence, the unified activity of "march" suggested here by both the musical and the visual as a result of the successful campaign — which itself required unified action, as indicated in the exchanges between Walker and Pyle — indicates Walker's success, and so, his ability as a leader. While he can share their individual yearnings, he can also unite the men for a unified purpose and inspire the requisite obedience and loyalty that such unification entails. And once again, his success, and so his competence in meeting his goal, is made clear by the score.

Narrative Cueing of an Entire Sequence

The preceding examples of musical function explain the extra-musical associations elicited by specific musical phrases, a vital component of traditional Hollywood scoring practice. But beyond its capacity to make meaning via the coding of specific musical phrases, another key component of the traditional film score is its facilitation of the unfolding of longer narrative sequences by illustrating the action, providing it rhythm and forward impetus, and avoiding ambiguity by representing the point of view of the characters (what Gorbman calls the "displeasure of uncertain signification" [58]). Just as the linear movement of plot depends on sequential exposition of visual and verbal components, so too does it depend on the score (or the silence) that is integral to them. In other words, the consecutive unfolding of the story elements — the cause and effect or the question and answer of the plot — is understood through the cumulative process created by appropriately arranged strings of words and images, not understood all at once, but via experience over time. Similarly, musical understanding is dependent on the cumulative effect which also must unfold temporally. As, for example, a certain action takes place onscreen, that action is illustrated musically; as a character or group of characters respond physically or emotionally to that action, the response is also represented by the score. This function was considered important enough by the composers of classical film music to allow it predominance over stylistically appropriate aesthetic properties of the music. That is, the illustrative function of film music often comes with a price. Gorbman points this out in discussing the example of the scores of Max Steiner. (It should be noted here that the Steiner model can be considered conventional for classical scoring practice in general.)

> Stiener's music often sacrifices its musical coherence to effect gained in coordinating with diegetic action. The formlessness and fragmentary nature of musical statements in his scores are perhaps the most easily recognizable mark of his style. [...] On several levels, then, the musical score exhibits a pronounced tendency toward hyperexplication. Stiener's intrusively lush dramatic music has an interesting effect — an effect common to all "realist" Hollywood cinema [...]. The music is an element of discourse that magnifies, heightens, intensifies the emotional value suggested by the story [97].

In *The Story of G.I. Joe,* a good example of "coordinating the diegetic action" of a long narrative sequence is one in which Walker demonstrates his dedication and concern for one of his men, Sgt. Warnicki, first, by worrying over his overdue return from battle, and then by his response to Warnicki's subsequent emotional collapse — following which Walker leads the troops to "do something about that" by mounting an attack and rousting heretofore immovable German troops from the rubble of a bombed-out monastery.

Time and again throughout the film, Warnicki tries to repair an old phonograph to play a recording his wife sent him of his toddler son Junior's first words. Thus far, his attempts have yielded only gibberish. Having begun as a series of comedic episodes, these attempts soon become obsessive, indicating Warnicki's single-minded desire to do whatever he must so he can return to his family. He has told Walker that each mission brings him closer to that goal — "Every step forward is a step closer to home," he says. Hence, he volunteers to lead more than his share of scouting parties against the German occupiers despite Walker's concern for his physical and mental well-being.

In response to Warnicki's late return from one such mission, we see Walker waiting, pacing anxiously. But when Warnicki returns at last, it is reason for alarm rather than relief: he is physically and emotionally exhausted. "Tough time getting back, sir," he says, passing Walker, who must support him so he does not fall as he makes his way to the dug-out shelter. Before he enters the shelter, he pauses, punching out bizarrely at the air as if he is fighting an unseen foe. In the shelter, he snarls uncharacteristically at the other men and puts the record on the phonograph, as is his habit. At long last, he hears Junior's voice repeat the words *"Hello Daddy, Hello Daddy."* This is the first time he has managed to make the recording intelligible. But just as his return did not produce the anticipated response, so too is his response to this success unexpected. Wild-eyed, he looks up from the record: "I'll kill 'em," he says. "Them, them! If it wasn't for them I'd be home with Junior!" He rushes violently out of the shelter, ready to attack the monastery single-handedly, striking out at all who try to subdue him, including Walker, who finally knocks him out. Walker has Warnicki taken away to the medics, assembles the troops, and leads a successful assault on the ruined monastery. Such is not an unusual response for male soldierly representation. Emotional responses to fallen or wounded comrades often take the form of "dedicating the next enemy kill to a deceased comrade or by generally raising the level of mayhem" (Donald 133).

The episode lasts approximately five minutes, and a close reading of the score demonstrates how principles of classical Hollywood scoring function within the mise-en-scène of this combat film: how the "fragmentary nature" of the score follows the narrative in a linear manner, building a cumulative effect for the audience.

In reading the analysis of this sequence, it is important to keep in mind that I do not mean to suggest that a given musical design will always signify in precisely the same way. My previous reference to music as a leaky system of signs is worth recalling here. To suggest that musical language (using the term *language* in its broadest sense) is in some way parallel to verbal language may be a compelling metaphor, but it can never be a literal equivalent. Just as Donis Dondis has suggested that "Visual literacy cannot ever be a clear-cut logical system similar to language" (12) because it is not subject to the same man-made systemic rules of communication that verbal language is, so too we must admit a certain subjectivity when analyzing music with regard to its capacity to communicate a specific message. While certain designs are indeed conventionally coded (according to both syntactic and non-syntactic parameters) by repeated use (recall Gorbman's discussion of lush string arrangements and Woman as Good Object) the subjective process of making meaning from the score is one that is dependent upon the simultaneous experience of all the filmic components including music, sound, dialog and image. If I suggest, for example, that a musical phrase in a minor key played in a very low register by the contra-bass lends an ominous atmosphere to the shot, I am not therefore suggesting that such a design will always "mean" *ominous*. The meaning is not necessarily *in* the music. It is in what the viewing-listening subject makes of the music as the music coordinates with all of the additional sign systems she experiences with it. In placing Susanne Langer's ideas about music and meaning into the context of film music, Royal S. Brown puts it this way:

> It is, then, the merging of the cinematic object-event and the musical score into the surface narrative that transforms the morphological affect of music into specific emotions and allows us to "have them" while also imputing them to someone and/or something else, namely the cinematic character and/or situation. As Langer also notes, "music at its highest, though clearly a symbolic form, is an unconsummated symbol." In this sense, most music can also be considered to be unconsummated affect, and as such it is ripe as an art form for the consummation provided by the representational nature of the moving picture and/or of the specific, narrative situation [Brown 27].

Thus, while the conventions of film music "mean" according to their repeated and often clichéd associations (Adorno and Eisler 12–13), meanings also depend upon the other elements that accompany the score. With this in mind, while the discussion here and throughout this study allows for film music conventions, it also includes a necessary discussion of image and dialogue.

Music's Illustration of Walker's Response to Warnicki's Breakdown

The sequence summarized above begins with a long shot of the ruined monastery that the Germans are using as a fort to hold off Walker's unit.

An opening dissonant stinger[3] underpinned by an ominous, low bass line and coupled with a low angle long shot (which emphasizes the ruin's looming aspect) signifies the danger it represents. A single, high, wandering and tonally ambiguous line in the clarinet enters shortly after we cut to Walker, who is waiting anxiously for Warnicki to return from his scouting mission. The plaintive sound of the instrument in tandem with the shot of Walker pacing back and forth alone beneath the looming monastery signifies his concern visually and aurally. Like the painfully slow, uneven ticking of a clock, a chime-like repeating note enters, marking time as Walker paces, thus providing an aural metaphor and making palpable the length and weight of the passing moments he feels as his anxiety mounts. The repeating, chime-like note is *almost* regularly spaced, but not quite, and this temporal ambiguity exacerbates the tension we feel as the time it marks stretches on. Walker's apprehension is made explicit by a cut to the inside of the shelter where Dondaro asks, "Warnicki, ain't he back?" The question is punctuated by a low bass figure, which, again, illustrates tension and confirms the ominous tone. The film then cuts back to Walker accompanied by the high melodic material in the clarinet. Again, this material has a wandering quality; it enters and exits intermittently and is rhythmically and melodically ambiguous as if it does not know where to rest, and thus illustrates Walker's own uncertainty. Set apart by its contrasting timbre and separated by a relatively wide interval from its orchestral accompaniment, the melody stands alone, as Walker does from his men. It sounds unsure (so to speak) of its own outcome, just as Walker is unsure of what has happened to Warnicki. These characteristics lend the cue the air of an internal monologue, communicating Walker's state of mind as he continues waiting.

As Walker paces, the film cuts to three young soldiers drinking coffee, watching him. The full-face close-ups reveal each man's concern, and we hear a woodwind cue based on the melody of the vocal material sung by the male chorus during the main title. Recall that the lyrics expressed the singers' dismay at having had to leave home, but suggested that he would return, regardless of the obstacles. The sentiment expressed by the lyrics serve to baptize this leitmotif accordingly. The leitmotif accompanies the close up of each man and continues over a three-shot. Because the melody has been coded with a single message, and because it accompanies each of the men (including Walker and Warnicki) at various times during the sequence, it functions to unify the men within their common experience of having left their homes behind, wanting nothing more than to return. "You'd better take him some coffee. And keep an eye on him too," says one of the soldiers indicating Walker. Just as Walker is concerned for Warnicki (whose actions are driven by his yearning for home), his men are concerned for him and must "keep an eye on him" despite his rank. Thus we see that through the common bond they share, he has earned their respect as well as their concern. And again, it is the score that makes salient the overarching theme underpinning that concern — the unwelcome acknowledgment of a job that must be accomplished, and the desire to get it done and return home.

When one of the soldiers asks, "When are we gonna hit 'em again?" the question is accompanied by another dissonant stinger indicating that the apprehension about Warnicki's return is only part of the reason for anxiety. Following six measures of connecting material, there are two brief, quickly ascending flute phrases, made salient by the contrast in timbre with the muted trumpet preceding them. They accompany, respectively, a shot of one of the young soldiers leaning forward, looking into the distance as if for Warnicki, and a shot of Walker also looking into the distance. The upward movement of the musical phrase is similar to the inflection generally accompanying a spoken question and confirms the questioning aspect of the shot, the musical equivalent of "Where is he?" or perhaps "Was that him?" thus providing Walker's and the soldiers' point of view. As if in response to this unvoiced question, the look that comes over Walker's face and a drop of his arms and shoulders indicate resignation to the possibility that Warnicki will not return. Having given up hope, Walker stops pacing and is about to enter his shelter when a single woodwind voice states the "I've Gone Away" theme first heard in the opening credits (recall that it has been coded by its lyrics to indicate the idea of a return regardless of the difficulty — with obvious connotations for the present circumstance). At this point he hears a step behind him, turns, and sees Warnicki. He has indeed returned just as the music foretold. The shot-reverse shot construction cuts to Warnicki, whose image is accompanied by precisely the same ascending musical construction previously voiced by the flute which formed the question "Where is he"? It is stated this time, however, as a slower staccato phrase, deep in the bass register, and thus imbues the "answer" with an ominous quality. As we see Warnicki's desperate condition through Walker's eyes, the realization is confirmed by the remainder of this jumbled musical statement that jumps two and one-half octaves within the space of two beats moving abruptly from a low register to a high register, and then back downward to a mid register in less than two measures. These abrupt leaps in the space of a few pulses create a confused, even frantic, musical phrase that parallels Warnicki's own confusion. As indicated earlier, as he approaches the shelter we see him stumble and strike out at the air. Further, the chromaticism[4] of the music accompanying him as he makes his way into the shelter and once again prepares to play the recording of his son, destroys the sense of a key center (in other words, a listener's sense of where the music has come from and where it is headed) thus musically mirroring his own obvious instability.

As Warnicki places the recording on the turntable and spins the disk, the score stops, and here the absence of music is as significant a signifier as was its presence. "The effect of the *absence* of musical sound must never be underestimated. [...] [D]iegetic sound with no music can function effectively to make the diegetic space more immediate, more palpable, in the absence of that Muzak-like overlay so often thrust on the spectator's consciousness" (Gorbman 18). In this instance, the space "that is made more palpable by the lack of musical sound" contains, ironically enough, a sound reproducing device, the importance of which is made clear not only by the close-up which fills the frame with the phonograph, but by the absence of the score. This sudden lack leaves a sonic vacuum, previously filled by the score, thus creating anticipation in the audience for imminent sound from the device itself.

As indicated earlier, for the first time, Warnicki successfully hears his wife's and son's recorded voices. He becomes agitated and runs from the shelter as the score returns and once again follows each nuance of narrative action. This cue begins with a deep bass figure reflecting the ominous tone created by his agitated response. The musical activity then builds rapidly, as does the action on the screen, with the inclusion of sforzando brass, string flourishes and tympani roll as Warnicki rushes from the shelter and strikes out at all who try to subdue him. The rhythm of the fist fight is paralleled by the music, and Walker's final knockout punch is illustrated by a final brass and tympani sforzando as Warnicki hits the ground (such exaggerated illustration is referred to in film music jargon as "Mickey Mousing").[5] The soldiers help Warnicki to his feet, and as he mimics his boy's recorded voice ("Hello Daddy, Hello Daddy") we hear a single note played low in the bass and accompanied by a high tremolo in the violins—a musical convention indicating psychological stress or "uncanny suspense" (Adorno and Eisler 17)—(Bernard Herrmann's cue for the famous shower sequence in *Psycho* is a widely recognized example of this). As he is led away, we hear a lushly scored quotation of the "I've Gone Away" theme that leads into the brassy main military theme signifying, as before, triumphal military action as Walker rallies the men to "Do something about that." Because the main military theme begins at the end of Warnicki's breakdown sequence and continues into the beginning of the final combat sequence, it provides continuity[6] between the two sequences and points to the connection between what the war has done to one of Walker's men and the action Walker takes because of it.

Aftermath: Response to Battle and Its Consequences

Unlike many war films from the period, *The Story of G.I. Joe* does not depend on a single battle or campaign for its narrative climax. The intention is to create a sense of protracted struggle as opposed to many other examples of the genre which tend to make single battles "stand for" an entire war (Solomon 245). Hence *G.I. Joe*'s denouement does not come with the end of a battle, but with the end of the protagonist Walker; and with that end comes what is perhaps the most revealing representation of the relationship he had with his men. As discussed earlier, the overarching characteristic of this war film protagonist is embodied in that relationship — the combination of authority and commonality through which he accomplishes his missions and at the same time garners love and respect. I have already pointed to a few sequences demonstrating this two-faceted bond, but the response his men have to his death, particularly Dondaro's response, encapsulates it significantly.

Often, combat films include sequences in which soldiers comment on the death of fallen comrades (e.g., *Bataan, The Green Berets, Full Metal Jacket, We Were Soldiers*). Such accolades (or criticisms) usually come from the men as they are in the presence of the one who has fallen. The dead, of course, cannot agree with or refute what is said about them, nor can they reward or retaliate in response; such expressions, then, take on significant credibility. Thus, when the men stand over Walker's prone and lifeless body (they are shot from a low angle suggesting the dead man's point of view) and express their sorrow at his passing, their sentiments can be read as particularly genuine.

The sequence occurs near the end of the film when Pyle and the allied forces are en route to Rome. Pyle finds what is left of Walker's company resting by the side of the road. Following the greetings and the requisite war film wisecracking banter, the men grow somber at the sight of a line of mules, each bearing the body of a fallen soldier. Dondaro is leading one of these mules, which is carrying the body of Lt. Walker. Dondaro lays Walker's body beside other fallen men; and, as indicated above, just before the troops move out, some of the men pause to stand over Walker's prone body to express their sorrow. The soldier most affected by Walker's death, the man who stays with him the longest and sits by his body holding and caressing his hand, straightening his collar, and smoothing his hair after the others have left is Dondaro. Dondaro's response is significant, because of all the soldiers under Walker's command, he was the one most at odds with Walker and was the only one subjected to disciplinary action. Thus his sorrow and his reluctance to leave the body to rejoin his company is a particularly salient representation of the common bond and the respect that Walker has managed to effect. In other words, Dondaro's response is significant in representing the acceptance of both facets of Walker's character highlighted here — his paternal authority (recall that Dondaro is the only recipient of Walkers punishment) as well as the commonality Walker shared with the men.

Pertinent to Dondaro's response and responses like it is the following from Ralph Donald: "[O]verflow of emotion and affection is only permitted because one of the two men is either dying or already dead. Only then is a man allowed to cradle another man in his arms, or to plant a chaste kiss on his forehead." Donald furthers the point by quoting Antony Easthope's *What a Man's Gotta Do: The Masculine Myth in Popular Culture*:

> In the dominant versions of men at war, men are permitted to behave towards each other in ways that would not be allowed elsewhere, caressing and holding each other, comforting and weeping together, admitting their love. The pain of war is the price paid for the way it expresses the male bond. War's suffering is a kind of punishment for the release of homosexual desire and male femininity that only war allows [134].

Thus Walker's death and the condition of war release Dondaro and the other soldiers from the constraints of "the manly credo" (Donald 133). Similarly, it releases the viewing subject from the gender-specific constraints placed upon his often cited "look" first identified by Laura Mulvey with such profound influence in her essay "Visual Pleasure and Narrative Cinema." The point is that Walker can now receive our gaze because he has been "feminized" by his death, which renders him passive, and by his death wound, which renders his previously "masculine" (thus impenetrable) body penetrable. Perhaps it would not be a stretch here to suggest that this death wound can be seen as analogous to the feminine "bleeding wound" of Mulvey's article.

In other words, then, an overt demonstration of respect and admiration is now permitted — a demonstration that would have been avoided while Walker lived because of the necessity to disavow the appearance of homosexuality within the homosocial world of the battlefield. But the point I wish to make here is not that we can now gaze upon Walker's body without risking discomfort because of Walker's feminization, but that the possibility of such feminization has profound implications for the way Walker can now be represented musically, i.e., this feminization-in-death is congruent with the character of the score that accompanies our last look at this protagonist.

The score here functions very much as it does in the sequence preceding Warnicki's breakdown—"illustration to the minutest detail" (Gorbman 88). Its structure is, as before, a musical collage, cohesive only in the presence of the visuals it accompanies. For example, we hear a solo diegetic harmonica followed by a plaintive reed melody leading up to an appropriately placed stinger as the camera cuts to the donkey carrying a body, another stinger as one of the men in the company recognizes Dondaro leading the donkey and still another as one of the men recognizes the body on the donkey as that of Captain Walker. Between these musical exclamation points, we hear appropriately repetitive connecting material "filling gaps" (Gorbman 73) and suturing the shots that move from soldier to soldier as they sit waiting for the mule to be unloaded, realizing, each in turn, who is on its back. It is not necessary—in fact it would be a redundant recapitulation of the previous discussion—to analyze each separate phrase and reiterate the illustrated affect or narrative action. But what is important here is the overall "musical design that evinces [...] expressions of emotion" (Elliott 199) accompanying the shots of Walker's body and of the men looking at it. In the previous sequence, the last one in which we see Walker alive, he is accompanied by a bombastic and rhythmic brass arrangement as he directs the charge on the monastery. Such instrumentation, says Katherine Kalinak, has "connotations of the military [and] are a classic convention for the heroic" (98): a style I refer to as "tarun-ta-raa music," an apt description for the film's main theme, first heard as the main title. But in sharp contrast to this musical representation of the living Walker is the lush string orchestration that illustrates the emotional response of Dondaro and the others as his lifeless body is laid beside other fallen soldiers. Such lush string arrangements are not unlike those identified by both Claudia Gorbman (80) and Katherine Kalinak (77) as conventionally representative of virtuous women. The significant point here is that it is not only the nurturing image that represents men at war released from, as mentioned above, their stoic, unemotional behavior towards each other. Musical conventions borrowed from representations of women (common in classical cinema melodrama) support this "feminization" of the soldier in his capacity to finally give way to his emotional response in the presence of suffering and death. It is as if (to re-purpose Gorbman's description of the "representation of Woman") "the emotional excess of this presence must find its outlet in the euphony of a string orchestra" (80).

Classical Scoring Practice and the Combat Film

This chapter has been an attempt to work through the scoring practices of classical Hollywood cinema as they pertain to a representative combat film made during the period when employing the conventions of such practice was at its peak. The intention is to situate a point of departure for comparison to determine if, and to what extent, scoring practice has taken other directions as the representations that it facilitates have themselves evolved over time.

The preceding analyses do indeed demonstrate that the score of *The Story of G.I. Joe* functions categorically according to traditional principles as identified by Claudia Gorbman and others (e.g., Adorno and Eisler, Brown, Chion, Cooper, Kalanak, Sabaneev) and that these principles are as essential a narrative apparatus for combat film as they are for melodrama. It is worth noting that I have chosen to use Gorbman's terminology (at least for the most part) in the interest of consistency. Her book *Unheard Melodies: Narrative Film Music* brought order to terminology that identified the various film music functions and thus offers a coherent system of reference. Nonetheless, it is worth keeping in mind that scoring principles are often identified differently by different writers. For example, the concept of *narrative cueing* as used by Gorbman is referred to by Cooper as *isomorphism*. Further, unlike Kalinak and Brown, Gorbman prefers the term *theme* over the term *leitmotif*, which she seems to avoid, and what she has called *melodic convention* and *connotation* are derided by Adorno and Eisler as *stock music* or *clichés*. For my own part, I find myself referring often to *musical metaphor* as a more specific variety of *narrative cueing*, though both can refer to essentially the same kinds of signification in practice.

It is also worth noting that some of these principles (regardless of what we choose to call them) are less significant with regard to representation of characters and the meaning we make from that representation than others. But such would be true for any genre; and the significance or prevalence of any given scoring principle will change from motion picture to motion picture as it will from composer to composer, director to director, and so on. For example, while they are indeed demonstrated throughout the film, the principles of "invisibility" and "inaudibility," are primarily structural. They function as an integral part of the apparatus meant to create the cinematic illusion — the apparatus concerned primarily with rendering the medium itself transparent — rather than as an agent affecting our response to the characters themselves. With this in mind, I have concentrated on examples of those principles that directly influence our readings of the protagonists Pyle and Walker — "narrative cueing," "signifier of emotion," and, to some degree "unity" and "continuity."

Regarding narrative cueing, Gorbman provides two sub categories:

— *referential/narrative:* music gives referential and narrative cues, e.g., indicating point of view, supplying formal demarcations, and establishing setting and characters.
— *connotative:* music "interprets" and "illustrates" narrative events [73].

The musical function in a number of the sequences discussed above fit the description of referential/narrative in its capacity to provide us with information about the characters and their point of view. To reiterate briefly, these include (but are not limited to) the camp sequence in which the "narrative's geographical and temporal setting" is indicated by the "cultural — ideological information" (Elliott 186) embedded in the diegetic Artie Shaw tune "Summit Ridge Drive." The score provides the men's subjectivity as they face the coming battle via the song "Linda," which becomes coded as a leitmotif, used to such advantage throughout the film to indicate longing for home — a clear example of Gorbman's description of "thematic association repeated and solidified during the course of the narrative, orchestration of music that was previously sung by or to the character" (83).

The main title is connotative — it contains an interpretative component in its function to provide the viewer an idea of what the narrative is based on. Connotative cueing is also indicated within every moment of the long sequence analyzed above during which Walker waits for Warnicki's return from his scouting mission, and subsequently reacts to Warnicki's breakdown. It "anchors the image in meaning" in its capacity to illustrate Walker's anguish as he waits and paces. It "imitate[s] and illustrate[s] physical events on the screen" (84) through its rhythmic paralleling of the fight sequence and its illustration of the painfully slow passage of time and of Warnicki's confused inner turmoil that finally causes his breakdown.

Music's function as a signifier of emotion is exemplified unequivocally in the sequence depicting the sadness, respect, and love Dondaro shows Walker after he has been killed. The slow violin solo and the lush string arrangement which gives way to a choir of voices are all clearly coded signifiers of affect.

Music works to create a sense of narrative unity (or cohesion) through repetition of thematic material over the course of the film as well as in specific sequences (e.g., in joining the separate shots of the men in their tents thus reinforcing the audience's understanding of the men's common bond). Finally, the continuity function serves not only to smooth the transition between scenes, but to indicate the narrative connection between them.

Battle Aftermath: Protagonist's Response

This reiteration of the various musical functions of Applebaum's score could go on, but the point is made: in each case the music is clearly within the functional domain of the scoring principles conventional to classical Hollywood movies. While the plot of *G.I. Joe* is not entirely typical in that it depicts a protracted struggle rather than an encapsulated one, the individual sequences themselves, as has been seen, do indeed follow familiar narrative patterns germane to many combat films. True to form, the final sequence, which provides insight into the struggle and kudos to the participants, is far from unusual. In it, Pyle's voice-over (in some combat films the voice-over is replaced or accompanied by rolling copy), which expresses sadness and reverence for those who have lost their lives as well as hope and encouragement with regard to the final inevitable victory, is accompanied by a return (another example of the scoring practice of unity) to the material first heard in the main title — both musical themes once again juxtaposed as if to reiterate the two simultaneous narrative themes that inform the film's ideology. This time, however, the performance is slower, more subdued and less brassy as if to represent the more jaded melancholy of the soldiers who are marching, if not into the sunset, at least toward the horizon, now seasoned by the price of inevitable victory — war's just as inevitable suffering and death.

II

The Vietnam Conflict Scored as a Conventional War Film: John Wayne Plays John Wayne in *The Green Berets*

I have noted that depictions of a given war usually take on the ideological cast of the times during which the depiction is released. With some exceptions, the preponderance of films released between 1941 and 1945 that laud, in one way or another, World War II — the "good war" waged by "the greatest generation" — generally ascribe just motives to the U.S. and its allies as well as heroic and honorable characteristics to the soldiers and officers who served them. Well over 100 American motion pictures were made about World War II during the years that the war was in progress, at least 32 of which were combat films (Basinger 281–294). The number rises dramatically if one adds World War II films released following the war, and despite the fact that Hollywood was approaching the end of its so-called Golden Age, and that film production in general had plunged markedly, the period has been referred to as the "golden age of the war film" (Cawley 74). Given the sheer number of these films both during and immediately following the war that contained positive representations of American soldiers, and given that these films are firmly situated within the conventional mechanisms of classical Hollywood storytelling, it follows that the scores used to facilitate the soldierly representations were themselves firmly coded by the end of the war, and that the codes, by and large, were meant to facilitate positive attitudes about the represented soldiers and the moral necessity of the war they fought. Thus, just as the "Virtuous Woman" and "the Fallen Woman" were usually accompanied by music with common identifiable characteristics — e.g., mellifluous string arrangements or sultry jazz saxophone, respectively (Gorbman 80, Kalinak 120–122) — so too, at least to some degree, were the "Heroic Soldier" and the

II. Vietnam Scored as Conventional War Film: *The Green Berets*

situations he found himself in also musically coded with common elements. As indicated in the previous chapter, these characteristics include densely orchestrated, brass-heavy narrative cues that often employed Mickey Mousing[1] to illustrate the heat of battle, and steady, firm and predictable march-like meters. That work-horse of Hollywood scoring practice the leitmotif was also common, though generally reserved for specific situations (e.g., battle, death, romance) rather than specific characters, unless those characters were women and fell into one of the categories identified above.

These musical codes did not disappear with World War II. Popular culture in general, and the Hollywood motion picture industry in particular are not known for re-inventing the wheel, and any narrative device that can be easily unpacked by the audience, thereby saving time, effort, and (most importantly) money, is endlessly recycled. Thus the musical codes of Hollywood combat films made conventional by motion pictures about the Second World War are also common in films depicting the Korean War and beyond (as indicated below), at least when the intent is to cast a positive light on the represented conflict. Indeed, common stylistic strategies[2] informing classical Hollywood scoring practice did not change very much until the American public's disillusionment with its heroes and the battles they engaged in began to find a place in popular cinema.

I have argued for the pivotal role of the Vietnam War as a primary factor in the devolution of the American soldierly myth in popular representations, and will show how this devolution affects musical representation in subsequent chapters. Here, it is important to note that the patterns of popular culture never change all at once, nor is there an absolutely distinct linear progression to the evolution of a film genre (as evidenced in the conventional scoring of such historical re-writes as the *Rambo* series). Indeed, change comes reluctantly to genre films, which is, of course, why it is usually a significant indication of a change in cultural climate or attitude; and despite the fact that it was released at precisely the time that popular support for the war in Vietnam began to plunge, *The Green Berets* (1968) maintains the Hollywood tradition and follows the path of traditional combat film storytelling.

The Narrative

Directed by Ray Kellogg and John Wayne, *The Green Berets* follows Col. Mike Kirby (John Wayne) through two adjacent though distinct narrative sections. In the first, Kirby fights to secure a recently established

American base in Vietnam, the security of which is plagued by frequent shelling from the Viet Cong—a demonized enemy that takes supplies and recruits from local Montagnard villages through a process of brutal intimidation. Their tactics include pillage, torture and rape; and, beyond his efforts to help secure the camp, Kirby also works to provide security for one of these indigenous groups by convincing them to take refuge inside the American camp.

George Beckworth (David Janssen) is a journalist for an American newspaper. During a stateside press conference in the opening sequence, Beckworth makes clear his skepticism regarding American involvement in Vietnam, and Kirby suggests that it is impossible to understand the American role without experiencing the situation first-hand. Beckworth accepts Kirby's implicit challenge and travels with him to the jungle camp to investigate and report on the American action in Southeast Asia.

In the narrative's second part, Kirby leads a group of Green Berets on a successful, covert mission to kidnap the enemy general Phan Son Ti (William Olds) with the help of Lin (Irene Tsu), a Vietnamese model who blames the general for the murder of her father and brother. She traps the general by agreeing to a tryst at a secluded chateau. While the general is in bed with Lin, a special operations unit led by Kirby overpowers the guards and takes the general prisoner. As they flee with their prize, Sgt. Petersen (Jim Hutton), a third protagonist, is killed by a booby trap.

The film ends on a military airfield, where we see Beckworth, now fully supportive of the American presence, marching in his new olive green fatigues, typewriter in hand, to "where the war is." The film's final sequence takes place on a beach where the airfield abuts the South China Sea. As the sun sets in the east, Kirby consoles Hamchunk (Craig Jue), a young Vietnamese orphan boy, about the death of his friend Sgt. Petersen, whom the boy had adopted as his surrogate father.

Score Overview

As noted earlier, until recently at least, Hollywood has generally been squeamish about producing movies critical of a war while that war is in progress. Thus, it is not surprising that *The Green Berets* (1968), the only narrative film about the Vietnam War released during the war, is an homage rather than an indictment. Additionally, the well-publicized political agenda of its director-star John Wayne is also undoubtedly a contributing

II. Vietnam Scored as Conventional War Film: *The Green Berets*

factor to the film's patriotic fervor. I make this observation neither to applaud or condemn, but to establish a point regarding the film's traditional approach to scoring practice as related to traditional thematic and narrative patterns common to the genre, and conventional roles within those patterns. With this in mind, I will argue that the score for *The Green Berets* is firmly situated within the tradition of classical Hollywood cinema. With a few exceptions the music functions well within the bounds of the seven principles of traditional scoring practice identified by Claudia Gorbman[3] in *Unheard Melodies: Narrative Film Music*. Once again, these principles systematize the most prevalent conventions of classical Hollywood film music.

One explanation for the score's conventional function is that composer Miklós Rózsa was himself a veteran of Hollywood's Golden age, that period falling roughly within the 1930s and 1940s, when, among other filmic conventions, those of traditional scoring practice were encoded (Gorbman 71). A chronologically-ordered tally of his over 100 film scores reveals that more than half were composed during this time; thus his stature and output during this period situate him as an important contributor to film scoring in the classical Hollywood style.

Regarding the character of the representations in *The Green Berets*, however, there are other pertinent reasons for the conventional musical treatment; and to understand these reasons, it is useful to understand something about why other models of scoring practice would be appropriate for other kinds of representations. While many contemporary films continue to employ the conventions of classical Hollywood scoring practice, in others these conventions are not obvious, not present, or are inappropriate. For example, I have made previous reference to Anahid Kassabian, who has noted that when representations of feminine roles depart from those conventionally coded during Hollywood's Golden Age (specifically the role of "good wife" or "fallen woman") classical cinematic scoring practice, coded to signify those conventional roles, is no longer meaningful (Kassabian 70–71). In other words, the coding, originally created to signify one thing, cannot now signify another without doing damage to the quality of the intended representation. In subsequent chapters we will see that the same can also be said for masculine representations; i.e., when an unconventional representation of a masculine role is present, so too is a non-traditional approach to scoring for that representation. The point is that in terms of its representation of the American war hero, *The Green Berets,* like the *Story of G.I. Joe,* exemplifies a standard against which such departures can be measured, and because the representation is clearly traditional as compared to films in which such representations were coded, the score itself is necessarily traditional.

The "Traditional" War Hero

As indicated previously, Ralph Donald provides a thumbnail description of the quintessential, cinematically-mediated soldier. He suggests that such representations are "essentially melodramatic portrayals of men performing virile, courageous deeds designed to protect helpless civilians from some sort of aggressor" (Donald 126). That the description is apropos of John Wayne's Col. Mike Kirby is beyond question, and regardless of whether one accepts the reductive popular soldierly myth of the American hero as described by Donald and others (e.g., Basinger 71), it is clear that the filmmakers position Col. Mike Kirby within that tradition. Whether scorning the paperwork associated with his new post in favor of putting himself in harms way in his eagerness to "take a look at those forward camps," or braving Viet Cong booby traps and ambushes to provide safety to Montagnard villagers, his representation embodies precisely those attributes to which Donald refers.

Again, given John Wayne's well-documented politics and his star-system coding, such cinematic representation is by no means surprising. To some extent it is John Wayne's star quality as "an actor whose screen persona overwhelmed (and thus determined) his individual roles" (Schatz 250) that contributes to the representation's traditional qualities. His position as the archetypal combat hero had already been firmly encoded by Wayne's Sgt. Stryker in *Sands of Iwo Jima* (Wills 156) and given his highly conventional portrayal of the myth of the American soldier, it is unthinkable that such a representation be accompanied by anything other than a traditional, conventionally-coded, composed score.

Col. Mike Kirby: For God, Country and Mom

The ideology from which this film proceeds, and which is, by extension, firmly attached to the protagonist Col. Mike Kirby, is unequivocally informed from the start by Barry Sadler and Robin Moore's chest-thumping "Ballad of the Green Berets" which accompanies the title sequence — film credits superimposed on a series of still photographs tinted green or orange. The melody of markedly regular and repeating eighth-note phrases is set to a military march tempo, thickly orchestrated for a predominantly brass band and sung by a male chorus, the sound of which is fattened by the unison vocal arrangement. The final attack of each eighth-note phrase is invariably separated from the beginning attack of the next by precisely three pulses, marked by the predominant thump of the bass drum. The cue also contains field drum and snare drum, instruments traditionally associated with military marching bands. Eight of the nineteen vocal lines (nearly half) contain the word *men*. Given the style, orchestration and the lyrics, then, the overall association with the spectacle of a patriotic parade is unmistakable, and the signification from the start is masculine, dominant, triumphal and patriotic.

Beyond the culturally-prescribed associations with military pageantry and its attending attributes of masculine power, camaraderie, loyalty, and patriotism, the structure of the song is also a metaphor for the structure of military life in general and, in his capacity as an embodiment of that structure, of the character of Mike Kirby in particular. The military's characteristic structure of regularity, predictability, adherence to strict, undeviating guidelines and discipline are comparable to analogous formal elements in the song, particularly the regularity in the design of its temporal and melodic phrasing, repeating orchestral figures, and, of course, the unwavering pulse provided by the drums. These formal elements function, then, not only as signifiers of ideology, but are illustrative of the narrative as well, specifically, of the military context within which the narrative unfolds. Such comparisons are not unusual in traditional film scoring practice. For example, in "Leitmotifs and Musical Reference in the Classical Film Score," Justin London comments similarly on musical representation for Mildred and Veda in *Mildred Pierce*: "One cannot resist commenting how the tonal stability or instability of each of these two themes is analogous to the constancy and steadfastness (or lack there of) of the characters to which they respectively refer" (93).

The lyrics of "Ballad of the Green Berets" reflect the formal elements and their attendant signification and make explicit the myth of the American soldier. According to the song, the Green Beret are honest, straight-talking and brave. They routinely win medals and are the unique few selected from the best of American manhood. They value family, honor their mothers, and willingly sacrifice their lives for their country.

The politics of the song, clearly associated with the film because of its position as main title, also become associated with Col. Mike Kirby, not only because he is the most recognizable figure in the opening stills, but also because of his position as the primary narrative agent. These ideological underpinnings are then reinforced by the sequence immediately following the main title, a press conference at the John F. Kennedy Center for Special Forces at Fort Bragg, North Carolina. As the conference begins, the group of Green Berets designated to answer questions march to their places before a panel of reporters and onlookers, and the song ends abruptly. This first performance stops significantly on the line "Men who mean just what they say." It is important to underscore that this line, which occurs mid-verse, is not a natural stopping point. Rather than fade out, the music and vocal halt abruptly, and there is no reduction in volume leading up to the ending. Normally, any number of formal mechanisms would be employed to maintain what Gorbman refers to as the principle of inaudibility, which suggests that the viewer should not be entirely conscious of non-diegetic music (73). These mechanisms include a gradual decrescendo or attempts to distract the audience by ending the song on an action (e.g. an abrupt movement, a slamming door, an explosion, etc.). The principle of inaudibility is linked to the overall processes of continuity editing, a convention of classical Hollywood style, which works to make the specific mechanisms of classical cinema transparent, and that the rule is broken here — that there is no attempt to make the cue's end inaudible as is usually the case with traditional Hollywood film music — immediately foregrounds the music and specifically the line itself, which hangs prominently in the air because of the sonic vacuum created by the abrupt ending. Regarding my intention to demonstrate the score of *The Green Berets* as consistent with traditional scoring practice, I should note that Gorbman's principles allow for violation if the violation is "at the service of the other principles" (73). And indeed, such is the case here.

The line "Men who mean just what they say" is a particularly pertinent way of characterizing the marines participating in the press conference, and as American involvement in Vietnam is handily defended by their responses to the reporters' questions, Kirby looks on approvingly. Thus his own ideology is situated firmly, once again, via the mechanism of the title song, which makes salient the pertinent line and reflects Kirby's blunt, no-nonsense honesty.

A Man Without a Theme

I have argued that this narrative represents Mike Kirby as the traditional war hero and that the main title contributes significantly to that coding. Beyond this, however, there is little in the way of musical signifi-

II. Vietnam Scored as Conventional War Film: *The Green Berets*

cation which refers specifically to Kirby. I have discussed the function of the leitmotif in a previous chapter; nonetheless, it is helpful to revisit that discussion here as well as some other points made earlier. Often, traditional scoring practice assigns the protagonist his or her own theme that recurs throughout the narrative and facilitates the viewing subject's reading of whatever emotional or ideational associations are appropriate for the accompanied narrative situation. Such recurring themes are called, once again, *leitmotifs* "after Richard Wagner's elaborate use of a similar system of musical tokens in his operas" (London 85), and are discussed here defined as "a musical phrase, either as complex as a melody or as simple as a few notes, which, through repetition, becomes identified with a character, situation or idea" (Kalinak 63). I am not suggesting that all protagonists at all times in all situations are assigned a leitmotif. However, the extent to which such devices are used in classical film music — according to Michael Chion, following its inception, the principle "would subsequently dominate nine out of ten film scores" (51) — makes the fact that Kirby does not receive such signification noteworthy. Noteworthy, too, is that while the representation of the protagonist in this film is not facilitated thus, other, less important characters in the film (e.g., Petersen, Hamchunk, the Montagnard chief's daughter) are. According to Leonard Meyer in *Style and Music*, "Works of art are understood and appreciated not only in terms of what actually occurs, but in terms of *what might have happened* given the constraints of the style and the particular context in which the choice was made" (6). If what Meyer suggests is true, our understanding of musical function in Kirby's representation can be facilitated by asking why "what might have happened" did not.

To address the question I would like to return a previous point. I have noted Anahid Kassabian's assertion that when representations of feminine roles depart from those conventionally coded during Hollywood's Golden Age (i.e., the good wife and the fallen woman) classical cinematic scoring practice, coded to signify those conventional roles, is no longer appropriate. One solution Kassabian discusses is the compiled score — scores comprised of pre-existing, often popular music in place of the more traditional score composed specifically for a particular sequence in a particular film (Kassabian 61). The strategy in such cases (beyond creating a more marketable soundtrack) is to call upon associations an audience has previously formed with preexisting music to create "paths of identification," thereby allowing the subject wider (and more flexible) understanding of a given character than would be possible using the more narrowly constrained significations available within the codes of classical scoring practices. A key concept for Kassabian is the interpretative variety or flexibility the compiled score offers, based upon the variety of associations with a musical selection a varied audience might bring to the film. To expand upon this idea, we can say that Kassabian is in effect suggesting that the more unfamiliar an audience is with a particular representation the more crucial flexible musical signification becomes to that representation, thus allowing a diverse audience a means of identifying with that representation. If such is the case, then the reverse must also be true; i.e., the more traditional or familiar a representation, the less flexible (or the more conventional) a score should be. To expand on this idea even further, I would argue that given a *very* familiar representation, no specific musical interpretation is necessary simply because no further clarification is needed. Similarly, Claudia Gorbman has suggested that a key role of film music is to "ward off the displeasure of uncertain signification" (58). Thus, to turn this around, we might say that where the signification is certain, the musical reference can become less direct because there is no "displeasure" to "ward off."

Recalling my previous argument positioning John Wayne's Col. Mike Kirby firmly within traditional representations of the American war hero, I would suggest that he does not require specific musical signification precisely because "in the context of debates around masculinity [he] provides perhaps the most longstanding and oft-cited example, a figure whose meaning seems absolutely fixed" (Tasker 234). Thus, his signification is certain without musical clarification. This is so based not only upon the character he plays in this and other films, but also based upon his coding within the Hollywood star system. The certainty of Wayne's representation is well documented. He is "more than a character in this or that film; he is, even dead, an evolving idea of a hero (Kolker 79). Indeed, according to Garry Wills's *John Wayne's America*, Wayne has been seen consistently as the symbol of "American manhood" (Wills 30). Of his representation of the American soldierly myth, Wills writes: "Though Wayne never served in the military, General Douglas MacArthur thought he was the model of an American soldier, the Veterans of Foreign Wars gave him their gold medal, and the Marines gave him their 'Iron Mike' award" (12).

In her discussion of music as a signifier of emotion, Claudia Gorbman identifies the places within the diegesis where music is and is not most appropriate as an aid to the narrative — what Michael Chion would call "added value" (5). Her discussion speaks directly to the question at hand regarding why Kirby is not represented with his own theme. Music, according to Gorbman and others (e.g., Elliott, Juslin, Kassabian, Kalanak, Meyer, Sloboda, to name just a few) functions effectively as a signifier of emotion, and as such, belongs to the realm of the irrational. She points to a series of polarities, differentiated according to whether or not they belong to the realm of music. Because they are germane to this discussion, I include them here.

As a general signifier of emotion, Gorbman suggests the following (the left column belongs to the non-musical realm):

Logic	The Irrational
Everyday Reality	Dream
Control	Loss of Control

In her discussion of music as a specific representation of Woman, she provides the following (again, the left column belongs to the non-musical realm):

Man	Woman
Objectivity	Subjectivity
Work	Leisure
Reason	Emotion
Realism	Romantic Fantasy [Gorbman 79–81].

While I do not mean to suggest that men are never represented musically (such is clearly not the case) I am suggesting that in all respects, John Wayne's hegemonic representation of the traditional war hero lines up tidily on the left—those elements to which musical representation does not necessarily lend itself.

Characterizing Wayne's Mike Kirby as a representation of hegemonic masculinity—as a "compound idea of what American manhood is in the minds of the vast majority of Americans" (Wills 30)—suggests another approach to explaining how this protagonist aligns with Gorbman's left-hand, non-music column. Hegemonic masculinity is a socially constructed ideal enabling a certain class of men to maintain dominance over women and other kinds of masculinities (e.g., non-white, homosexual, working class). Such masculinities tend to defy specific characterization because hegemony is fluid, necessarily changing over time as the groups it seeks to dominate themselves change. Nonetheless, it is universal to the concept that whatever form hegemony takes to maintain dominance, its characteristics are mediated as "normal," "natural," and "commonsensical" (rather than constructed), and that the characteristics are embedded in, and disseminated through, various mediated contexts, including, of course, cinema (MacKinnon 9–10). Thus, the "naturalness" of the heroic characteristics of Mike Kirby line up tidily alongside Gorbman's non-musical column. That we are expected to understand Kirby as a "normal" representation of the model American hero makes extensive use of signification via musical function superfluous.

But despite the dearth of dedicated musical signification for Kirby, it would be a mistake to suggest that he — or more specifically what he does — is not represented or facilitated musically in more general ways. As I have already noted, Miklós Rózsa's score contributes to the narrative using traditional scoring principles. Because he is an active narrative agent, this narrative cueing represents Mike Kirby by extension as he drives the narrative overall. It is therefore appropriate to look at significant examples of this narrative cueing in sequences within which Kirby's role is significant.

Kirby and the Correspondent

Particularly revealing components regarding the representation of war film protagonists are those that indicate the protagonists' motives for participation in the depicted war and their attitude toward that participation. Such components regarding Col. Mike Kirby emerge from sequences depicting his interactions with journalist George Beckworth. They reveal Kirby's unwavering devotion to the American presence, the experience upon which that devotion is based, and the persuasive power of that experience with regard to Beckworth's own change in perspective regarding the war.

The sequence introducing Beckworth outlines the opposition between two war-time ideologies — Beckworth's, inclined against American involvement in Southeast Asia; and Kirby's, convinced of the necessity for continued involvement. The sequence, which immediately follows the opening credits, is a press conference at which Beckworth reveals his bias against the American presence and suggests that the conflict should be left exclusively up to the Vietnamese people. I have argued above that the main title unequivocally situates both the film and Kirby's place in it as pro-involvement, and that the manner in which the main title ends (on the line "Men who mean just what they say") points to characteristics of the panel of marines being interviewed, and, by extension (as he looks approvingly on) to Kirby's character as well. Paradoxically, the main title and the salient line are also pertinent to George Beckworth's representation. Note that he is introduced almost immediately following the line, and is the first to ask a confrontational question regarding American involvement. The musical and dialogical representation, then, suggest that he too is a man who means what he says. Given that both men are characterized thus by the main

II. Vietnam Scored as Conventional War Film: *The Green Berets*

title, and that their opposition is clearly established at the outset, the audience is immediately aware that their interaction will be key in revealing the overall argument of the film; and whatever the outcome of the ideological struggle, both participants (who "mean what they say") act from this position of credibility established by the score.

The next pertinent sequence takes place at the American outpost camp in Vietnam. It reveals the men's oppositional attitudes within a more specific context. A Viet Cong infiltrator has been discovered, and Beckworth, having witnessed the interrogation process, complains bitterly to Kirby, accusing him of sanctioning an "inquisition." Although we do not witness the interrogation — the display of harsh treatment of prisoners was prohibited by the Defense Department in return for their cooperation in making the film (Wills 232) — we can assume from Beckworth's response, and from the shot leading up to the interrogation, that physical coercion was used. The exchange occurs when Beckworth exits the building in which the interrogation took place and finds Kirby standing outside:

> BECKWORTH: Is that what you do? Sponsor an inquisition over here?
> KIRBY: Is that what you're gonna tell the people?
> BECKWORTH: I'm gonna tell the people the facts — the facts of what I saw in there.
> KIRBY: That was nothing.
> BECKWORTH: I don't call brutality nothing.
> KIRBY: That man was lining us up for a V.C. mortar crew.
> BECKWORTH: There's still such a thing as due process.
> KIRBY: Out here, due process is a bullet.

At this point, Kirby tosses a cigarette lighter found on the infiltrator to Beckworth. It is engraved with the name of a medical specialist who was decapitated and mutilated while returning to camp after having delivered a Montagnard baby. When Beckworth begins to press his point about brutality, Kirby cuts him off: "Tell it to Captain Coleman," he says, "but you better shout it loud because Arlington Cemetery is a long way from here."

The exchange reveals Kirby justifying the "brutality" based upon the infiltrator's actions, and although the sequence is not scored, it is, nonetheless, tightly bracketed by music which functions connotatively as narrative cueing. Thus the cue that surrounds the sequence prepares viewers for the exchange and comments upon it when it is done: "express[ing] moods and connotations which, in conjunction with the images and other sounds, aid in interpreting narrative events and indicating moral/class/ethnic values of characters" (Gorbman 84).

The formal, syntactic elements of the musical cue immediately preceding this sequence anticipate its narrative significance by building suspense via sequential repetition of a brief motive[4] at ascending intervals, a technique commonly used to build suspense and to prepare the viewer for an emotional or climactic moment: "Sequential progressions — each restatement of a motive beginning a step or a third higher than the last — build tension incessantly and relentlessly" (Gorbman 77). Most interesting in this case is not the interval by which the motif ascends, but the intervallic relationship created between the voices. Each statement of the motif is answered in the other voice at a pitch which creates either the tri-tone or the minor ninth. In this case, then, the motif's signification of suspense via repetition is further intensified because the motif is repeated at intervals conventionally considered particularly unstable and dissonant in diatonic Western harmony: the augmented fourth (or tri-tone) and the minor ninth. This tonal instability creates an aural tension paralleling the ideological tension that informs the representation of the two protagonists, and just as these musical constructions seek resolution and initially find none, the same can be said of Kirby and Beckworth. Music's capacity to function metaphorically as discussed above, i.e., via syntactical or formal properties which can, through the use of imagination, create "fictional worlds," has been explored by Kendall Walton. He argues that within a listener's imagination, musical structures can assume the role of characters or plot elements (63–65). This is precisely the case here in that the music, in addition to underscoring the tension leading up to the interrogation, structurally parallels the resulting conflict between the two men. To clarify the point, I am suggesting here that the unresolved tension between Beckworth and Kirby is mirrored by an analogous musical tension created by our aural expectations.

A further (though perhaps more subtle) example of this function is created by the intervallic relationship (the space between one note and another) between the lowest and highest notes within these repeating motifs. The first time we hear the motif, for example, the lowest and highest notes create a perfect 4th. But when the motif is "answered" by the bass voice, the interval between these notes is an augmented 4th, that is, the motif's high point is one-half step higher the second time we hear it. In other words, the motif's construction fluctuates between a perfect fourth and an augmented fourth. If the listener were a musician with very good ears, he or she may hear this subtle change clearly. Chances are, however, for most listeners, such a change would not be obvious, but the listener would, nonetheless, respond to the tension created by the ambiguity in the same way that they might respond to, say, singing "Row, Row, Row Your Boat" in rounds and having one of the singers hit a slightly wrong note every time they sang the first *merrily*. The deviation occurs more than once during the cue and, again, this fluctuation sets up its own ambiguity and instability. Because the intervallic relationships in the repeating motifs are neither exactly similar nor clearly different, our reading of the melodic material is frustrated by that ambiguity. By way of explanation, we can borrow from Gestalt theory as it applies to visual semiotics. For example, Donis Dondis suggests that "Visual ambiguity, like verbal ambiguity, obscures not only compositional intent, but also meaning. [...] The Gestalt law of perceptual simplicity is greatly frustrated by such an unclear state of difference [...]" (28). Here again, the music becomes a metaphor for the ideological clash — the aural ambiguity created by the *almost-but-not-quite* similar intervallic relationship is associated with the unresolved ethical issue of the interrogation methods sanctioned by the Americans, and the representation of these two protagonists at loggerheads is thereby facilitated.

After Kirby gets the last word and stalks off leaving Beckworth to contemplate the significance of the engraved lighter, the motif returns briefly, sounds firmly and summarily, and ends on a clear point of rest (where before it had simply faded out) as if to punctuate Kirby's words. In this way, the score places a musical period, so to speak, after Kirby's angry reference to Arlington.

To summarize the narrative function of the score in this sequence: As the narrative sets the confrontation in motion, the music reinforces the tension and illustrates the unresolved differences. Once Kirby ends the discussion by turning his back on Beckworth and stalking off, however, the ultimate resolution of the musical material that closes the sequence leaves no doubt about the bias of the film (and that of its actor/director). Beckworth is left holding the lighter, evidence of VC brutality, and the finality of Kirby's words are underscored by the finality of the music.

Beckworth's Conversion

Beckworth reverses his opposition to the war in a key sequence during which he discovers the body of a murdered Montagnard child. He had become emotionally attached to the child during a previous encounter when the camp medic treated a foot wound she had received from a punji stick (a Viet Cong booby trap). The village chieftain, the child's grandfather, brought her to the camp for medical attention. During that encounter, the child receives her own leitmotif, a pentatonic[5], faux-Asian melody scored for electric sitar and G alto flute (Wrobel 24), which enters precisely on a cut to the child as Beckworth kneels to examine her foot. Although the theme is clearly the child's (coded as such by its "Asian" modality and instrumentation), it is important to note that it only sounds when Beckworth is present, usually when he interacts directly with her, e.g., when he talks to her, gives her an amulet she sees him wearing, or carries her from her grandfather's arms to a litter for their return to the village. Consequently, the theme does more than just represent the child — it is baptized as a "Beckworth-caring-for-the-child" leitmotif. In this capacity, when its characteristics change (as discussed below) it represents both what has happened to the girl as well as Beckworth's emotional response.

On the day following their initial interaction, the soldiers arrive in the child's village to escort the villagers to the safety of the military camp. They discover, however, that the Viet Cong have ravaged the village and killed the chief. Beckworth asks after the little girl and learns that she was taken to the jungle by five Viet Cong soldiers, who did not bring her back. When he and the doctor find her dead in the brush and the doctor returns Beckworth's amulet, her theme enters; and again, the formal elements are changed to parallel the narrative. The melody is now scored for woodwind and electric sitar and is markedly slower than the first time we heard it during the sequence in the American camp. The darker reedy sound of the woodwind and the slower tempo imbue the visual with a grim, plaintive atmosphere as compared to the previous performance, which created the opposite effect. Most importantly, however, the salient characteristic in facilitating the atmosphere, and thus Beckworth's response to it, is the ambiguous and unusual modality. While the melody retains the same shape[6] as its previous pentatonic performance, the mode on which the melody is built creates an ambiguous key center. The accidentals suggest E-flat Aeolian (or natural minor), but the melody of the first eight bars seem to suggest the Locrian mode,[7] a rarely used, unstable, dark-sounding tonality. The bass pedal sets up a drone of non-descript pitch, thus it does not anchor the woodwind melody to a specific key center. A characteristic of the Locrian mode is that the tonic (the note named for the "home" key on which the melody would normally find rest or resolution) is particularly unstable because the Locrian scale is built on the seventh degree[8] of the major scale, and is therefore subject to a constant "pull" from its second degree (the structural root of the far more familiar major scale). In simpler terms, the melody is constructed so that it insists on coming to rest in one place while our ear wants it to rest elsewhere (because repeated exposure to the musical relationships within the major scale has conditioned us to expect that the melody "should" rest on a particular note). Such ambiguity is unsettling, because our aural expectations are not met. Even if one discounts the Locrian "reading" here, the passage remains disturbing because of the ambiguity created by the drone (a low rumble, which is felt more than it is actually heard). Regardless of how one "hears" it, this harmonic and melodic ambivalence parallels Beckworth's own mixed feelings as he faces the "reality" of the Viet Cong's brutality and is thereby led to reexamine the ideology that informs his opposition to the war. In this way, the signification of the recast motif not only points to the sadness of a single murder and the loss of an innocent child, but to the deeper conflict taking place in Beckworth. In other words, the musical dissonance mirrors the cognitive dissonance Beckworth is experiencing because his previous bias against the war is now at odds with his emotional response to what the enemy has done to the child, by whom he had been profoundly moved. The cognitive dissonance is resolved by his decision to embrace the American struggle rather than oppose it; and again, the score is constructed to inform the narrative.

Significantly, as soon as the doctor carries the girl away and Kirby enters, the musical ambivalence disappears. The drone is replaced by conventional (and therefore no longer "foreign") tertian[9] harmonic voicings and diatonic counterpoint; consequently, the melodic centers sound stable and the musical form in general sounds more familiar. Too, the "exotic" instruments (e.g., the sitar) are replaced by a string section thus situating Kirby's presence as representative of Western ideals. Just as Kirby represents the same resolve that Beckworth is moved to embrace, so too does the music resolve the ambiguity within its own structure upon his entrance. If Kirby is nothing else, he is, like the music that accompanies his entrance, predictably unambiguous. His response to Beckworth's feelings drives home the point of the enemy's depravity with an unspoken and sympathetic "I told you so." The exchange reaffirms Kirby's support for the war and is perhaps the final straw sealing Beckworth's conversion to his way of thinking. Kirby says:

> It's pretty hard to talk to anybody about this country until they've come over here and seen it. The last village that I visited, they didn't kill the chief. They tied him to a tree and brought his teenage daughters out in front of him and disemboweled them. Then 40 of them abused his wife. And then they took a steel rod — broke every bone in her body. Somewhere during the process she died.

Beckworth, convinced now that American engagement is necessary and just, refuses Kirby's offer of a ride back to (we assume) Da Nang. "I'm staying," he says, indicating his desire to participate in what he had, until now, criticized. Thus the opposition between the men is over, and the hard-edged cynicism Beckworth had harbored toward American involvement has been abrogated by his feeling for the child, by his anger and sadness about what has been done to her, as indicated by the presence of the girl's theme — the "Beckworth-caring-for-the-child" leitmotif.

The scores for the three sequences discussed above reveal Kirby's pronounced characteristic of unwavering conviction in the struggle against the Viet Cong. Beckworth's role in revealing this conviction is the contrast his character provides, i.e., his ideological shift as compared to Kirby's ideological stasis. Both men "mean what they say," and there is no reason to doubt that Beckworth's initial bias against the war is any less rooted than is Kirby's opposite bias. Consequently, Beckworth's conversion reinforces both the argument of the film as well as the representation of Kirby as a man of intractable values.

The motivating force for both men (and this will become even clearer for Kirby later in this chapter) is their philanthropy toward an oppressed people, a theme which becomes the central argument of the film. One could suggest an interesting paradox, then, with regard to both representations — that on the one hand, Kirby and Beckworth are represented within the context of traditional, aggressive and violent masculinity (MacKinnon 11–13): Kirby by his unflinching support of the brutal treatment of a demonized enemy and Beckworth by his determination to oppose that brutality. On the other hand, they are motivated by a tendency toward nurturing — a tendency, interestingly enough, historically attributed to the realm of femininity (MacKinnon 10).

Kirby and Beckworth in Combat

The central combat sequence in *The Green Berets* depicts a long anticipated Viet Cong attack on the American camp. Petersen has told Beckworth that if the camp is overrun, the Viet Cong will kill everyone, including women and children, thus further demonizing the enemy. Night falls. The Viet Cong approach. The camp prepares for attack. The feeling of tension is increased by the juxtaposition of two musical cues. As we see the Viet Cong approach through the darkness, their theme indicates their presence via conventional Hollywood coding using Asian and Western instruments playing a melody in a minor mode, a Hollywood scoring convention that "means" exotic. When we cut to the inside of the camp and view the soldiers taking positions along the walls, we hear an appropriately ascending musical motif performed by conventional orchestral instruments accompanying the shots of the dark fortifications. Such ascending material, as discussed previously, is often used to build tension (Gorbman 77). We crosscut to Kirby in his chopper returning from Da Nang, where he had delivered Montagnard villagers wounded in the Viet Cong assault on their village. The chopper is shot down. Kirby is rescued by an American platoon. He takes charge of his rescuers and they secure a landing zone to be used by the special operations Mike Force on its way to help defend the camp. Meanwhile, back at the camp, the battle is by now well underway.

A significant event in this protracted sequence occurs when noncombatant Beckworth joins the battle. Although the score does not accompany Beckworth's decision to do so, it has nonetheless played a significant part in representing his ideological movement from opposition to support. It is important to note his final step from reluctant sympathizer to committed participant because of how that movement informs Kirby's representation.

In this sequence, Beckworth is led to a pit for safety when the shelling begins. Petersen and another soldier are operating a rocket launcher from the pit. When they kill a group of approaching Viet Cong soldiers, Petersen turns to Beckworth and says: "That's what it's all about Mr. Beckworth. You gonna stand there and referee or are you gonna help us?" "What can I do?" Beckworth asks, and, at Petersen's suggestion, begins feeding the men ammunition.

Significant here is that Beckworth has repositioned himself from active critic to active participant, and again, the reversal is a powerful testament to Kirby's unwavering, single-minded dedication to the American effort. Given his personal skepticism as well as the pressure brought to bear by the liberal bias of the newspaper he works for, Beckworth's conversion confirms Kirby's commitment and furthers the ideology that informs the film. Kirby's position has been that once Beckworth understands the situation first-hand, his opposition will dissolve. Thus the ideological "rebirth" represented by Beckworth's conversion lends much currency to Kirby's position. So too, interestingly, does the somewhat more subtle change in Peterson's approach to his military involvement as demonstrated by the fervor with which he eventually engages the enemy.

Petersen's movement from his preoccupation with securing his own comfort to his dedication to the war effort is important to note for its reflection on Beckworth and Kirby. Its reflection on Kirby is much the same as is Beckworth's; that is, in its capacity to lend credibility to Kirby's steadfast, unwavering dedication to a cause. Its reflection on Beckworth is two-fold. First, it is Petersen's invitation that instigates Beckworth's final step to participation; and second, Petersen's conversion echoes Beckworth's in that each man becomes dedicated to the war because of a paternal bond formed with a Vietnamese child. To understand Petersen's conversion it is necessary to consider our initial introduction to him.

Petersen: Before and After

Unlike Beckworth, Petersen does not oppose the war; he just tries to ignore it. Until well into the film, he is represented as a figure of fun, a light-fingered con man dedicated to not letting his duties interfere with his creature comforts. We see him first as he is caught pilfering supplies from Kirby's outfit to deliver to his own. As Kirby, Sgt. Muldoon (Aldo Ray) and others watch from Kirby's office window, Petersen loads the back of his jeep with various items lifted from a supply shed. A cartoon-like, comic musical cue accompanies his actions. The melody is scored for oboe, two clarinets, and xylophone — instrumentation that often introduces comic characters (Gorbman 82). Positioned by the shot-reverse shot construction, the audience shares Kirby's bemused response to Petersen's activity, a response primarily informed by the cartoon music. Kirby has been interviewing and selecting soldiers to join his company for the Vietnam mission. We learn from the dialog that Kirby admires Petersen's tenacity and would like to recruit him. As they watch from the window, Sgt. Muldoon expresses reservations:

SGT. MULDOON: Are you sure about this soldier?
COL. KIRBY: What do you mean?
SGT. MULDOON: Well, I checked his jump record, and every time he goes up the jumpmaster has to push him out.
COL. KIRBY: That's why I want him. He won't quit.

In the next sequence, Kirby leverages Petersen to "volunteer" by threatening to bring charges against him based upon his pilfering. He promotes him to sergeant and orders him to "steal back" everything he has taken. Petersen's unhappiness with his new assignment, and his subsequent elation at realizing he has been promoted, is accompanied by the same comic motif that accompanied his pilfering; and again, we see him as a likeable though less than serious character.

In a sequence that occurs after Kirby's outfit has reached the American

II. Vietnam Scored as Conventional War Film: *The Green Berets* 61

camp in Vietnam, Petersen walks into a practical joke set by the Vietnamese orphan boy Hamchunk (for whom he becomes a surrogate father) when he falls over Hamchunk's tripwire (foreshadowing the Viet Cong booby-trap that ultimately kills him). "Ha ha, you funny," exclaims the delighted boy pointing at Petersen. Here again, Petersen's actions are accompanied by a cartoon-like woodwind melody.

In at least two more sequences, Petersen is represented in this light vein. One, in which he airlifts a pallet of roofing tin from beneath the nose of a pompous officer at a nearby naval base, and another in which Muldoon comments incredulously on Petersen's plush living quarters (to which Petersen replies significantly, "I'm not a marine; I believe in my comfort"). Each sequence is accompanied by some variation on the comic cue which we might call the "Petersen-as-comic-relief" leitmotif. The point is that this is a very different man than the one who tells Beckworth that the fighting is "what it's all about" and the one who ultimately dies in the end of the film because he has volunteered to "take the point" despite having been assigned to bring up the rear.

Once Petersen loses his obsession with his creature comforts, he is no longer represented with specific musical signification. This omission recalls the previous argument regarding the acceptance of "normal" masculinity without the need for the further explication that music can provide. Once the man who had previously decorated his quarters with curtains, throw rugs, and a bright red rocking chair becomes an aggressive soldier, he no longer belongs to Gorbman's right-hand column of musical signification. The disappearance of the comic motif normalizes Petersen's masculinity as rational and thus the emotionally descriptive function of music would be superfluous.

Kirby's insight into the characters of Petersen and Beckworth reflects significantly on his representation. He understood that once the men experienced Vietnam as he has, both would become important converts: Petersen as a dogged military asset, and Beckworth as a bridge to the skeptical stateside civilians, made particularly credible by his conversion. This knowledge leads him to allow Beckworth to accompany him to the outlying American camp and to manipulate Petersen into his unit. Thus Kirby's belief in the American effort — his unwavering and aggressive pursuit of his cause — is reflected in and validated by the conversion.

Throughout the combat sequence Kirby demonstrates his unwavering control at all times — barking orders, evacuating Montagnard refugees and leading troops to safety when the camp is inevitably overrun by the Viet Cong. Although, once again, Kirby does not have a dedicated musical theme, the situations within which he moves or to which he responds are nonetheless illustrated by the score, demonstrating that its function remains situated within the context of classical scoring practice. And again, if the score does not represent Kirby specifically, it nonetheless represents the situations within which he reacts, and, by extension, his character is revealed through musical signification. A representative example of such function is contained in the sequence during which Kirby's chopper is downed as he returns from Da Nang. The score works to illustrate and anchor the image — what Gorbman has termed "connotative cueing" (84), a classical scoring approach already discussed at some length in the previous chapter. Its presence here, then, provides an example of the same approach working within a newer film.

A loud and dissonant brass stinger[10] sounds when the chopper is hit. The stinger is followed by a high, dissonant, descending chromatic passage played by flutes and strings which culminates in a cacophonous brassy blast (another stinger) as the chopper hits the ground and explodes into flame. The dissonant chords and the shape of the chromatic melody are a clear example of "Mickey Mousing."[11] The descending chromatic line illustrates the downward spiral of the chopper and the opening and closing stingers illustrate the explosions. In addition to this illustrative function, the subjectivity of the characters and the confusion and fear they experience as they plummet downward is illustrated by the melodic and harmonic dissonance.

During the rest of the sequence, the score parallels the narrative and provides rhythmic support to the rapid editing. The pilot's terrible death (we see him stumble from the chopper engulfed in flame) is illustrated by a tortured melodic phrase distorted by an over-blown trumpet. Illustrating sequences of parallel editing, which move the viewer from the threatening Viet Cong platoon to the American forces and reveal shots of Kirby, the chopper crash survivors, and MIKE Force, are musical cues coded for each side during the sequence leading up to the attack on the base. Within this musical and visual cacophony, despite the downed chopper, the burning pilot and the approaching Viet Cong troops, Kirby remains in charge. He takes command of MIKE Force. They capture a landing zone and then return to the camp to evacuate the refugees and to rally the troops. Because the music is confined to illustrating events and is not coded to represent Kirby himself, it never suggests inner turmoil or indecision on Kirby's part; thus, while it works to illustrate the fog of war, Kirby remains separate from its signification, and it therefore works to confirm his cool-headed competence within the midst of the confusion it signifies.

Kirby's Response to Fallen Comrades

A convention of the combat film genre's narrative pattern are sequences depicting soldiers giving solace to dying comrades. Such sequences can function significantly in representing characters. A particularly salient example in *The Green Berets* occurs between Sgt. Provo (Luke Askew) and Col. Kirby. Provo has requested Kirby's presence and, in a clichéd masculine bonding ritual common to a number of classical combat films, asks him to "take a touch" of bourbon with him. When Kirby asks the doctor why Provo had not been "put on a chopper" Provo responds "the wounded go before the dead, sir." It is clear, then, to Provo, the doctor, and Kirby, that Provo does not have long to live. "They zapped me good, sir," he says with a labored chuckle.

Earlier in the film, Provo remarks upon the various military facilities that bear the names of fallen soldiers and expresses the desire to be similarly memorialized. At the time, though, he was undecided about the kind of building that should bear his name. Here, he whispers to Kirby his choice, and we learn in the next sequence that he has requested that a latrine bear the name "Provo's Privy" because "it sings."

Of such sequences, Ralph Donald makes a number of pertinent observations, which are borne out by this one. Donald suggests that it is considered un-soldierly (and of course un-manly) to be consumed by grief for a dead friend, to allow such grief to interfere with the performance of one's duties, or to give in to fear for one's own life. One way a soldier's fears of death are assuaged is through the promise of immortality (132–133). Donald also notes that in the presence of death, certain conventions that customarily mark men's relationships — conventions meant to disavow the suggestion of homosexual attraction — can be dispensed with. Behavior demonstrative of love and tenderness becomes acceptable (134); and only in the presence of death is "a man allowed to cradle another man in his arms." In this sequence, grief and immortality are, respectively, disavowed and assured by the joke of Provo's memorial. And regardless of whether or not one chooses to accept Easthope's assertion that "War's suffering is a kind of punishment for the release of homosexual desire and male femininity that only war allows," (Easthope qtd. in Donald 134) this sequence, during which Kirby cradles Provo's head, speaks tenderly to him, and promises to honor his final request nonetheless "feminizes" the men in significant ways; and, as we shall see, the score plays a significant part in this feminization.

To further understand the function of the score in this context, and to expand upon a previous point, it will be helpful to point to Stephen Cohen's discussion of male feminization. Calling upon Kaja Silverman's psychoanalytic definition of "conventional masculinity," as well as anthropologist Françoise Héritier-Augé's accounts of sexual difference according to various tribal myths, Cohen makes the point that in defining masculinity as an opposition to all things feminine, the hard, armor-like male body "with no orifices to make it vulnerable to penetration" becomes a particularly significant symbol as does the "control of blood as a means of maintaining the illusion of bodily wholeness" (Cohen 104–105). Once that "armor" has been pierced on the battlefield, and once the soldier consequently loses control of his own bleeding, he becomes penetrable, passive and dependent — precisely the characteristics Laura Mulvey and others after her have ascribed to feminine roles in classical Hollywood cinema. I would suggest that this role reversal, this feminization, is commiserate with the musical characteristics that accompany the sequence.

This study has pointed often to Claudia Gorbman's discussion of musical signification for "Woman as romantic Good Object" (80). What is interesting here is that the musical characteristics identified by Gorbman as belonging to this variety of feminine representation now facilitate the representation of the dying male soldier who has been "feminized" in terms explored by the previous discussion — his body penetrated and his bleeding uncontrolled. Rózsa's military theme, which has accompanied the men as they perform routine duties or march toward battle, is recast here in a performance that takes on many characteristics Gorbman has identified as signifying such femininity (80). What was previously a medium to fast bombastic piece scored primarily for brass, is now gentle and plaintive, performed at approximately half the original tempo. The scoring contains the lush harmonies Gorbman has identified as signifying the "emotional excess of this [female] presence" (80) and the melodic material, previously scored primarily for brass instruments, is now stated by the string section. The point, of course, is that the "feminizing" behavior and the presence of the "bleeding wound" (Mulvey 834) are supported by Gorbman's and Kalinak's terms of classical scoring practice.

But despite these observations, and despite the score's character, the performance of hard masculinity is nonetheless redeemed, however tenuously, in a number of ways. As indicated, Provo submerges a response to imminent death by making light of his wounds; the exchange of meaningful conversation is replaced by the exchange of a "touch" of bourbon; and even the desire for immortality is reduced to a bit of bathroom humor.

Rather than respond openly to Provo's death, Kirby picks up his weapon, turns immediately away, and walks off to his other duties at the sound of the strong final cadence. One might even go as far as to suggest that the finality of the cadence (signifying, of course, the finality of death) which comes to rest firmly on the tonic[12] as the doctor confirms Provo's death ("That's it," he says) along with the image of Kirby retrieving his weapon, suggests that whatever emotional response he has is dispensed with here. "That's it," says the doctor, and indeed it is.

Kirby's Relationship to Women

Absent from the representation of Col. Mike Kirby is any suggestion of current or previous personal relationships with women. Whatever personal interest he has in women is confined to what Laura Mulvey has identified as "scopophilia" or "pleasure in looking" (Mulvey 835). Kirby expresses this pleasure on two separate occasions — once to Sgt. Provo when he says in a crowded Da Nang marketplace, "There's nothing wrong with looking at pretty girls," and again when he sees Lin (Irene Tsu) for the first time in a Da Nang dinner club and comments to Col. Cai (Jack Soo) "What is there not to like?" One result of such comments is the explicit disavowal of sexual ambiguity within the homosocial world that constitutes the combat film. But his subsequent interactions with Lin, who becomes an operative in the scheme to kidnap the Viet Cong leader General Pham Son Ti, is revealing in other, more significant ways. Thus Lin's role and the musical signification that marks her are important to explore at length because of their bearing on Kirby's representation.

> In most war films, men relegate women to three basic roles: mothers to revere and respect, chattel to acquire and use legally in marriage or illegally via rape and pillage, or whores to provide temporary satisfaction while men are away from home. In each case, women are clearly the "out group," a separate entity men find distracting to the task at hand, but a commodity to think, dream and make plans about [Donald 129].

The question here is which of these categories does Lin occupy, if indeed she falls into any of them. In many war films, including two that inform this study — *The Story of G.I. Joe* and *We Were Soldiers* — women who fall within Donald's first category represent a way of life underpinned by the ideology that the war is fought to preserve.

With regard to Donald's second category, it is the enemy, not the American soldiers, who are demonized as pillagers and rapists. Kirby has described one such incident to Beckworth with disgust as justification for the American presence.

Finally, with regard to Donald's third category, while Lin does indeed compromise her honor for the American cause (thus prostituting herself, at least in a broad sense of the word), it should be noted that there is only fleeting, non-specific reference to prostitution in the film.

With all of this in mind, particularly interesting about Lin's representation is that while she does not adhere neatly to any of these roles, her function within the film is dependent upon all three. Her motive for acting as a sexual lure to ensnare the general is related to the reverence and respect she has for her own family (though here, the reverence is for a murdered father and brother rather than a mother), which motivates her desire to avenge them. To do so, she exchanges sex for the general's capture; and in so doing, compromises her own standing as the "good" wife of Col. Cai's brother. Thus, Lin straddles a number of conventional positions of cinematic femininity, and just as her role is therefore non-traditional, so too is the music that marks her.

Despite the fact they specifically refer to the war film genre, the roles Donald ascribes to women are not substantially dissimilar from those identified by Kalinak, Gorbman and Kassabian with regard to classical Hollywood films in general. In their discussion of film music's representation of femininity, both Kalinak and Gorbman reference the binary opposition between, on the one hand, "Woman as romantic Good Object" and "The Virtuous Wife," (including wives, mothers and girl friends); and, on the other hand, "femmes fatales" and "fallen women" (Gorbman 80, Kalinak 76).

As indicated elsewhere, both Gorbman (80) and Kalinak (77) have identified two possible musical representations of such roles: the romantic object, good wife, mother, etc., with a mellifluous and lush string orchestra and the femme fatale or fallen women with jazz or some musically "decadent" equivalent. Referencing these categories, Anahid Kassabian notes that when women depart from these stereotypical roles, musical signification must be sought elsewhere (71). Such is clearly the case with Lin (making her something of an anomaly in this otherwise conventionally scored movie), and it is important to note for the resulting ideological reflection on Kirby's representation.

We first see Lin in a Da Nang night club where Kirby is meeting with Col. Cai and Col. Morgan (Bruce Cabot). Kirby is about to learn of the plot involving Lin to kidnap the Viet Cong general. The sequence is structured to position Lin as a classic example of Mulvey's gaze (837). Col.

Kirby is the "bearer of the look" thus identifying Lin as a sexual object. She appears in the door of the club and pauses to display herself to Kirby's (and so, the viewing subject's) look. We cut to a full-screen image of her silk-clad buttocks as she sashays across the room to her waiting table. It is here that Cai says to Kirby, "You like?" to which Kirby replies, "What is there not to like?"

The sequence is accompanied by the film's only source music, the score's version of a French torch song called "The River Seine." While this functions primarily to provide a sense of place (it is performed "live" from the stage), it also further eroticizes Lin with its lyrics about rekindling a lost love affair.

Later in the film, following the protracted battle sequence discussed above, Kirby, Morgan and Cai meet with Lin in a Da Nang street cafe where she makes explicit the offer of her services to help kidnap the general. Here, Kirby does not look at Lin. She sits at a separate table facing away from the men to maintain secrecy. Thus she is marked as a member of Donald's "out-group" not only by her sex and her lack of uniform, but by the mise-en-scène (as well as by the fact that she is never identified by her full name and is known throughout the film only as Lin). She is further coded as "other" by her foreignness, underscored by the music that accompanies the meeting — a faux-Asian pentatonic melody performed primarily by nasal-sounding oboe and an electric sitar. A very similar though more lively version of this melody occurred early in the film during a sequence in a Da Nang marketplace as Kirby and Provo watched the "pretty girls" file out of an office building. It enters precisely as the sequence cuts to a close-up of Lin and is thus immediately associated with her. Similar melodic material characterized by the same pentatonic scale and exotic instrumentation accompanies Lin's seduction of the general in the bedroom of his chateau as Kirby's men surround it and prepare to take him prisoner.

The choice of music remains significant here and in the cafe sequence for its capacity to mark her, not only as "other," but also as deviating in some respects from Donald's traditional roles. It does so by departing from what Gorbman and Kalanak have described as traditional scoring practice for feminine representation. This departure is congruent with Kassabian's discussion regarding signification of non-traditional representations of femininity (71). Lin cannot be coded by "decadent" music as a "fallen woman" would, because, although she is in a sense prostituting herself, she is doing so for a "noble" cause. She cannot be coded with the lush Romantic strains of a string orchestra as the Good Romantic Object would be, because, cause or no cause, she is, after all, compromising her honor. Kirby's response to her, then, cannot be interpreted in either of these contexts, and it is interesting that he reveals as much by the way he treats her. After they have tied and drugged the general, and as they make their escape from the chateau via a rope from the bedroom window, Kirby says, "Where's the lady." She appears next to him, and he slings her over his shoulder and descends the rope. Significantly, he does not refer to her by name, but by the generic term "lady" much as he might refer to a piece of equipment that has been useful and must be retrieved; then, upon retrieving her, he shoulders her as he might shoulder a weapon or a duffle.

The last pertinent sequence involving Kirby and Lin comes as the unit is leaving the area following a successful airlift of the kidnapped general. It is clear from ambivalent glances that pass between Cai and Lin that Cai is having a difficult time reconciling himself to the nature of his sister-in-law's participation. Kirby understands the gathering emotional undercurrent and suggests to Cai that Lin's whole future within the social structure of her Vietnamese family and community is dependent upon Cai's response to what she has done. Kirby says as much to Cai and thereby instigates forgiveness and reconciliation (as well as transplanting his Western values, replacing Cai's own culturally motivated misgivings).

In sum, then, during the first meeting with Lin, Kirby is made to appreciate (and objectify) her based upon her usefulness as a sexual commodity. In the second meeting, he learns how he can use that sexuality to further the American cause — his one unquestioned, single-minded purpose. Thus Lin is further objectified as her sexuality, in Kirby's mind, becomes weaponized. During the third interaction, he retrieves Lin-the-object ("the lady") from the operation as he might any piece of military equipment that needs to be slung over the shoulder and carried away. And finally, once her usefulness as sexual weaponry has been exhausted, he returns her to the position of "Good Wife" by encouraging her brother-in-law to assure her that there is no shame in what she has done. Significantly, just as Cai speaks to Lin to absolve her of her "guilt" the exotic instrumentation that has marked her so far is replaced briefly by a lush string section — precisely the convention that Gorbman and Kalinak identify as signifying feminine virtue.

Other than brief directives, there is no direct interaction between Lin and Kirby, and when he does refer to her, it is in terms of a categorization ("the lady") as if she is an additional piece of war machinery. In his single-minded desire to further the American effort, Kirby is willing to exploit Lin the loyal family woman, employ Lin the sex object, transport Lin the valuable weapon, and finally defend Lin the wife to her brother-in-law

Col. Cai against the suggestion of dishonor her actions bring to her and her family. Although it is arguable that in this final instance Kirby is acting on behalf of Lin the person, I would suggest that because she has so clearly been marked as "other," by sex, by culture, and particularly by the score, that she becomes metonymic of the Vietnamese culture itself, the preservation of which is precisely what Kirby uses to justify the American effort; and Kirby's effort to rescue Lin from disgrace is analogous to his desire to rescue her country from the Viet Cong. This reading is commiserate with the final sequence in the film as well as with Kirby's final words.

Battle Aftermath: Protagonist's Response

By the final sequence of *The Green Berets* the film's position on the war has been confirmed in a number of ways — by the demonstration of the depravity of the enemy, by the plight of hapless Vietnamese natives (particularly children), and by the resulting conviction of Petersen and Beckworth, both, in their own manner, having been converted to Kirby's cause. Remaining most consistent throughout the narrative is Col. Mike Kirby's belief in the justness of this position. Unwavering resolve is the single most defining characteristic in the representation of this war film protagonist. At no time does he question his orders, and the only suggestion of disagreement is with civilian policymakers — the "politicians" who stood in the way of his keeping General Ti prisoner when Kirby first captured him (an event preceding this narrative).

Confirming Kirby's resolve and its ideological motivation is the end title[13] and the unfolding musical material that connects it to the final sequence. We see Hamchunk standing alone on the shore of the South China Sea which abuts the airfield where the returning marines have just landed. He is crying. He has just run to the shore from the airfield having learned that his "adopted" surrogate father Sgt. Petersen has been killed. The long shot of the little boy, an insignificant figure in the center of the frame dominated by sand and sea, underscores his isolation. We hear his theme. In the theme's first performance, introduced early in the film as Hamchunk sets a tripwire as a joke on Petersen, the theme is an Asian-sounding melody based upon a pentatonic scale and played on cheng (or zither) and sitar. For this final performance, the instrumentation and melody are similar, but for the third and fifth degree of the scale, which are flatted. This lends the melody a minor quality — a clichéd (nonetheless common) film music convention generally signifying sadness and loss.

Interestingly enough, in Western terms, the flatted 3rd and 5th, when used in pentatonic scales, are often referred to as blue notes, associated with American blues, based upon scales that are in part derived from European tradition as well as from African tradition (Collier 38). Thus Hamchunk's otherness is marked here not only by the Asian connotation of the pentatonic melody, but also by a more subtle associations of cultural otherness signified by the blue notes and the sadness associated with having the blues.

Kirby approaches, and kneels near the boy to discuss his friend's death. As he does so, the melodic center shifts to the related natural minor and the cheng melody is doubled by a lushly scored string section. The drone-like line performed by the bass section, another factor in creating the passage's exotic Asian feel, now becomes more active. Thus the key center, the instrumentation and the orchestration become less exotic, more "Western" sounding. Following this culturally coded shift in tonality, the cheng disappears entirely and a number of bars of connecting material follow. These are scored for full orchestra. This connecting material builds in volume and climbs in register culminating finally in the final verse of "Ballad of the Green Berets" which emerges seamlessly from the connecting material and provides a return to the chest-thumping main title.

The musical movement of this final sequence, then, represents a gradual process of "Westernization," a process that is immensely significant in its relationship to Kirby's overall view of the conflict and his (and America's) place in it. As we see Hamchunk alone, we hear the Asian cue played only by the cheng and the drone-like bass. When Kirby kneels next to Hamchunk and tells him of Petersen's bravery, the Western instruments overpower the thin voice of the cheng — an interesting metaphor with regard to one culture supplanting another — thus representing Kirby's presence and the ideological associations it brings to the sequence. As Kirby puts Petersen's green beret on Hamchunk's head, the cheng disappears entirely, and the passage that connects the score of the final sequence to the end title — the final verse of "The Ballad of the Green Berets" — is performed entirely by Western orchestral instruments. This final section of the cue also functions to transition the piece out of C natural minor to C major, the key of the end title. Thus the Asian implication of the natural minor (or Aeolian mode) is now supplanted by the American song "Ballad of the Green Berets" performed in C major. This final shift from Rózsa's score to the final verse of the ballad which opens the film (the main title) occurs precisely (and significantly) as Kirby answers Hamchunk's question,

II. Vietnam Scored as Conventional War Film: *The Green Berets*

"What will happen to me now?" "You let me worry about that, Green Beret. You're what this is all about," responds Kirby.

In tracing the effect of this cue, I would suggest that Hamchunk is initially marked by his "otherness" just as Lin was earlier. His representation in this sense transcends that of just a little boy who has lost his friend. As a little boy in the process of growing into his own future, accepting the struggle and loss that such growth implies, he becomes metonymically associated with Vietnam struggling for its future, which is, for Kirby, the motivation for the conflict as a whole. And the Westernization of his theme parallels Kirby's explicit shouldering of the burden that Hamchunk represents.

Ultimately, Kirby has to be seen as protector and liberator. His personal motive and, by extension, his justification for the American presence in Vietnam, springs from the desire to take on the patriarchal burden of the conflict represented by Hamchunk. As the role is situated within the realm of patriarchy, it is thus "normalized" and therefore does not require the defining characteristics of specific musical signification. Nonetheless, the return to the main title, "The Ballad of the Green Berets," is significant in its representation of Kirby's unyielding belief. The implication is that Kirby exits the narrative in precisely the same ideological position that he occupied when he entered it. Recall that Beckworth's initial position during the press conference that opened the narrative was that this was a Vietnamese conflict and that the United States had no business interfering. In the final sequence and the end title analyzed above, the question is answered musically. The movement of the Asian theme that codes Hamchunk as a signifier for the Vietnamese struggle to the theme for the American military positions the struggle inexorably as an American concern, while, at the same time, representing Kirby's steadfast resolve.

III

The Ambivalent Hero: Major Heroic Malfunction in *Full Metal Jacket*

The Narrative

The war film protagonists represented in the previous chapters have been broad-stroked and uncomplicated, adhering tidily to Donald's description — men who demonstrate virility, courage and protectiveness (125). Perhaps this is so because consistency and clarity of purpose inform the narratives they inhabit. Perhaps, too, because there are demonstrably traditional elements in each representation, previously formed expectations borne out by the narrative facilitate our identification with its characters. However, in the case of Private Joker (Matthew Modine), the protagonist in Stanley Kubrick's *Full Metal Jacket* (1987), such broad strokes are elusive to say the least. In his case, and in the case of the narrative he inhabits, the most constant characteristic is inconsistency. He is adrift, without an ideological center and offering no indication that he is searching for one. Just as Joker seems to exhibit a certain trait, something happens to skew the reading. Just as, for example, we appreciate his empathy, we witness his brutality; just as we feel we have finally cleared a path through what at first seems like a protective cynical facade to the "real" man, the cynicism reemerges twofold. Such ambiguity is acknowledged, indeed it is applauded, by Kubrick himself. In a rare 1987 interview for *Rolling Stone* magazine, Kubrick says the following of *Full Metal Jacket*:

> Some people demand a five-line capsule summary. Something you'd read in a magazine. They want you to say, "This is the story of the duality of man and the duplicity of governments." I hear people try to do it — give the five-line summary — but if a film has any substance or subtlety, whatever you say

III. The Ambivalent Hero: *Full Metal Jacket*

is never complete, it's usually wrong, and it's necessarily simplistic: truth is too multifaceted to be contained in a five-line summary. If the work is good, what you say about it is usually irrelevant [Cahill].

Private Joker, then, is in many ways an intentional departure from the traditional protagonists explored thus far — not surprising in light of the film's creator, an auteur who, by his own admission, resists characters who reside comfortably within five-line descriptions such as Donald's. I will argue that this departure results in a score that also veers from (though never abandons entirely) traditional practice, and that although the score does indeed function at times in terms of Gorbman's principles of traditional scoring practice, even when it does so, the formal elements of the music are by no means traditional because they are charged with representing something and someone who is not.

Joker's representation emerges from a narrative with two distinct parts. The first part takes place on Parris Island, South Carolina, the site of his basic training. Here, we are introduced to Joker, the new recruit, whose most salient characteristic is his compulsion to obscure from his peers and superiors (and the viewing subject as well) any meaningful clue as to the kind of person he is — his motives, values, beliefs, etc. — behind a wall of wise-cracking cynicism. His first dialog in the film is an impersonation (and a not particularly good one) of John Wayne: "Is that you John Wayne? Is this me?" he says, as the drill instructor dresses down the recruits. Thus even as an impersonator he questions the identity of his own impersonation and at the same time questions what it means to be a war film protagonist — to be a "John Wayne" — during the Vietnam War.

Joker becomes squad leader by impressing his senior drill instructor Gunnery Sergeant Hartman (R. Lee Ermey) with his "guts" because he is unwilling to appease the sergeant by reversing his professed disbelief in the Virgin Mary. The irony here is that he is not standing firm because of personal conviction — his "guts" are in fact a result of fear. When the drill instructor strikes him and commands him to profess belief in the Virgin Mary, Joker says "Sir, the private believes that any answer he gives will be wrong and the senior drill instructor will beat him harder if he reverses himself, sir." He is spared, then, as well as "rewarded" because of his understanding that *there is no right answer* — a premise that underwrites the entire film.

Attendant to his new position as squad leader is the responsibility of tutoring Pvt. Gomer Pyle/Leonard Lawrence (Vincent D'Onofrio), an irredeemably inept recruit incapable of avoiding the drill instructor's wrath. The drill instructor, in turn, visits that wrath upon the rest of the squad.

Joker seems to take his task seriously. He patiently instructs Pyle in all matters of basic training from how to dress to how to shoot. But like so many elements in this film, what at first appears to suggest one thing quickly engenders a suggestion of its opposite, creating a second condition that abrogates the first. Joker's "success" in turning Pyle into an exemplary recruit in fact empowers Pyle to destroy the drill instructor and himself. What Joker and the drill instructor had interpreted as Pyle's success is in fact Pyle's "world of shit," a world he escapes by killing the drill instructor and himself in the barracks latrine. Thus the trajectory of the first narrative segment of *Full Metal Jacket* ends in death and ambivalence. The same is true of the second part.

Immediately following Pyle's murder-suicide there is a direct cut to Vietnam, where we follow Joker through various sequences as a combat correspondent. Joker, who wears a peace button on his uniform and the words "born to kill" on his helmet cover, is ostensively writing "feel good" propaganda pieces for *Stars and Stripes*. Eventually, he reunites with his Parris Island friend Cowboy (Arliss Howard) and tags along with Cowboy's outfit the Lusthogs as they patronize hookers and "liberate" bombed-out cities. In the penultimate sequence Joker kills a young, wounded, female sniper who is pleading in agony for death. Once again, the act is steeped in ambivalence. We can believe that it constitutes a mercy killing, yet the other members of the squad interpret it as an act of pure "hardcore" brutality. And again, nothing is as it seems. There is no ideological center — no "right" answers.

Score Overview

Full Metal Jacket contains a true combination score: part composed, part compiled. While the same could be said for the other films analyzed here, the compiled portion of the score for *Full Metal Jacket* functions less as part of the setting (an incidental indicator of time and place) and more as an integral part of the narrative. Much of the musical analysis in previous chapters has pointed to closely analogous relationships among the image, the dialogue and the score. These close parallels are possible because large portions of the scores are composed expressly to accompany, anchor and facilitate the image's capacity to "tell" the story. Such is not — indeed cannot — be the case when the film employs cues compiled from music that pre-exists the film. As indicated previously, the compiled score makes meaning more loosely, by way of a far more flexible (and less predictable) signifying process than does the composed score (Kassabian 70). By using both approaches, the score of *Full Metal Jacket* can function in traditional ways where appropriate, only to "turn around" (so to speak) and in effect disavow that traditional approach. In a broad structural sense, then, the score is itself a reflection of Joker's duality. Just as Joker's uniform displays opposing and irreconcilable ideologies, the score is comprised of both traditional and non-traditional scoring methods. This is not to suggest that inclusion of popular music and composed film music in the same film are irreconcilable in the same sense as are Joker's "born to kill" slogan and his peace button; however, as will be discussed here, this formal approach allows inclusion of simultaneously irreconcilable musical elements.

Preparation for Combat: Joker in Training

The training sequences that comprise the first part of *Full Metal Jacket* are just over forty-five minutes long. Only about seventeen and one-half minutes of these (including the title sequence but not the diegetic drill routines) contain music. Yet the dearth of musical signification is not surprising when one considers that in light of the narrative material here, music's absence is far more meaningful than would be its presence. The most widely agreed-upon function attributed to music in film is that of a signifier of emotion. No matter what else they suggest the score may do, there are few writers on the nature of film music who do not point to music's power to communicate affective response. But most important to the narrative here is not emotion, but its suppression. It is this emotional vacuum that accounts for the absence of music, emotion's principal signifier. The training sequences which enact "a systematic, controlled dehumanization that strips the Marines of identity" (Rasmussen and Downey 184) often do so through intentional suppression, even perversion, of individual emotional ties. Christmas is celebrated with a rendition of "Happy Birthday" (dear Jesus), and the recruits are told by the stridently cynical drill sergeant that the sing-along is to be followed by a magic show. God is said to appreciate the Corps because it keeps heaven stocked with fresh souls. Parental relationships are routinely denigrated in drill calls and dialog. At one point, for example, Sgt. Hartman tells Pvt. Pyle that "the best part of you ran down the crack of your momma's ass and ended up as a brown stain on the mattress!" Romantic love is vulgarized beyond recognition. "Your days of finger-banging ole' Mary Jane Rottencrotch through her purty pink panties are over!" Hartman tells the recruits, and in the same sequence instructs them to sleep with their rifles and to give their rifles girls' names "because this is the only pussy that you people are going to get."

Just as such haranguing is meant to strip the recruits of all emotional attachment, so too is the diegesis stripped of music as an emotional signifier. Music's function is confined primarily to communicating a sense of place as well as providing rhythmic impetus to the training sequences via martial-sounding drums accompanied by "low musical tones [that] increase tension" (Rasmussen and Downey 184). Beyond this, there are two key sequences in the first part of the film for which music provides key insight into Joker's responses.

Joker "Motivates" Pyle

As previously indicated, Joker is charged with Pyle's instruction and appears to be making progress until Hartman discovers a jelly donut in Pyle's footlocker and retaliates by vowing to punish the platoon for Pyle's mistakes so that they will help him "motivate" Pyle. This motivation comes in the form of a late-night beating that follows a series of sequences in which we see the marines being punished in various ways for Pyle's mistakes. The beating is a turning point for Pyle, and it does indeed motivate him to devote himself to training—training that culminates in the murder-suicide that closes the film's first section. Most significant about the sequence is that Joker, once again, represents a protagonist unwilling or unable to demonstrate personal values traditionally expected of a war film protagonist.

Night has by and large drained the mise-en-scène of color, and we see a barracks bathed in hues of deep blue—a visual atmosphere without warmth. The recruits wrap bars of soap in towels, and while four of them pin Pyle to his bunk with a blanket stretched over his body, the others file past one by one and strike him in the chest and stomach with the loaded towels. Cowboy, Joker's closest friend on the island, gags Pyle with a towel. Joker hangs back watching—clearly reluctant to take part until his friend Cowboy tells him to "do it." When he does it, when he lets loose and strikes Pyle, he attacks with more violence than did the others, each of whom struck Pyle only once or twice as they filed past the bunk. Joker strikes him six times despite Pyle's escalating cries of pain.

The violence in the sequence builds as the blows become more frequent, yet as Pyle's muffled screams become louder and more frantic (particularly when he sees Joker take part) the musical cue, performed entirely on synthesizer, remains constant, as if it transcends the action like some ominous presence — observing, perhaps influencing, but never responding. The cue begins with low, sustained notes which repeatedly spell a single tri-tone.[1] These tones are doubled by an un-pitched, prominent, synthesized "breathing" noise. Intermittently, a second voice enters a third above the bass tones, sometimes in parallel motion and sometimes as a three-note contrapuntal figure.[2] This figure has been heard in a previous sequence, discussed later. Above it is an arrhythmic percussive sound (similar to a wood block) which is "struck" seemingly at random. While it is clear that the score adds a distinctly ominous cast to the already grim atmosphere of the image, the precise process of signification is less traditional and somewhat more complicated. In previous chapters I have pointed to ways in which the music works as an analogue to the narrative, illustrating events by paralleling their rhythms and intensity, illustrating settings through various musical conventions or associations. Here, however, conventions are compromised by the method of composition and performance. Again, the score is composed and performed on a synthesizer, and beyond the percussive wood-block effect, the lack of similarity to real instruments removes the possibility for conventional associations we might ascribe to that part of the musical design.

Conventional tools of traditional scoring practice depend upon specific emotional or geographical associations the audience has learned to make with certain instruments. Such conventions are so ubiquitous in film music that they are sometimes derided as cliché (Adorno 16–17). Too, because the sounds' sources are not identifiable as musical instruments, human agency has been removed from them. This instrumental ambiguity is exacerbated by the ambiguous key center created by the unresolved, repeated tri-tone, which informs the unsettling feeling of the colorless sequence. Also disturbing is the association of steady breathing suggested by the noise component of the sound. This provides an unmoved and unmoving organic quality, as if to suggest life without affect. The fact that the score does not change in intensity as the violence of the sequence increases seems to underscore this lack of affect and intensify the cold, sterile quality of the barracks, an overall atmosphere signified visually by the cold, blue cast. As the sequence comes to a close, the men have returned to their bunks, and Pyle is left alone, crying with pain and humiliation. In the bunk beneath him we see Joker, eyes shut, covering his ears to shut out Pyle's cries as the mechanistic emotionless "breathing tri-tone" steadily continues.

Thus composer Abigail Meade (a pseudonym for Vivian Kubrick, Stanley Kubrick's daughter) has created a cue that does indeed illustrate the narrative, a traditional signifying function of film music. But the materiality of the signification is not itself traditional. Its creation on the synthesizer, its predominant dissimilarity from traditional instrumentation and its steady, unchanging nature removes the performance from human agency just as the sequence, taken as a whole, represents the dehumanizing intention of Kubrick's version of basic training. At the same time, the machine-like quality of the score is made organic by the noise which suggests the sounds of breathing, a musical reflection of the goal to make the marines organic "killing machines" unencumbered by emotion.

The sequence effectively reveals Joker's conflicted and fragmented values. Up until now we have seen a protagonist who, on the surface, displays at least some empathy for Pyle. Even after the jelly donut incident (but before the beating), which precipitated Hartman's decision to hold the entire squad accountable for Pyle's mistakes, Joker tries to reassure Pyle that he is not hated by all of the others and insists, as he infantilizes Pyle by buttoning his shirt and straightening his collar, that he is trying to help him. However, in the "motivating" sequence discussed here, once he strikes Pyle — once the dam bursts, so to speak — he strikes Pyle more times and with more violence than any of the others. Following the beating, he covers his ears, consciously disavowing the regret resulting from his own actions. Thus while the cue, in one sense, represents the dehumanizing purpose of the film's Parris Island segment, that dehumanization is particularized in Joker as we see him move from empathy to denial.

Another noteworthy musical function not to be overlooked is the cue's operation as a leitmotif. It is subtly baptized as such in a previous sequence in which Pyle, flanked by Joker and Hartman, is jogging — lagging far behind the rest of the squad. Hartman is goading Pyle onward while Pyle, clearly exhausted, is supported and pulled forward by Joker. Berating Pyle mercilessly, Hartman says, "Pyle, are you going to die on me? Do it now!" Just as Hartman utters these prophetic words, the three-note motif discussed above enters, supported by a simple bass drum-like pulse on the strong beats of the measures. Welded via the process of synchresis[3] to the image of Pyle's agonized expression, to Joker's tense struggle to keep Pyle from collapsing, and to Hartman's haranguing litany, this motif becomes a signifier of Pyle's pain as well as of Joker's involvement in that pain — whether Joker is trying to help Pyle avoid it (as in the training sequences) or whether he is a party to it (as in the "motivation" sequence). That the motif first enters on Hartman's prophetic words is significant for its coding of the leitmotif to foreshadow Pyle's ultimate psychological disintegration. At the same time, it identifies Hartman and Joker as complicit in that disintegration, which culminates in the last sequence to take place on Parris Island.

Fire Watch: How Joker Survives Pyle's Major Malfunction

It is the marines' final night on the island. Joker is on watch, patrolling the barracks. We hear the same ominous cue that initiated the beating sequence, and the same blue cast envelopes the mise-en-scène. Joker discovers Pyle sitting alone on a toilet in the latrine. Breathing slowly and heavily, a human echo of the machine-made breathing sound embedded in the cue, Pyle loads a live magazine into his rifle, says that he is in a "world of shit," and loudly recites the "prayer" to his rifle, a litany Hartman requires the marines to recite upon retiring: "This is my rifle. There are many like it but this one is mine. My rifle is my best friend. It is my life. I must master it as I must master my life. Without me, my rifle is useless." The disturbance awakens Hartman who enters and confronts both Joker and Pyle, interrupting Pyle's chant.

Although they are both trying to do the same thing — to diffuse the threat posed by Pyle — the sequence reveals the striking contrast between Joker as the embodiment of inconsistency and Hartman as the (destructive and ineffective) embodiment of traditional, aggressive and unyielding masculinity. Hartman's response is consistent with his approach to all the recruits and particularly so regarding his previous interaction with Pyle. He challenges Pyle aggressively, orders him to surrender the weapon while peppering him with humiliating insults: "What is your major malfunction, numb nuts?" he yells, "Didn't Mommy and Daddy show you enough attention when you were a child?" Still breathing in a rhythmic pattern not unlike the one set up by the cue, Pyle responds by shooting Hartman in the chest. Then he raises the gun slowly and points it at Joker. Joker's response is precisely the opposite of Hartman's. His tone is quiet and placating, and despite his obvious fear, he exerts the control necessary to keep it so. "Easy Leonard," he says. "Go easy, man." At this point, rather than kill Joker, Pyle slumps to the toilet seat, turns the gun on himself, puts it in his mouth and pulls the trigger.

While one could make the case that Joker's approach to Pyle's madness is consistent with his previous approach to Pyle's ineptitude, and that this approach indicates compassion or sensitivity, I would suggest that a deeper look indicates otherwise. Joker has already demonstrated his willingness to sidestep principle for expediency. While the immediate appearance of sensitivity toward Pyle may allow the audience to identify positively with Joker, there are many indicators that Joker's sensitivity is only a component of the dehumanizing process under which he is bending. Joker has just seen Pyle's response to Hartman's confrontational approach and has already indicated in an earlier sequence his belief that Pyle is not able to handle such abuse. Thus, his response is just as defensive as is Hartman's, motivated by precisely the same thing—not sensitivity, but the desire to escape a dangerous situation. The score supports this reading.

Once again, as the sequence opens and we see Joker on fire watch walking the barracks, the deep breathing-tri-tone cue begins. Significantly, the beginning of this performance is nearly identical to the previous one heard during the beating sequence, though what had been the middle voice is now is performed an octave higher. As before, the pitch, "instrumentation" and dynamics are static: inhuman, unresolved and organic without affect. That the cue remains constant during both Hartman's "traditional" approach and Joker's more "sympathetic" strategy confirms the lack of real concern for Pyle's tortured psyche from either man. Its steady and unchanging performance signifies the emotional vacuum discussed previously, suggesting that Joker feels no more sympathy toward Pyle now than he did as he struck him earlier with the soap-laden towel. His only real concern is to maintain the emotional disconnect necessary to survive Pyle's madness, the madness of his training, and later, the madness of the war itself. The cue further suggests that Hartman also feels no differently toward Pyle now than he did during the forced march when the three-note leitmotif was baptized. Both men are simply seeking a way through the present danger created by Pyle's breakdown. Hartman's anger, as real as it may seem, is standard issue. His response to Pyle's brandished, loaded weapon—"What is your major malfunction, numb nuts?"—is a performance delivered with precisely the same level of outrage, the same practiced "affect," as his response to Pyle's jelly donut—"You are a disgusting fat-body, Private Pyle!" As he walks slowly toward Pyle, Hartman is an audio-visual echo of a John Wayne gunfight, and as he says "Now you listen to me Pyle, and you listen good" and tells him to put his gun on the "deck" and step away from it, the barracks latrine becomes a dusty Western street; only this time, John Wayne and the traditional masculinity he embodies are destroyed, and it is Joker's ambivalence that survives the showdown. Once again, I would suggest that this ambivalence is the essence of this war film protagonist. It is what distinguishes him from traditional pictures of masculinity just as it is what distinguishes him from Hartman. He is neither for nor against aggression; he is neither for nor against compassion. As we shall see, what he is *for* is survival.

It would be easy to discount some of what is suggested here by pointing to Joker's apparent empathy toward Pyle; nonetheless, the motivation behind it is analogous to the motivation behind Hartman's intractability. Although we expect such sympathy from a protagonist and are thus more willing to accept it at face value, we do not have to look far beyond appearances for reason to question Joker's sincerity. He has demonstrated his willingness to waffle — his emotional disconnect — too often. For example, in an earlier sequence, while cleaning the latrine with Cowboy (the same sterile setting in which his life is now threatened), he anticipates the current crisis when he expresses "concern" for Pyle, suggesting that he "can't cut it" and may be a "section 8." But just as we think his concern might be genuine, without missing a beat, he jumps to an obscene reference to Cowboy's sister: "I wanna slip my tube steak into your sister," he says. "What'll you take in trade?" Both comments are delivered with the same matter-of-fact tone and are immediately juxtaposed suggesting that both carry precisely the same weight or, to be more precise, lack thereof. In other words, Joker's level of concern for Pyle is as insignificant as his obscene reference to Cowboy's sister. Just as he does not actually expect Cowboy to barter for his sister's favors, just as he does not actually expect to act upon his professed desire to have sex with her, so too does he not actually demonstrate regard for Pyle's well being. His "concern" for Pyle in the murder-suicide sequence is not more genuine than it was in the latrine with Cowboy. He is simply adapting to a situation for purposes of survival; and, in so doing, he underscores the profound ambivalence we associate with his representation throughout the film.

Ironically, then, Pyle's is the only unequivocal representation of sincerity here, demonstrated by his murder-suicide which ends the first section of the film. Pyle's "major malfunction" is his inability to submerge his characteristic sensitivity; it is precisely what causes him to lose his sanity — or to kill himself to keep it — just as Joker's ability to do so (recall him covering his ears at Pyle's cries of pain and humiliation in the bunk above him) enables him to keep his. Significantly, Pyle's breakdown is the first and only sequence thus far in which musical signification of emotion is appropriate. As indicated above, the cue remains constant throughout nearly the entire sequence and nearly identical to its emotionally-drained previous performance that accompanied Pyle's beating. However, when

Pyle turns the gun on himself and our attention shifts from Joker to him, the cue deviates significantly from its steady, drone-like characteristic. The dynamics increase, and new voices enter — layered so as to make the piece more rhythmically and harmonically complicated. Pyle's increasing cognitive dissonance is signified by the harmonic dissonance set up by the entrance of a bass pedal,[4] which creates a very dissonant minor second with the tone beneath it as well as a dissonant major ninth with the tone above it. The three-note leitmotif mentioned earlier is doubled by a synthesized violin an octave above. This doubling of the violin voice is harmonically and rhythmically ambiguous, because it is displaced temporally from the voice it doubles sometimes lagging behind it by an eighth note (1/2 beat) and sometimes by a quarter note (1 beat). The displacement creates a feeling of a nearly-but-not-quite doubling with the lower voice.

The musical metaphors are clear. Just as Pyle cannot resolve his psychic dissonance, just as it becomes too overpowering to handle, so too does the music become dissonant. Just as Pyle's mental equilibrium becomes hopelessly out of sync, so too does the asynchronous voice enter in the synthesized violin. It should also be noted that this synthesized violin is the only instance of an identifiable instrument (save for the percussive effect) in the entire cue. As such, it is the only substantial sound that we might ascribe to human agency. The fact that it enters precisely as Pyle turns the gun on himself is a tragic signifier of his humanity vis-à-vis Joker's lack thereof. The fact that it is rhythmically displaced illustrates that Pyle's humanity is in crisis. And so, Pyle's emotional overload serves, via the contrast it sets up, to demonstrate Joker's emotional bankruptcy.

Joker in Vietnam: Structural Disorientation

The ambivalence that most accurately describes Joker's character is represented again and again throughout *Full Metal Jacket* through juxtaposition of contrasting images, characters, behaviors and, of course, music. We see the ambivalence in his flexibility compared to Hartman's intractability; in his kindness vs. his brutality, in his cynical rebellion standing against his fear-inspired acquiescence, in his near-simultaneous expression of sensitive compassion immediately abrogated by his insensitive vulgarity. As the film lurches from the first section to the second, from Parris Island to Vietnam, we see it expressed in formal elements as well. Just as Joker's conversation with Cowboy in the latrine jumps abruptly from his "concern" for Pyle to his "lust" for Cowboy's sister, thus bestowing both comments with similar weight so that the import of one is drained by the triviality of the other, so do we jump abruptly from the first part of the film's final sequence — Hartman's murder and Pyle's suicide — to the second part's initial sequence — a Vietnam street where Joker watches a young prostitute sashay toward him to sell her body for ten dollars. The result of such Eisensteinian juxtaposition forces the viewing subject to consider both settings simultaneously, and the dark psychological underpinnings of the first are trivialized by the moral bankruptcy of the second. Equally significant to the effect is the jolting leap from the ominous and darkly synthesized composed score to the banal 1966 pop tune "These Boots are Made for Walkin'." In this world, however, the image of Nancy Sinatra's blond-maned, mini-skirted body strutting across a variety show stage is replaced by a dark-haired, tubercular Asian prostitute crossing a congested Vietnamese street. The incongruity is vivid; the clash of the former association with the latter image intensifies the audience's sense of displacement regarding the very young soldiers, the settings they find themselves in, and the skewed values implicit in the scene. The lyrics, too, are part of the effect. The song is about a woman inconsolable because her man has cheated — because he is promiscuous. Here, it is paired with the image of a woman who makes her living by facilitating sexual promiscuity.

I have suggested that the juxtaposition of these sequences, that is, the visual dissonance created by a jarring leap from the darkened and violent latrine to the sun-bathed Vietnamese street, is Eisensteinian in its effect. I am referring to Eisenstein's belief that the process of trying to reconcile two or more seemingly incongruous shots would "make the viewer see something greater than the individual shots alone" (Kolker 50). I have also suggested that the juxtaposition of two very different musical cues, dissimilar in style (the dark synthesized composition and the banal pop tune) and also dissimilar in scoring practice (the composed score vs. the compiled score) have an analogous function. In this sense I am borrowing from Eisenstein's theory of montage and applying it to the structure of the score. A similar extension or "borrowing" is appropriate with regard to Rasmussen and Downey's term "dialectical disorientation." They argue that in *Full Metal Jacket* and other films of the period (e.g., *Apocalypse Now, Deer Hunter, Platoon*), the American mythology of war has been subverted by "dialectical disorientation ... a confrontation between two powerful, incompatible, and complementary world views." They contend "that the films' systematic undermining of the *purpose* and *value* intrinsic to the mythology of war negates the [American] myth's viability" (177). I am suggesting that in many instances, the purpose and value of the score in the second part of *Full Metal Jacket* is used to the same end. This process of disorientation can be demonstrated again and again in the film's second part by examining the choice of popular song that accompanies seemingly incongruous narrative or visual material. The following discussion works through possible functions of the compiled score; it seeks to demonstrate the extent to which the choices in *Full Metal Jacket* are or are not congruent with the images they accompany and what this means to Joker's representation.

Popular Music's (Mal)Function in *Full Metal Jacket*

Regarding *Full Metal Jacket*'s compiled score, David James writes:

Low-grade forms of rock and roll, as distinct from the more musically progressive hippie music of the late sixties, are used to denigrate the Tet offensive (the Dixie Cups' "Chapel of Love") and the fighting at Hue (Sam the Sham and the Pharaohs' "Wooly Bully"), while the use of "The Mickey Mouse Club Song" at the end of the film completes the sardonic nihilism [90].

This seems to suggest that the viewing subject's response to the war is informed by some subjective assessment of the quality or artistic value associated with the musical accompaniment — that the "low-grade" associations with the musical genre become a metaphorical comment on the value of the battles. I have no quarrel with this argument, but I think that the negative responses the score may bring are more directly related to the context within which the viewer would *expect* to hear such pop tunes as opposed to the context within which they are experienced here. In other words, the meaning is created by contrast rather than by comparison — by context rather than by quality. For example, if my culturally inscribed associations with "Chapel of Love" (regardless of whether or not I think it is a "good" song) involve youthful romance (my relationship with, say, Mary Jane Rottencrotch) as the song's lyrics suggest, then its superimposition over the sequence containing an image of Joker and other combat correspondents lounging in their barracks discussing battle experience creates a disorienting incongruity. This incongruity would support my reading of Joker as ambiguous and of his behaviors as irreconcilable. Given the setting, the case could be made that a traditional view of masculinity is subverted by the pajama-party-like dialog suggested by the song, thus feminizing the men and trivializing their discussion. Such a reading is interesting, but perhaps too subjective to be entirely satisfying.

Elsewhere, I have discussed Anahid Kassabian's suggestion that one function of popular music in film scores is to create what she has called "paths of entry for identification" (73) between the viewing subject and the film's characters. These paths are flexible, according to Kassabian, because they are based on viewers' previously-made associations carried with them to the filmic experience. In *Thelma and Louise,* for example, Kassabian suggests that the audience recognizes the enjoyment of the protagonists singing pop songs as they ride in the car. Kassabian's point is that if the audience has experienced similar pleasures in similar settings, then a pathway to identifying with the characters is created via common, pleasurable activity. Yet for such a process to occur, intra-diegetic acknowledgment of the song would be necessary, and that is clearly not the case here. Further, one would be hard-pressed to map such an identifying path to Joker's desire to get back "into the shit" along the saccharine strains of "Chapel of Love."

Yet another possible explanation for the choice is to view the song as diegetic — to assume, for example, that it issues from some unseen radio. If such were the case, it could function traditionally according to Gorbman's principle of referential narrative cueing (83), and the song could be said to simply situate the scene in time. This would seem appropriate enough as the song was released approximately four years before the Tet offensive. But this explanation does not address the question of choice (why *this* particular song) as there are certainly more appropriate tunes from the era that would serve the same temporal function, while signifying the soldierly representations more coherently. Further, it is a common sound technique to reduce a song's fidelity in relation to the rest of the soundtrack when it is meant to be understood as issuing diegetically from a radio, thus mimicking what would be heard from a small speaker. Such is clearly not the case here.

Another avenue of explanation that must be discounted for obvious reasons would be ascribing to the music an expressiveness of emotional response based on its resemblance to accustomed patterns of speech or gesture (Kivy 52). Clearly, the soldiers' discussion of being "in the shit" of battle and their subsequent apprehensive dash to their stations when the base falls under attack is in no way parallel to the bouncy sock-hop rhythm or pop-tune instrumentation of "Chapel of Love."

Ultimately, then, in trying to reconcile the musical choice with the image, we keep returning to its irreconcilability, which supports the reading of Joker's character as ambiguous and ambivalent. We have seen how his own behavior supports this reading time and again, and the barracks sequence is no exception. As the correspondents continue chatting and the Dixie Cups' "Goin' to the Chapel" plays on, Joker complains of boredom and says he "can't wait to get back into the shit." Another soldier challenges his statement and suggests that he has never seen real combat and instead of denying the charge, Joker hides behind his impersonation of John Wayne to make light of the soldier's remark. When an attack suddenly comes and an alarm sounds, the men rush out to assume their defensive positions. As the attack begins, Joker says, "I hope they're just fuckin' with us. I ain't ready for this shit." Once again, Claudia Gorbman tells us that

> Whatever music is applied to a film segment will *do something*, will have an effect — just as whatever two words one puts together will produce a meaning different from that of each word separately, because the reader/spectator automatically imposes meaning on such combinations [15].

The interesting thing here is that "Chapel of Love" does not "*do something.*" Indeed, it does not seem to *do anything*; thus, we are left confused as to what it is doing here at all. And this confusion, I would suggest, is precisely the point.

The next sequence scored with a popular song subjected to similar scrutiny yields a similar conclusion. Domingo Samudio's song "Wooly Bully" recorded in 1965 by Sam the Sham and the Pharaohs is as out of place in its context as was "Chapel of Love." Based on a bouncy 12-bar blues progression, the song is about urging Hattie not to be a square (an "L-7") and to learn a dance called the Wooly Bully (a name borrowed from Samudio's cat). It accompanies a sequence in which Joker is reunited with his friend Cowboy in a gutted building while covering the assault on Hue City for the *Stars and Stripes*. He exchanges the accustomed banter with Cowboy about having hoped never to see him again; he claims to have had sex with Cowboy's sister; Animal Mother (Adam Baldwin), a member of Cowboy's squad the Lusthogs threatens to tear Joker "a new asshole"; and Crazy Earl (Kieron Jecchinis), the squad leader, introduces Joker to his "best friend," a dead Viet Cong soldier propped up in a legless arm-chair against the wall where the Crazy is resting. This introduction to the Lusthogs presents an unsettling picture of the American fighting men, and again, trying to track a pathway for identification by seeking an explanation based upon principles of traditional scoring practice or by finding some analogous association between the musical or lyrical content and the accompanying image is futile. Once again, we come away from the representation with the same sense of ambiguity as in the previous sequences.

III. The Ambivalent Hero: *Full Metal Jacket*

The Response to Death

As indicated in previous chapters, the sequence in which a war film protagonist responds to the death of fallen comrades is as much a part of combat films as is combat itself. We have discussed, for example, Walker's sadness at writing condolence letters and journalist Ernie Pyle's hope that the sacrifice will lead to a better world in *The Story of G.I. Joe*. We have explored Kirby's anger and stoicism in *The Green Berets*. We will explore Moore's guilt and his tears in *We Were Soldiers,* and his insistence that Galloway "tell the folks back home" about his men's bravery. Joker, however, presents a very different response; and commiserate with what I have discussed thus far, it is a non-response.

In his discussion of the score accompanying the battle of Hue in *Full Metal Jacket* David James writes:

> [T]he summary figuration of the superimposition of Kubrick's cynicism about the invasion over his critique of films about it occurs during the battle for Hue, when the appearance of a medevac helicopter cues the Trashmen's "Surfin' Bird" and recollection of the surfing "birds" of [...] Kilgore and the helicopter pilots of *Apocalypse Now*. In the immediately following scene, Kubrick parodies Coppola's staging of Kilgore's attack, in which Coppola represented himself as a journalist filming it. As the idiotic staccato chant of "Bird is the word" accompanies the machine guns at Hue and the dance of Kubrick's news crew, Coppola's "realism" is mocked by Kubrick's marines, who articulate the spectacularization and media self-consciousness Kubrick foregrounds all through [90].

Once again, I have no quarrel with James's argument; however, the function of "Surfin' Bird" in this sequence provides more than an opportunity for parody, particularly when considered within the context of the sequence that immediately follows it. While the reference to Kilgore and his helicopter pilots is clear, the function of the "idiotic staccato chant" superimposed over the deadly serious activity of battle is noteworthy for other reasons, and its function in the scene needs further unpacking. To appreciate just how banal the "idiotic staccato chant" of "Surfin' Bird" is, keep in mind that the line referred to by James is repeated in rapid-fire fashion 20 times, and is followed by an even more nonsensical verbal construction which is repeated approximately 29 times.

I would suggest that the weld between the image and the score in this instance is somewhat more pertinent than in the choices of popular music discussed above because of the sympathetic rhythm set up between the chant and the ambient gunfire. There does seem to be a contextually-appropriate, narrative function here after all, whereas the previous examples of popular songs discussed above seemed intent on subverting the context. Given the clear anti-war bias of this film, the meaninglessness of the idiotic, banal chant of "Surfin' Bird" comments clearly on the "meaninglessness" of the gunfire, and so, on the representation of mortal combat. Once again, we can see the inanity of "Surfin' Bird" superimposed over the assault on Hue as a kind of dialectical disorientation. Its presence undermines the dire seriousness of mortal combat, just as the film (and others of this period) undermine the American mythology of war.

But the meaning-making function of "Surfin' Bird" does not end there. In the sequence that immediately follows the song, we see a low angle shot of each squad member, one at a time, as they stand over their prone comrades killed in the battle. The low camera angle within the shot-reverse shot construction suggests the point of view of the slain soldiers; consequently, as the Lusthogs look down at them, they seem to be addressing the dead men directly. Some of the soldiers utter traditional words of condolence or encouragement: "You're goin' home now" and "Semper fi," for example. Others have less sympathetic comments. A key exchange takes place between Animal Mother and Private Rafterman (Kevyn Major Howard):

> ANIMAL MOTHER: Better you than me.
> RAFTERMAN: Well, at least they died for a good cause.
> ANIMAL MOTHER: What cause was that?
> RAFTERMAN: *(spoken with uncertainty)* Freedom?
> ANIMAL MOTHER: Flush out your head gear, new guy. You think we waste gooks for freedom? This is a slaughter. If I'm gonna get my balls blown off for a word, my word is *poontang*.

Juxtaposed as it is with the immediately preceding word-nonsense of "Surfin' Bird," the sequence indicates that the signifying power of words has broken down completely. The men die for words, and their deaths lack meaning because the words that should rationalize their deaths lack meaning: Surfin' bird, freedom, and poontang are all interchangeable. Previous war film protagonists' rationalizations for death in battle — e.g., *Bataan*'s Sergeant Dane who says, "It don't matter where a man dies as long as he dies for freedom," or *The Story of G.I. Joe*'s Ernie Pyle who envisions a "reassembled" world in "a pattern so firm and so fair" or even *We Were Soldier*'s Joe Galloway who suggests that "in the end they died for each other" — are sardonically recast in *Full Metal Jacket* as getting one's "balls blown off" for "poontang," a base sexual reference. For his part, our protagonist has no comment at all. Clearly aware of the futility of words,

Joker looks down at the soldier's prone bodies wordlessly, and in light of his role as a combat correspondent, in light of the fact that words are his stock and trade, we are faced with the irony of his silence. He does not join the others who either wish the dead well or comment on noble or ignoble rationalizations regarding their deaths. Earlier in the film, standing over a group of murdered Vietnamese civilians while gathering information for a story, his voice-over provides his only commentary — a commentary that clearly suggests the futility of seeking justification; he says, "The dead know only one thing — that it is better to be alive." Significantly, then, this man of words has found none to affirm or denounce the value of death in battle.

Man and Machine

The clichéd title of this section points to the fact that masculinity is so traditionally associated with machinery and technology that the association has become "normalized" to the extent that such clichés exist. One consummate representation of the relationship between man and machine — of man's dependence upon machines for his survival — is that of war, and the representations of war and warriors in *Full Metal Jacket* are cases in point. Marines are referred to as "killing machines"; they are instructed to sleep with their rifles; and one of their common litanies suggests that their rifle is their "best friend" — that they are nothing without it (just as it is nothing without them). Thus, men are not only dependent upon machines, they are meant to become machines — a point made earlier in my discussion of a previous cue containing both organic and machine-like components. Susan McClary has pointed to the man-machine relationship with regard to traditions of musical signification and performance art. She writes that "[...] it is supposed to be *Man* who gives birth to and tames the Machine" (138). And recall Susan Linville's discussion of *Courage Under Fire* during which she points to Robyn Wiegman's reference to "the exteriorization of the masculine body as technology" (104). Thus in combat films, machines and men are inseparable, and in some cases, they are one and the same. In the practice of war, they work together or they do not work at all. The composed musical cue for the sequence discussed next makes significant use of this relationship, and in this particular case, the relationship is clearly dysfunctional.

The Lusthogs are lost in the ruins of Hue City, pinned down by an unseen sniper who is picking them off one by one. At this point, the squad's command structure breaks down — Animal Mother argues in favor of rescuing two wounded soldiers in an open area, and Cowboy, who is now squad leader, insists that it is a trap and that the sniper is trying to draw them out into the open. Repeatedly, Cowboy admonishes the Lusthogs to hold their fire; repeatedly, they disregard his requests and return fire. Animal Mother disobeys Cowboy's direct order, tries to rescue the fallen soldiers, fails, and subsequently finds cover closer to the sniper. The others follow. As they try to decide on the next move, Cowboy is shot and dies in Joker's arms. When Animal mother says "Let's go get some payback," Joker agrees. As the squad nears the sniper's position, a cut places Joker in the center of the frame. He makes a 180 degree turn holding his rifle. At this point the score (perhaps more sound-design than musical score) enters.

The difficulty of notating or verbally describing the "music" in this sequence is exacerbated by a number of components characteristic of this synthesized score: the electronically designed sounds do not mimic identifiable instruments; the "rhythms" are not constrained by a time signature; and the pitches are not only indefinite, but they do not conform to the traditional 12-note structure of our Western pitch system. With this in mind, I would suggest that what we hear as Joker makes his 180 degree turn is best described as the sound of twisting or rending metal accompanied by a deep repetitious thumping sound as if someone is striking their fist absent-mindedly against an empty oil tank. A not-quite-regular pulse is maintained by a metallic groaning sound and all this is punctuated intermittently by what sounds like metal tubing striking a concrete floor. I understand how subjective this is, and can only effectively combat the charge by urging that the reader listen to the score for him- or herself. In any event, the cue I am describing is not unlike the sound of broken or badly damaged machinery. If one accepts these suggestions, then the metaphor becomes clear — significant in light of the relationship between man and machine in combat films. Not only has language as a vehicle for justifying the soldiers' participation in the battle broken down, but the mechanism for actually doing battle has broken down as well, indicated by the sounds of tortured machinery as Joker and the rest of the Lusthogs approach the sniper's hiding place. Although I have suggested that this reading of the score could be construed by some as somewhat subjective, it is, nonetheless, a reading supported strongly by the mise-en-scène. As we hear the metallic sounds of twisting and grinding metal, we see the squad moving through buildings gutted by bombs, which have exposed much of the ruined, twisted re-bars and rent metal girders — the understructure of the destroyed buildings. Strewn throughout are burnt, stripped and overturned vehicles — tortured machinery iconically mirroring the sounds of the score. Just as the understructure of the buildings have been destroyed by this war, so too has the "understructure" of the myth of the American soldier-protagonist and his relationship to the machinery of war. Further confirmation is provided when Joker confronts the sniper. Here, his automatic weapon jams and he is unable to fire. If it were not for the backup provided by Rafterman, who shoots the sniper, Joker would be killed. Thus, during the only time in the film that Joker takes his role of "killing machine" seriously, as he seeks revenge for the death of his friend, the machinery of war is broken; and, as the litany discussed earlier says, without that machinery — without his rifle — Joker is nothing. The traditional relationship between man and machine is severed, and the break is indicated by both the narrative and the score.

Joker's Kill

The sniper is a young woman, perhaps not yet out of her teens. As she lay dying, the squad surrounds her, watching her gasp for breath while she prays unintelligibly. A shot-reverse shot between her and Joker cues the final composed section of the score. The music is in many ways structured similarly to the cues in two other sequences: the latrine sequence in which Pyle commits suicide as Joker looks on, and the barracks sequence in which the squad beats Pyle with the soap bars wrapped in towels. The cue's salient three-note melodic motif has also been heard in the earlier sequence during which Joker physically props up the anguished and exhausted Pyle as Hartman forces him to march and asks him if he is "going to die." The previous coding of the cue, therefore, necessitates a comparison of its previous function with its function here, as well as a comparison of the previous performances with the subtle though distinct differences contained in this one. In its first appearance, the three-note melodic motif is overpowered by the martial drum accompaniment. It is very soft and is quoted only twice. The second time we hear it (in the beating sequence) it is more prominent, layered above the less overpowering, breathy, tri-tone bass line discussed earlier in this chapter. In its third performance (the suicide sequence) it is more pronounced still, also layered above the bass line, but now mirrored in the upper synthesized string section. In the present sequence, it enters alone and is the first component of the cue we hear as Joker and the young dying girl regard each other.

I have argued that both Joker and Hartman share responsibility for Pyle's death — that both, in their own way, facilitate Pyle's descent into his "world of shit," which creates the psychic turmoil impelling him to murder Hartman and kill himself. I have also suggested that the motif was baptized as a representation of that complicity in its first performance, again, the sequence during which Hartman forces an exhausted Pyle to march as Joker physically supports him. In the present sequence, Joker once again shares the responsibility (this time with Rafterman) for another's death, and this time, more directly. Joker's direct responsibility for killing the sniper (as opposed to his less direct responsibility for Pyle's madness) is perhaps the reason that the melodic motif is more prominent here.

If it is true, as I have suggested, that in the previous instances Joker's actions are not a result of his own values but are, instead, a result of his lack thereof, precipitated by the desire to survive, then the motif's presence here should indicate a similar state of mind. The motif is present in each previous instance during which Joker reacts to the pressure of the moment based upon this desire: instructing Pyle so as to deflect Hartman's anger from himself and the rest of the platoon, beating Pyle in a bow to peer pressure, and trying to calm Pyle to prevent his own murder in the suicide sequence. That the same motif is present here suggests that we should look beyond the obvious reading of Joker's motivation as a compassionate response to the sniper's agony and her repeated plea to be shot. In the process of looking beyond this surface, the cue, taken as a whole, renders a particularly complicated view of Joker's response as it relates to his overall representation.

As the three-note melodic motif continues, the bass enters. It is constructed, as before, upon a repeating tri-tone; and again, the ambiguity and instability of the interval is analogous to Joker's ambivalence about how to respond to the situation. Significantly, however, the tonal quality of this line is far more identifiable as a bowed contra-bass, so much so, in fact, that it is difficult to determine whether it is produced electronically or by the actual instrument. Thus the perception of human agency in performing the score is now present where it was not present before. Coupled with the fact that the breath-like noise is no longer part of the cue (a sound that I argued earlier produced an unmoved and unmoving organic quality, as if to suggest life without affect) we now read Joker's response not in terms of some organic machine, but as a response generated by real human emotion, regardless of how conflicted that emotion may be. The gradual build-up of Joker's internal conflict is illustrated by the string voices and

III. The Ambivalent Hero: *Full Metal Jacket* 93

set off by Animal Mother's suggestion that Joker kill the sniper. Note the behavior of the score as indicated within the following exchange between Joker and Animal Mother:

> ANIMAL MOTHER: Okay. Let's get the fuck outta here.
> JOKER: What about her?
> ANIMAL MOTHER: Fuck her. Let her rot. *(three-note motif enters)*
> JOKER: We can't just leave her here.
> ANIMAL MOTHER: Hey asshole, Cowboy's wasted. You're fresh out of friends. I'm running this squad now, and I say we leave the gook for the mother lovin' rats.
> JOKER: I'm not trying to run this squad. I'm just saying we can't leave her like this. *(volume subtly increases and bowed bass enters)*
> ANIMAL MOTHER: You wanna waste her? Go on, waste her.
> *(Strings begin building in layers and in intensity, building to a crescendo as Joker stares into the snipers face. Joker shoots the sniper. String crescendo ends abruptly and the cue begins to fade.)*
> ANIMAL MOTHER: *(Giggling)* Joker — we're gonna have to put you up for the congressional medal of ugly.
> MARINE: Hardcore man. Fucking hardcore.

Significantly, the melodic motif enters precisely as Animal Mother sets Joker's conflict in motion by suggesting that the Lusthogs leave the sniper to die. The motif indicates (according to the way it has previously been coded) that Joker is once again under pressure to acquiesce to another's demands and thereby become complicit in another's suffering. Joker's statement that they should not "leave her like this" is met with Animal Mother's hostility and his challenge that Joker should "go ahead and waste her," and at this point the motif is mirrored in the string voice. Note that in the previous murder-suicide sequence, this is the voice that paralleled Pyle's internal conflict and psychic anguish as he lowers the weapon he had pointed at Joker, sinks to the toilet seat, and prepares to take his own life. In the suicide sequence, the parallel is created by the motif's steadily increasing volume. In the present sequence the parallel to Joker's intensifying inner conflict is created by the entrance and layering of additional string voices, which not only steadily increase the cue's overall volume, but steadily increase the dissonance in the upper voices as well. In both cases the music continues building to a dissonant climax until the shot is fired at which point the volume and dissonance end abruptly and the cues reach resolution.

This sequence is the copestone for the ambiguity of Joker's representation, an ambiguity created by the questions left unanswered. Did Joker feel that the Lusthogs should have taken the sniper prisoner and transported her to the base where she could have received treatment? Was the execution carried out as an act of compassion or as an acknowledgment that he had no support left among the Lusthogs and therefore had no other choice? Was it a response to Animal Mother's challenge, and as such, an act of "hardcore" brutality as suggested by the marine's comment? Joker's look after he kills the sniper (a look that could have been precipitated by any of the above) may be shock, it may be anger, it may be pity, it may even be machismo; and the musical cue which illustrates his intensifying inner turmoil could be illustrating turmoil caused by any one or any combination of these possibilities. The reason that there *are* so many possibilities is that in all of the narrative leading up to this copestone moment we have been given no clear ideological ground with regard to what makes Joker tick. Thus we cannot hang his present response on any single, cogent stereotype. Although the score is clearly functioning with regard to Gorbman's principle of narrative cueing, it is only partially functional in those terms because it fails to "anchor the image in meaning" (84) or "ward off the displeasure of uncertain signification" (58). Because we never discover his long term response to the execution, just as we never discovered his response to Pyle's suicide, we are forced to accept the ambiguity and move on, just as the film moves on to the final sequence.

Battle Aftermath: Protagonist's Response

The final sequence of *Full Metal Jacket* shows the platoon at night moving through the ruined city amidst billowing smoke, gutted buildings, and ubiquitous fire, hellishly backlighting the marines and rendering their images as silhouettes. Brimstone would be right at home here. Joker's voice-over informs us that they have "nailed [their] names in the pages of history enough for today," and that they "hump down to the Perfume River to set in for the night." As they march, they sing the "Mickey Mouse Club Song" with slightly altered lyrics.

The superimposition of the children's song over the marching silhouetted troops set against the hellish backdrop of burning buildings presents the viewer with visual and aural components that at first seem disturbingly irreconcilable. Indeed, the combination could not be more ironic had Fred Rogers provided a voice-over welcoming us to his neighborhood. A cursory glance at this musical choice could suggest that the song supports the overall ambivalence of the film and of Joker via the seeming disconnect between it and the visual, and I would agree that on one level this is certainly the case. But there are other elements at work in both music and lyric that bear closer scrutiny.

The form of the song is pertinent. The strong steady tempo and the repeating melodic and lyrical phrases clearly situate it both melodically and rhythmically as a march. Branch of service aside, it bears uncanny resemblance in both musical and lyrical structure to the Army infantry march "The Caissons Go Rolling Along." For example, compare "Then it's hi! hi! hee! / In the field artillery / Shout out your numbers loud and strong" with "Hey there! Hi there! Ho there! / You're as welcome as can be... / forever let us hold our banner high!" Structurally, then, the song is not an inappropriate choice for "Hump[ing] down to the Perfume River to set in for the night." Further, the lyrics contain many references to ideas clearly appropriate to the myth of the American soldier — working in harmony, following a leader, familial belonging, and so on. But while the literal stuff of the song may be appropriate, its context here, as opposed to the context in which one would normally place it, muddies the waters considerably. In its original context this is a children's song, meant to be sung by children as they play. It belongs to a children's television show — a show intended for entertainment and perhaps to espouse a moral lesson or two in the process. As have so many elements of this film, such preformed associations work to disrupt a traditional reading of the narrative in terms of the American military myth, and I would suggest that choice is an overall indictment of the war effort in general. Just as Drill Sergeant Hartman asks upon bursting into the latrine during the closing sequence in the first section of the film "What is this Mickey Mouse shit!" so are the marines answering with their own indictment of their activities. Consider, for example, the line in this altered version: "Who is marching coast to coast and far across the sea? M-I-C-K-E-Y M-O-U-S-E." Thus the myth of the American soldier is subverted by the suggestion that marines are nothing more than cartoon characters, and that their missions can be characterized as "Mickey Mouse shit."

I have pointed earlier to the combat film convention of ending with an explicit, thematic summation of the narrative. Such summation can take a number of forms — the protagonist's voiceover, rolling copy, end title lyrics — and is present in many combat films (e.g., *Bataan, Wake Island, Gung Ho, A Walk in the Sun, Jarhead*) including those that are the focus of this study. Usually, it limns some overarching context for the narrative: eulogizing the dead with regard to sacrifice for a grand purpose, situating the narrative within the context of some larger canvas. True to form, Joker also provides a concluding voice-over in *Full Metal Jacket*, and as the "Mickey Mouse Club Song" disrupts the American myth through association, Joker does so via the voiceover:

> We have nailed our names in the pages of history enough for today. We hump down to the Perfume River to set in for the night. My thoughts drift back to erect-nipple wet dreams about Mary Jane Rottencrotch and the great homecoming fuck fantasy. I am so happy that I am alive, in one piece, and short. I am in a world of shit, yes. But I am alive. And I am not afraid.

Unlike the other examples listed here, and unlike the other films contained in this study, Joker's is not a discussion of the dead, their sacrifice, or the overarching purpose of the struggle. Joker's only explicit comment on the dead is reinforced: that all they know is that "it is better to be alive." Perhaps this is the one consistent characteristic that Joker represents throughout the film, this belief that survival, even if it means inhabiting a "world of shit" is the only thing that makes sense.

IV

Vietnam Redux: Scoring the Conflicted (Post–9/11) Hero in *We Were Soldiers*

Following *The Green Berets*'s failed attempt in 1968 to claim for Vietnam the moral imperative of World War II, and following the spate of films that began releasing about ten years later giving belated voice to the anti-war cauldron that had started to boil over even as *The Green Berets* was released, Leo Cawley wrote in 1990, "It is in films that the important work is going to be done of forcing the facts of the Vietnam War into the mold of national myth and reconciling the country to its first defeat in war." One could argue that the round-pegged, square-holed fact-forcing of such action fantasies as *Rambo II*, *Lethal Weapon* and *Die Hard* (to name only a few) were just such attempts. Yet these did not seek reconciliation so much as they placed blame, deflecting responsibility for the defeat away from the American military and onto liberal or corrupt politicians and the corporate interests they served. But, perhaps for the first time, *We Were Soldiers*, completed (ironically enough) just a few months before 9/11 and released in 2002, presented a real attempt to find honor in the sacrifices made by American soldiers in Vietnam while at the same time acknowledging the nation's lingering discomfort with the war itself. For this reason, regardless of whether or not one thinks *We Were Soldiers* is a good movie, its protagonists represent yet another significant shift in heroic representation, and therefore require our attention: not for their chest-thumping, hard-bodied righteousness as represented by Col. Kirby, and not for their trembling, self-serving ambivalence as represented by Private Joker, but because they represent conflicted heroes to whose commitment popular culture offers respect while it simultaneously looks askance at the cause to which they are committed.

Conflicted Heroes

The combat sequences in Randall Wallace's *We Were Soldiers* re-present the 1965 battle between United States forces and the North Vietnamese Army in the Ia Drang Valley — the first battle, we are told, between U.S. forces and the NVA. These sequences are intercut with those set in Fort Benning, Georgia, the military base where the protagonist, Lt. Col Harold (Hal) Moore (Mel Gibson), his wife Julie (Madeleine Stowe), and his five children take up residence immediately preceding Moore's departure for Vietnam. Thus the narrative follows Moore interacting with his men as well as his family, allowing an exploration of the score's characteristics as it works to represent the same protagonist in two very different narrative spaces. In concert with the score, this parallel structure works to differentiate Hal Moore in significant ways from other protagonists discussed in previous chapters. It is not unusual for combat films to contain domestic sequences. Such sequences give dimension to characters and underpin a dramatic intensity borne of regret at leaving loved ones behind, thus raising the stakes with regard to what is being sacrificed. Usually, however, domestic scenes precede the hero's departure. Here, the crosscutting that takes place even as the battle is underway heightens the dramatic intensity, providing an ongoing complexity which contextualizes the conflicted nature of this post 9/11 hero.

Moore's foil Joe Galloway (Barry Pepper) appears during the film's second half. He is a photojournalist, the only journalist present during the actual battle. He is a bridge between military and civilian life. Galloway explicitly identifies his personal mission in Vietnam as an effort to help himself and "the folks back home" understand war.

Score Overview

Of the preexisting music used in the film's combination score, Joseph Kilna MacKenzie's "Sgt. MacKenzie" is the most significant with regard to its overall narrative function. Released in 1999 by MacKenzie's Scottish band Clan An Drumma, it was orchestrated for use in various contexts within the film. Thus, it differs from other examples of compiled music discussed here in that it is integrated into larger composed pieces of original film music. (A familiar example of this scoring technique is *Casablanca*'s "As Time Goes By"). For purposes of clarity, I refer to its various performances within the film by its original title.

The cues based on "Sgt. Mackenzie" and two other composed themes comprise most of the film's music. "What Is War" functions throughout as a leitmotif, coded (as discussed at length below) to recall and transfer Hal Moore's various concerns, his spirituality and his searching nature. Similarly, "Mansions of the Lord" is associated with a young lieutenant with whom Moore identifies because he voices the same kinds of questions that Moore has obviously wrestled with.

Good Husbands, Good Fathers, Good Soldiers

The characteristics that Lt. Col. Hal Moore values in a soldier are inseparable from those that he values in a family man. This is made particularly clear by way of the structural crosscutting mentioned above, which conflates interactions within familial and military settings. The structure foregrounds the support Moore takes from his home space even when we see him engaged in mortal combat half-way around the world, and his behavior as soldier and commander is made inseparable from his behavior as father and husband. These two characteristics are welded at the film's outset via both visual and musical components. In the opening sequence, we are introduced to Moore and his family within the closed, shared space of his station wagon. This effectively unifies the family as they travel toward Moore's new military assignment. The camera pans slowly from the back seat to the front seat until the frame encompasses Moore, his wife, and the children at once. At no time during this introduction sequence do we see Moore framed by himself, thus his identity as an individual is subsumed beneath his identity as a family man. Significantly, the same unifying, enclosed area that connects him to his family, moves Moore toward his post, suggesting that his family life is integral to his professional life. This suture is confirmed by the diegetic soundtrack. As they travel together in the car, Moore's wife and children sing "The Bear Went Over the Mountain" and "BINGO." The activity of group singing in the car further attaches Moore to the family unit both visually and musically: "Rhythmic motion and patterned tones are traditionally used in situations to elicit group solidarity in action" (Zuckerland qtd. in Scott 230).

The songs are significant not only as group activity, but as songs that have been culturally coded to create interaction as traditional sing-alongs — an interaction that Moore is obviously enjoying. It is also worth noting that "The Bear Went Over the Mountain" is sung to the tune of "For He's a Jolly Good Fellow," and given the positive interaction among Moore, his wife, and his children, he is clearly represented to us in this light.

As the title sequence continues, the camera shifts our point of view to an establishing shot of the car's exterior as it enters the military base. We hear the children singing "BINGO," over which is now superimposed the sound of martial drums. The overlapping musical themes — one military, the other familial — attaches the family to their new military surroundings. As they unpack their rented trailer, moving into their new home, the children have stopped singing, but the martial drums continue. Moore's youngest daughter climbs the front stoop wearing Dad's marching boots, as if the process of unloading the family's belongings is itself a military drill. Thus, the family unit, to which Moore has already been connected by filmic space, is now connected to Moore's career by the diegetic soundtrack.

The family-military connection is so integral to Moore's identity that he not only connects family life to military life, but he also interprets his relationship with his men and their relationship with each other in familial terms; and, once again, the score is vital in signifying this relationship. As is conventional in combat films, martial drums occur often throughout *We Were Soldiers*, usually during training sequences or during establishing shots of soldiers on the move. Their conventional function is to provide sequences with forward impetus via rhythm or as indicators of place or activity. Regarding connections made between military unit and family, a martial drum motif identical to the one identified above brackets a significant training sequence. We hear the drum score as Moore leads the men jogging through the woods. They enter a clearing where a member of another group of trainees has taken advantage of "atmospheric bounce" to tune a field radio to receive the sounds of an actual battle from Vietnam. The drums stop, replaced by the tinny, staccato sound of artillery fire coming from the radio's small speaker. The sounds of gunfire and barked orders create anxiety among the trainees. The aural vacuum created by the score's abrupt end foregrounds the sound of gunfire and Moore's words as he uses the moment to instruct the men about what they hear. His comment indicates both his erudition as well as the value he places upon family ties. He says:

> When Crazy Horse was a baby, he nursed from the breast of every woman in the tribe. The Sioux raised their children that way. Every warrior called every woman in the tribe "mother." Every older warrior, they called him grandfather. [...] they fought as a family. Take care of your men; teach them to take care of each other. Because when this starts, [Moore indicates the

speaker from which the battle sounds issue] each other is all we're gonna have.

The sequence ends with a long shot of the men continuing through the woods, and the martial drums resume. The score functions on two levels here. Conventionally, it illustrates the narrative by creating a military atmosphere congruent with the images and provides forward impetus for the sequence. Additionally, however, it has also been baptized within the diegesis to recall the opening sequence during which the drums were first heard as Moore and his family moved into their home. That these drums, coded now with both military and familial associations, bracket the sequence during which Moore characterizes the relationships between the soldiers in familial terms, confirms Moore's sense of the significant connection between military activity and family relationships.

Moore acknowledges the suture between his domestic and military life in an early sequence. He enters to congratulate Jack Geoghegan (Chris Klein), a young lieutenant praying in the hospital chapel, whose wife has just given birth to a daughter. The lieutenant, clearly conflicted, asks Moore, "What do you think about being a soldier *and* a father?" Geoghegan has come to the chapel for spiritual guidance — trying to rationalize the compatibility of the very components essential to Moore's identity. Moore's response, then, is particularly telling with regard to the characteristics his representation embodies. He says, "I hope that being good at the one makes me better at the other." In this way, Moore rationalizes Geoghegan's conflict — to which, we must assume by his ready answer, he has devoted some previous thought — by suggesting that the characteristics allowing success in both roles are precisely the same.

Key questions raised by all of this speak to Moore's criteria: what characteristics are embedded in the narrative that constitute that amalgam of values, beliefs and behaviors that Moore considers "good" with regard to his military and familial self? In other words, what precisely does he have to be "good" at with regard to the "one" that also makes him "better" at the "other"? The salient feature of this and other sequences is Moore's representation (and later Galloway's) as a man who consistently and constantly interrogates his own behavior and the motivation that precipitates it. This process of inquiry is *the* defining characteristic of this war film protagonist. The representation, then, may validate viewers' own nagging questions regarding American involvement in the war. We see protagonists who implicitly acknowledge the lingering distaste for the Vietnam War but whose own questioning nature works to provide a mechanism by which viewers who also harbor distaste for the conflict may nonetheless identify with the men who engage in it. In other words, our identification with the common process of inquiry allows identification with the protagonists despite negative feelings about what they are doing.

Moore accepts the responsibilities of his career, but his reasons regarding the necessity of placing others in harm's way, his concerns about the wisdom of his superiors, his commitment to his duty and to his men — these are not matters of unquestioned patriotic or ideological fervor as they were, for example, for John Wayne's Mike Kirby in *The Green Berets*. Thus, he pursues justification and affirmation within himself, within the tenants of his religion, in historical research and from the support he derives from his family. For Moore, then, there is no such thing as a "gut" response. His inspiration, leadership skills, duty, and so on, are often generated from sources outside of himself, and he is represented as one who actively seeks guidance from those sources. This is not to suggest that Moore's action is entirely predicated upon the rational. To do so would be to disavow the motivation of loyalty, responsibility and faith. But within that framework, Moore is methodical and rational about the way he makes decisions within the context of family and career. The discussion that follows shows how selected sequences represent Moore in this light, and how that representation emerges from image, dialogue, and, most particularly, from the score.

A Spiritually Guided Academic Pussy

Moore holds a master's degree in International Relations from Harvard University, and there is some indication that his scholarly bearing is not entirely accepted — perhaps deemed incongruous or unconventional for a warrior. In the title sequence discussed above, he carries stacks of books into his new home while on-looking soldiers discuss whether he is "one of those academic pussies." The pairing of the words *academic* and *pussies* speaks volumes, of course, vis-à-vis conventional representations of masculinity within the military, and this is not the only time Moore's behavior is associated with this vulgar and pejorative reference to femininity.

The title sequence ends as Moore sits in his darkened study, a man alone with his books and his thoughts — if not purely an academic, nonetheless a man thoroughly engaged in methodical inquiry. He is familiarizing himself with the design of the helicopters — the yet untested warfare technology he is to pioneer — and perusing an historical account of the failed French campaign in Indochina, *Les Guerres en Indochine*. As he turns to a photograph of a battle, the non-diegetic soundtrack indicates his internal conflict. The muted sounds of war, artillery fire and shouting men that offer a ghost-like comment on the image in the book, represent an internal, psychic monologue indicating his anxiety. The sequence is important for its representation of Moore's tendency toward studied preparedness. Whether he succeeds or fails, the outcome will not be based on bravado or some implied masculine "essence." It will be a result of skill and knowledge. This tendency is also evident in the considered responses Moore customarily makes to his men. As previously noted, for example, when Geoghegan asks his question during the chapel sequence, Moore has an answer at ready; and the implication is that he has asked it of himself many times.

As a signifier for this searching aspect of Moore's (and later Galloway's) character, the scoring of the chapel sequence is particularly significant. It is here that two of the film's most salient musical themes, "Mansions of the Lord" and "What Is War" are initially coded to function as leitmotifs with associations that remain pertinent throughout the narrative. Beyond this coding within the diegesis, certain qualities of the cues are also noteworthy for their extra-diegetic associations.

Both themes are reminiscent of sacred music, primarily for the slow tempo coupled with the chapel setting in which they are heard. Structurally, too, they contain elements traditionally associated with church music. "Mansions," for example, ends with a plagal cadence[1] and "War" ends with the picardy third.[2] Both of these cadences have inherited religious connotation from their use in sixteenth century sacred music (Kivy 134, Hall 78). Further, the sustained bass notes in "What Is War" are reminiscent of the pedal of a church organ as is the sustained chordal structure of the piece as a whole. Both cues are introduced as the men are engaged in seeking answers to profoundly troubling questions about their places in the military and the part they must take in armed combat. "Mansions" enters as the camera tilts downward from the chapel's stained glass window — an image of Mary — to Jack, sitting alone, meditating and praying. When Moore enters, he leads Jack to the alter to pray, which cues "What Is War." Thus both cues are associated with Jack and Moore, respectively, and both are associated with the process of inquiry into the grand issues of life and death.

Recounting for Moore a previous experience as a Peace Corp volunteer, Geoghegan recalls witnessing heinous acts against children by tribal warriors. Moore suggests that they ask God for guidance, and as Moore begins praying, the "What Is War" theme enters and is thus coded to be associated hereafter with narrative situations in which soldiers question their role in war, how they will face the enemy, how they will behave when in mortal danger and how they can justify killing (O'Brien 62). The cue, then, not only references Moore specifically, but also his questioning nature as well as the questions themselves. Clearly, such questions are not insignificant, and the spiritual context of the music as well as its formal qualities suggest that the question is meant to transcend the particular, and is thus elevated to the realm of myth. Claudia Gorbman writes:

> Music, especially lushly scored late Romantic music, can trigger a response of "epic feeling." In tandem with the visual film narrative, it elevates the individuality of the represented characters to universal significance, makes them bigger than life, suggests transcendence, destiny.[...] The appropriate music will elevate the story of a man to the story of Man [81].

The music, then, and the questioning to which it refers, connotes spirituality and therefore transcendence. Although the style may not be specifically Romantic, it is nonetheless a "lushly orchestrated" string arrangement, and provides, for this and the other reasons discussed here, a clear example of "epic feeling." The transcendence is evoked because of the activity the piece accompanies and the location in which it is experienced. I would suggest that in each of the subsequent sequences in which a performance of this cue occurs, similar references are triggered, regardless of whether or not Moore is "present."

Moore's search is represented as introspective, spiritual, and personal, but at the same time it can also be methodical and scholarly. In a series of sequences immediately following the chapel scene, we hear a much extended performance of "What Is War" as well as variations, all of which remain similar to the initial performance, not only harmonically and melodically, but also in meter, tempo, rhythm and orchestration. The first of these takes place when Moore's young daughter asks the question from which the theme takes its name. "Daddy, what is a war?" she asks, as Moore prepares to read her a bedtime story. "Are they going to try to take your life away, Daddy?" Moore tries to answer so as to allay her fears as the musical theme continues, suturing this sequence to the next in which Moore lies in bed beside his sleeping wife. The leitmotif's associations paired with Moore's restlessness indicates that his daughter's question continues to plague him, evinced not only by his facial expression, but by the entrance of a ponderous and therefore ominous bass line. His discomfort forces him from his wife's side to his study, where he consults his books, records his observations, and tries to work through them methodically.

Thus, as indicated above, Moore's process of inquiry encompasses both the spiritual as well as the practical. In his study, he examines, side by side, an account of the French campaign in Indochina and an account of Custer's last stand. On a pad, he lists a series of mistakes, errors in judgment, and tactical disadvantages that plagued the original French campaign. The list is set up as a kind of equation, culminating with the word *Massacre*, which he underscores with two heavy pen strokes. While one purpose of underscoring *Massacre* may be to increase dramatic tension — foreshadowing the possibility of defeat — the score suggests something more subtle. "What Is War" is clearly not typical of the heavily orchestrated style that we might normally associate with abrupt dramatic emphasis as we would, for example, a discordant stinger after traditional Hollywood scoring practice (e.g., the abrupt series of diminished 7th chords that mark the men's discovery of the first casualty in *The Story of G.I. Joe*). Instead, the underscoring and the immediate cut to Moore's troubled pose, accompanied by the plaintive string section and the slow, close melodic intervals of "What Is War" signify Moore's questioning attitude and the increasingly acute sense of reflection packed into the cue's coding. Hence, at the risk of belaboring the point, Moore's characteristic process of inquiry is made clear by the leitmotif, an essential component of the representation, and once again, we are invited to identify with this conflicted hero — an implicit invitation that is based upon our own questions about the conduct of this divisive war.

Moore's concern is not driven by fear for his own safety, but for that of the men he is to lead in battle and, of course, for the wellbeing of his family. As the theme continues, Moore's wife enters the darkened study. He shares his concern for the "boys" he will lead, who remind him of his own sons (again, conflating military and family values). This ongoing familial theme is underscored yet again in the only sequence that contains popular music. A party to celebrate orders deploying Moore's command to Vietnam is scored diegetically with two popular soul hits: Sam and Dave's 1966 recording of "Hold On, I'm Comin'" and Mel Carter's 1965 version of "Hold Me, Thrill Me, Kiss Me." Both songs are apolitical. Both songs are clearly appropriate as dance numbers. Both were released during the represented time period (though "Hold On I'm Coming" actually postdates the events). Most obviously, then, they function as narrative cueing, situating the narrative in time and place (Gorbman 83). At the same time, their apolitical nature (lacking as they do ideological reference to 1960s counterculture) works against any suggestion that the fears represented implicitly in this sequence are to be taken as ideological opposition to the Vietnam War. The musical choice suggests that Moore's professed distaste for the method behind his orders and his obvious disdain for the bureaucracy responsible for them is not to be confused with rebellion in the ideological sense. He does not identify with the anti-war counterculture; he does not want to make love not war. In fact, he wants to do both. Common to each song is the professed yearning of lovers to stay close despite the knowledge that the closeness is threatened and tenuous. As "Hold Me, Thrill Me, Kiss Me" plays, we see head shots of the men and their wives dancing cheek to cheek. The camera lingers longest on Geoghegan (who will be killed in battle) and his wife — the first close-up — and on Moore and his wife — the final close-up. Ultimately, then, music not only functions to situate the sequence in time and place, not only to distance Moore from the ambivalent protagonists of the post–Vietnam period, but to support the ongoing weaving of the domestic space with the military one — the bridge between home and combat.

Another sequence in Moore's study immediately follows the party, and Moore's characteristic selflessness is demonstrated again via his concern for his wife and family. At the party, Moore is troubled by specifics that he learns of his mission and by the fact that his unit has been given the same name as Custer's massacred regiment, the 7th Cavalry. In his study, Moore signs his will, cueing the "What Is War" theme. To return to a previous point, the signing of the will could be read primarily as a dramatic device to foreshadow the possibility of defeat if it were not for the score, which signifies Moore's penchant for introspection, the questions regarding the nature of war and the awareness of inherent danger. That there is no dialog here foregrounds the musical component of the mise-en-scène, which continues to inform the rest of the sequence. After Moore signs the will, he looks once again at side by side images of Custer's and the French troops' massacres. In the darkened doorway behind him, we see his wife. This time, however, she chooses to leave him alone with his questions, and the cue continues as she backs away into the shadows of the darkened house.

In sum, the study sequences are significant for their representation of Moore's three-pronged approach to inquiry — his introspective nature, his scholarly investigation of history and technology, and his willingness to seek counsel from others (here, of course, his wife). The questions that concern him are both practical and personal: his concern for his family should the worst happen, as indicated by his signature on his will; his concern for his men and his ability to lead them, as indicated by his question to Julie regarding his own boys; and his concern for the success of the mission itself as indicated by his study of the technical drawings and the historical material about the French campaign and Custer's 7th Cavalry. Imbuing all of these components with the atmosphere of inquiry so vital to the representation of this war film protagonist is the score.

A Soldier's Gotta Do What a Soldier's Gotta Do

Following the arrival of Moore and his men in the central highlands of Vietnam, following a briefing with the officers stationed there during which he is given his simple orders ("find the enemy and kill them"), Moore discusses the mission with his next in command, Sgt. Maj. Plumley (Sam Elliott)—a gruff, no-nonsense, one-dimensional caricature of traditional war film heroism. The discussion is grim. Moore characterizes the mission as an "ambush." He clearly wonders at the wisdom of the orders, unconvinced of the chances for success. Nonetheless, the words that close the discussion indicate his resignation to duty despite his misgivings: "Let's go do what we came here to do." At this point the theme "Sgt. MacKenzie" enters, connecting this sequence to the next, which does indeed depict the men doing what they came to do. It begins with an extreme close-up of Moore. His aspect is one of concern, read as such not only because of the conversation with Plumley, but because of the song's lyrics, which speak of certain death and of the determination to face the enemy bravely. We cut to a long shot of the troops, hear the order for them to board the choppers, see them rush to board and cut to a series of close-ups of the anxious faces of individual soldiers, many of whom are about to see battle for the first time. The score is absolutely vital to our reading of the sequence, and the selection is particularly significant because it informs our reading of the images in a number of ways. Hence, it is appropriate to describe it here in some detail.

Written and performed by the Scottish band Clann An Drumma, the song begins with a low wavering bagpipe or organ pedal drone which serves as harmonic accompaniment to the lyrics, written and sung in Scots dialect. The melody is Mixolydian,[3] common in traditional Celtic music (Czulinski 46).

The first level of meaning is, of course, suggested by the lyrics themselves, which "often contribute to the production of meaning in a sequence" (Kassabian 80). Again, these are a vow to maintain courage in the face of death. They provide a statement of Moore's obvious anxiety which is transferred by way of the mechanics of the film's form (e.g., shot-reverse shot) to his men. Somewhat more interesting, however, are the ways the unusual stylistic choice of this song build upon my previous reference to Gorbman's category of film music as a signifier of epic feeling. Consider that we have a modern American combat sequence occurring in a Southeast Asian country, accompanied by a song patterned after traditional Scottish folk music, sung in an antiquated dialect and orchestrated with a drone, an "archaic" form of accompaniment "doubtless known at least five-thousand years ago" (Sachs 99) and "a sound that for at least a couple of centuries has signified 'rustic' or 'primitive' to western listeners" (Taylor 172). I am suggesting here, just as I previously suggested for the chapel sequence, that the representation of Moore as the searching soldier is not the representation of only one particular soldier in one particular place reviewing his troops as he weighs the concerns with which his representation has thus far been freighted. Instead, the representation is of every soldier in every war troubled by epic questions of courage, justification for armed conflict, mortality, and so on. I am further suggesting that these larger-than-life questions are present primarily because of the score. The musical reference reaches back through time to encompass the epic questions regarding all armed conflict. It does so not only because of its obvious associations with antiquity that create temporal displacement, thereby moving the particular to the general, but by cultural displacement as well. By removing the American-Vietnamese conflict from America and Vietnam, the conflict itself becomes universalized, and thus, so do the questions that arise from that conflict. The displacement also serves to further quash negative associations an audience might bring to the narrative about this still-unpopular war.

The excerpt from "Sgt. MacKenzie" flows into the next cue, "What Is War" by way of sustained high string figures. We see establishing shots of the choppers careering over the mountainous jungle terrain intercut with full-face close-ups of Moore and his men. Hence, we are yet again made aware of the questioning aspect of the soldiers as they fly into battle. Whatever ambiguity there may be in reading the facial expressions is overcome by the previous coding of the musical material that accompanies them. The questions are made explicit by our first introduction to the journalist Joe Galloway by way of his voice-over. As the cue begins, he says: "It was a Sunday, November 14th, 1965. Before that day, the soldiers of North Vietnam and those of America had never met each other in a major battle." As Galloway speaks the word *battle,* the main melodic material of "What Is War" begins. Thus the questioning processes implicit in the leitmotif fuse the questions suggested by those explicit in Galloway's voice-over with the images of Moore and his men. The addition of the martial drums, a variation on the cue's initial performance, situate the concerns previously coded within this leitmotif in the context of the battlefield. Thus the cue makes meaning here on a number of levels simultaneously. With regard to Moore, it underscores his anxieties and his paternal concern for his men (his "boys"), as well as affixing those anxieties to the men themselves. Its juxtaposition with "Sgt. MacKenzie" further supports the previous suggestion regarding universalizing the question *what is war?*, "elevat[ing] the story of a man to the story of Man" (Gorbman 81). And finally, it places all of this within a combat setting.

Questions Unanswered

As previously suggested, the character of Joe Galloway, a UPI reporter and photographer, gives voice to questions implicit in the film as well as those implicit in the representation of Hal Moore. In a sequence that takes place before daybreak, during a lull in the battle which has been raging off and on since the morning of the preceding day, Moore is praying over the casualties. The mise-en-scène is grimly rendered, dominated by a deep blue cast illuminated at brief and abrupt intervals by brilliant flashes of artillery fire. Moore is kneeling in the foreground, surrounded by prone, dead soldiers. Behind him we can make out the vague forms of others collecting the dead and tending to survivors. Moore breaks off his prayers as Galloway approaches him.

> MOORE: You got a death wish, Galloway?
> GALLOWAY: No, sir.
> MOORE: Then why are you here?
> GALLOWAY: Because I knew these dead boys would be here, sir."
> MOORE: Why aren't you a soldier? You got the guts for it.
> GALLOWAY: ...Sir, Galloways have been in every war this country's ever fought. When it came to this one, I didn't think I could stop a war. Just thought I could maybe try and understand one. Maybe help folks back home understand. I just figure I could do that better shooting a camera than I could shooting a rifle.

Galloway, then, is clear about his purpose. He positions himself as a bridge between civilian life and combat, a liaison, so to speak; and instead of offering an ideologically freighted response about the current just cause as would have generally been the case in classic combat films (e.g., *Bataan* [1943], *Gung Ho!* [1943], *Wake Island* [1942]), Moore simply wishes him well (O'Brien 62).

Shortly following this conversation is an extended, particularly violent and graphic battle sequence in which Galloway takes part despite his non-combatant status. "Ain't no such thing [as a non-combatant] today, boy," says Plumley, thrusting a bloody weapon into Galloway's arms. But even as Sam Elliott's Plumley recalls John Wayne in *The Green Berets*, the echo here of civilian turned warrior after the example of journalist George Beckworth is fleeting. Galloway's "calling" is redeemed when, at one point during this battle, American planes act upon incorrect coordinates and a number of American soldiers are engulfed by friendly fire. One of these is Galloway's recent acquaintance Jimmy Nakayama (Brian Tee). During a brief lull in the fighting, Galloway carries the horribly burnt and disfigured Nakayama to a helicopter. Profoundly moved, Galloway falls to his knees sobbing, and buries his head in his arms as the helicopter departs. Wandering, aimless and disoriented, he stumbles upon his camera hanging from a limb. He drops the rifle Plumley has given him, retrieves the camera, and begins recording the battle—thus returning to his search for understanding and abandoning his short-lived role as fighter. What follows is a montage of black and white, still battle photographs over which are superimposed translucent moving images of Galloway shooting them. This compelling sequence crystallizes my argument that what is most significant about the representations in *We Were Soldiers* is the depiction of men as "questioning soldiers," neither embracing nor cynically rejecting their military role, but approaching it with grim resignation as they simultaneously struggle to understand it. This crystallization could not occur without the vital contribution of the score.

Given Galloway's stated objective—to understand war—it is significant here to note the soundtrack's function of drawing us into his thoughts. As Galloway carries his disfigured friend to the chopper, the music enters, and the ambient sounds of battle recede. It is a good example of Michel Chion's assertion that "suppression of ambient sounds can create the sense that we are entering into the mind of a character absorbed by her or his personal story" (89). (For another example, see the opening battle sequence of *Saving Private Ryan*.) The suppression of the ambient sounds also foregrounds the music, as does its volume and the void it fills relative to the absence or muting of the previously overpowering sounds of battle. The music is further emphasized by the abrupt absence of motion in the black and white static images that immediately follow vividly colored moving scenes depicting the frantic chaos of battle. These absences create a vacuum, filled as the perceiver redirects attention from the ambient noise and the frantic movement onto the music. Finally, because the preceding sequence did not include music at all, audience awareness of its presence is increased at its introduction. The point of these observations is that the narrative structure tells us that this music is important and alerts us to pay attention. As we are drawn into Galloway's "personal story," the associations we make with the now prominent score inform our response to that story.

Signifying Galloway's search for understanding — his purpose for photographing the war — is the restatement of the "What Is War" leitmotif. Some important differences in orchestration (and so, in signification) between this and the previous performance are noteworthy. The martial drums are gone, transferring the musically inscribed inquiry to Galloway the non-combatant — a search for answers by a civilian for civilians. At the same time, the omission of the drums and a markedly slower tempo (from *andante* to *largo*) makes the cue more reverent and plaintive, resonating appropriately with the images of fallen soldiers Galloway is photographing. The melody is stated by what sounds like an Irish whistle — stated in the whistle and then answered by the string section — and the use of this particular instrument recalls and thus conjoins the Clann An Drumma performance of "Sgt. MacKenzie" with this statement of the "What Is War" theme using comparable, culturally-coded orchestration. The messages of both themes are thus conflated — one coded to be associated with questioning and the other coded to suggest the temporal and cultural significance previously identified with regard to the "Sgt. MacKenzie" performance — universalizing the questioning aspect of Galloway's search for understanding. The joining of these two musical messages is supported by Galloway's discussion with Moore regarding his reason for participating. During that exchange (quoted above) he recalls his family's involvement in "all the wars this country has ever fought," and says that he wishes to understand "a war." Significantly, then, he seeks understanding of "a war" in general and not of *this* war in particular, placing Vietnam into a general context of war by his choice of words and by referencing all the past wars in which his family has fought. This universalizing of the personal, moving the quest once again from "the story of a man to the story of Man" (Gorbman 81) disallows our possible reading of the representations as supportive of this particular war and thereby circumvents this country's negative associations with the defeat in Vietnam. More importantly, if we accept that universalizing the question which asks *why do men fight* — if we accept that the narrative as a whole and the music in particular endow the question with epic status — we thus remove the ideological implications involved in a particular conflict. We are no longer justifying participation in this war based upon a specific nationalism.

Instead, largely because of the score's influence, we are searching for a more inclusive understanding. And if the representations in *We Were Soldiers* indicate a new "moral rearmament" (Doherty 1) or depict a "return to triumphalism," as has been suggested for *Saving Private Ryan* (Auster 1) (and which, hard on the heels of 9/11, might be even more expected here) then that moral rearmament and triumphalism is motivated by something other than a nationally-inscribed ideology. The myth of the American soldier as described by Donald (125) and Cawley (70) and referenced by Rasmussen and Downey (177) can emerge without the negative ideological baggage attached to Vietnam itself. In this light, we are able to appreciate the protagonist for his admirable qualities — appreciate him for who he is, which becomes divorced, in a specific sense, from what he has done within the context of a particular struggle.

My Enemy My Brother

Conventional in the end of most combat films are sequences that depict the response of the protagonist to the battle, the war, the loss of comrades-in-arms, or to all three. Such responses are significant for the insights they provide into protagonists' feelings of responsibility for their men, their ideologies regarding the war, and their motivation for taking part. Notable in *We Were Soldiers* are the following such sequences in which the score figures prominently.

The scoring of the final "victory" sequence in *We Were Soldiers* is perhaps as significant for what it is not as for what it is, and it is important to note what certain absences suggest about the characteristics of Moore and Galloway. "Works of art," writes Leonard Meyer, "are understood and appreciated not only in terms of what actually occurs, but in terms of *what might have happened* given the constraints of the style and the particular context in which the choice was made" (6). What might have happened with regard to style and context is, of course, somewhat speculative; however, we can suggest possibilities based upon examples of previous recurring patterns in the genre. We might expect, for example, as the soldiers realize victory and survival, that the music contain an element of bombast — brassy, loud and celebratory — what I have called "tarun-ta-raa" music. Such music is so common in battle sequences that depict the final charge of the "good guys" that even children at play can be heard creating an appropriate soundtrack by mouthing their own versions of "buglelike fanfares" (Kivy 134). Even anti-war films have followed this convention during battle sequences — "The Ride of the Valkyries," for example, in Coppola's *Apocalypse Now*. Here, however, as the cavalry (literally) appears over the horizon riding to the rescue, and as the automatic weapons mounted on the choppers cut down the advancing enemy troops, thereby winning the day and preventing the enemy from executing the massacre that has haunted Moore from the beginning of the film, we hear "Sgt. Mackenzie," once again, a slow, plaintive and introspective comment on the imminent death of the individual soldier. Instead of rejoicing in the slaughter of a demonized enemy, we see and feel Moore responding with empathy to the carnage wrought by his American rescuers. His empathic response is carried in his facial expression, his "pose," (a term borrowed from Roland Barthes who suggests that pose signifies via "a store of stereotyped attitudes which form ready-made elements of signification" (22)), and it is anchored by the score.

The previously coded musical signifiers discussed earlier regarding temporal and cultural displacement, which move the stuff of the narrative from story to myth, are in full play here. The song's connotations, previously packed with the questioning propensity of Moore and his troops, provide "anchorage" (Barthes 39) for our reading of Moore's look. This empathic look, however, is now directed toward the enemy, just as it was previously directed at his own troops in the earlier, similarly structured sequence which introduced the "Sgt. Mackenzie" theme. Instead of demonizing the enemy, then, we are led to consider them in the same light as we were previously led to consider the Americans — as we understand that Moore, as bearer of our look, considers them. As the plaintive musical and lyrical strains of "Sgt. Mackenzie" dominate the sequence's soundtrack, and as the ambient battle sounds are once again suppressed, thereby moving us into the protagonist's thoughts, full-screen shots of Moore's face reverse to lines of rushing enemy soldiers cut down in their tracks by weapons mounted on choppers. Thus the North Vietnamese Army is presented in a sympathetic light even as they are annihilated, and our protagonist's inquiry into the nature of war and his participation in it, once again, transcends his specific command, this specific battle and this specific war.

Of similar significance is the comparison, facilitated by the score, of the experience common to Moore and the enemy commander. In three sequences the "What Is War" cue overlaps intercut shots of Moore and the NVA commander: as they both introspectively regard the moon, as they both consider the possibility of massacre, and following the final defeat of the NVA forces when the NVA commander is informed of the defeat. Significantly, then, the activities of both commanders are conflated within the mise-en-scène and (most obviously during the sequence in which they both regard the same moon) their struggle transcends the particular and is thereby recast in epic proportions. In this light, a particularly remarkable sequence occurs as the NVA forces claim their dead following the departure of the Americans. In classic combat films, it is a narrative staple to show a commander cutting down and sometimes desecrating the flag of the opposing army when his troops occupy a territory previously occupied by the enemy. Here, by contrast, accompanied by the "What Is War" theme, the NVA commander respectfully regards a small American flag that has been left behind, carefully replaces it in the same place that he found it, and suggests to one of his troopers that this will be seen as an American victory, which will prolong the war but will not, ultimately, alter the outcome.

Heard for the first time during the final battle sequence is the last verse of "Sgt. Mackenzie." The singer-soldier speaks of finding strength to face certain death in his thoughts of home and utters a plea that those he leaves behind him will remember him in prayer. This solo, quiet-voiced, plaintive plea performed in a minor mode represents a very different characteristic than the loud, brassy chest-thumping chorus of the "Ballad of the Green Berets." The lyric returns us to my initial point regarding Moore as both soldier and family man, the performance of one role informing and supporting the performance of the other. One effectively becomes an extension of the other in that Moore's regard for his troops (as well as for those of the enemy) is not different in character from his regard for his own family. And what is particularly interesting is that the motivation for courage in the face mortality and strength to endure pain and loss is provided by individuals — by "thoughts of home" — rather than by love of country.

While one could argue that thoughts of home include love of country (and certainly there is no indication that Moore or Galloway do not, in fact, love their country) it is nonetheless significant that the final voice-overs provided by both Moore and Galloway discuss sacrifice only as it applies to individual relationships. During the film's denouement, Moore's voice-over, comprised of the text of his letter to Geoghegan's widow Barbara (Keri Russell), does not reference sacrifice for country. It expresses only sadness at the loss and asks her to take comfort in her husband's assured place in heaven. This shot, in which we hear Moore's letter in his own voice as we see Barbara reading it, is intercut with a similarly constructed image of a young Vietnamese woman whose photograph Moore found in the diary of a dead NVA soldier, who had nearly killed him.

Moore's words continue from one shot to the next as the camera cuts from Barbara to the Vietnamese widow. The juxtaposition informs the viewer that the sentiment Moore expresses to Barbara extends also to the widow of the unnamed NVA soldier, who we see reading the returned diary, a letter from Moore on the desk before her. The suturing of these two shots via the "What Is War" theme accompanied by Moore's voice-over suggest, yet again, that Moore's response to the battle transcends nationalism and elevates personal relationships.

Galloway's summation is more explicit in this regard. As the melody of "What Is War" sounds in a bugle-like voice (significantly reminiscent of "Taps"), we see the image of two returning soldiers, one pushing the other's wheelchair down a long, nearly empty airport corridor. The sequence is accompanied by Galloway's voice: "They went to war because their country ordered them to. But in the end, they fought not for their country or their flag. They fought for each other."

The representations of the male protagonists in *We Were Soldiers* must finally be read as elevating the bonds between individuals above all else, including nationalistic ideologies. The characteristics of responsibility and devotion represented in both Moore and Galloway are clearly fraternal and familial and are extended to all, regardless of nationality or era. The sentiment behind Moore's prayer in the chapel sequence early in the film, which included a request of God to ignore the prayers of the enemy "and help us blow those little bastards straight to hell" (an anomalous plea with regard to the tenor of the rest of the film), is summarily abrogated by his reaction to the dying NVA troopers during the final battle, by his comparison to the NVA commander and by the extension of his feelings of remorse for the widow (perhaps girlfriend) of the unnamed, dead NVA soldier. If, as I have suggested here, the representation of Moore and Galloway is also primarily that of men seeking reasons for their engagement in war, then these bonds provide the only answer, ambivalent as it is, that this film has to offer. In the end, Galloway is unable to help "the folks back home" understand the war. All he is able to do is to tell them how it feels.

V

Heroes Without a Cause: Scoring Practice and the Devolution of Combat Film Heroism in the Wake of Vietnam

"If men really disapproved of war, dear, we'd have stopped war years ago. Men like war." So said writer Adela Rogers St. Johns in an interview conducted by Warren Beatty for his 1981 film *Reds*. It is a bleak indictment, to be sure, and one that only rarely finds its way into popular culture's representations. We have considered scores that facilitate a number of representations: the dutiful reluctance of Capt. Bill Walker (Robert Mitchum), the American-as-savior Col. Mike Kirby (John Wayne), the discomforting ambiguity of Private Joker (Matthew Modine), and the conflicted paternalism of Lt. Col. Hal Moore; but we have not yet encountered a protagonist who actually *likes* war. While it is true that the protagonists considered here do not represent anything close to a full inventory of the kinds of protagonists offered up by the American combat film, it is also true that among the vast array of American war film protagonists — protagonists who depict surprisingly diverse feelings about, and approaches to, the conduct of war and the reasons for it — few actually *like* it. Most often, the American soldierly myth presents soldiers who "do what a man's gotta do," do it better than everyone else, but in the end are saddened by the necessary evil of having had to do it and are eager to finish the job so that they can return home to a far more mundane way of life. When we do see soldiers who look forward to battle, the common generic pattern displaying unseasoned soldiers' excitement at giving the enemy what for is almost always tempered with an eventual, sober reckoning of what it really means to kill, to be killed, and to watch friends get killed.

There are, of course, exceptions. Perhaps *Patton* (1970) is the most glaring of these. But General Patton provokes dramatic interest precisely because he is an anomaly. Too, the audience's admiration is alibied by the fact that Patton is punished throughout the eponymous film for his jingoistic behavior, and whatever support the mise-en-scène provides for his fervor is often ambivalent. Consider, for example, General Bradley's (Karl Malden) admonishment, "There's one big difference between you and me, George. I do this job because I've been trained to do it. You do it because you love it." But if the narrative suggests that we look askance at Patton's zeal, it also insists that we admire his success as it justifies the ends he achieves. Further, he answers popular expectations of heroism in enough other, traditional ways to facilitate the audience's positive identification, including, most importantly, his conviction that "A moral impulse is behind every American war," which, as Cawley suggests, is an essential ingredient in the myth of the American soldierly hero (70).

Other examples of soldierly representations who are explicit about loving war for its own sake are often secondary characters, whose affinity is usually represented ironically. Lieutenant Colonel Bill Kilgore in *Apocalypse Now* (1979), for example, who "love[s] the smell of napalm in the morning," the colonel in *Full Metal Jacket* who admonishes joker for his ambivalence and advises him that "We've got to keep our heads until this peace craze blows over," and Staff Sgt. Sykes (Jamie Foxx) who tells Swofford (Jake Gyllenhaal) in *Jarhead* (2005) that he isn't home making 100K a year "Because I love this job. I thank God for every fucking day he gives me in the corps, oorah."

Perhaps men are uncomfortable acknowledging an affinity for war, concerned it can be interpreted as a particularly distasteful component of their gendered selves; or perhaps St. Johns makes an unfair observation, only anecdotally defensible. Whatever the case, it is, interestingly enough, a woman who has addressed the characterization in a manner unadorned by irony or hubris. Kathryn Bigelow's *The Hurt Locker* (2008), then, foregrounds a very different kind of war hero. Sergeant William James (Jeremy Renner) does not see war as an opportunity to fight for his country, he does not see it as a chance to defend helpless civilians against oppressors, and he does not engage out of fraternal duty. For him, it's a recreational drug.

The Narrative: Boys Who Play with Fireworks

The Hurt Locker follows the activities of a three-member Explosive Ordinance Disposal (EOD) squad during the U.S.–Iraq War in 2004. The protagonist, Sergeant First Class William James (Jeremy Renner), has replaced Staff Sgt. Matt Thompson (Guy Pierce), who dies when he is liquefied inside his body armor when an explosive device he is working to disarm is detonated remotely. The film is structured as are most combat films, moving from periods of active combat to periods of down time during which the soldiers reveal themselves to the audience and to each other as they talk about women, think about home, and engage in various forms of physical or verbal horseplay. Here, however, the conventional, loud and chaotic combat sequence common to most combat films is by and large replaced by sequences fraught with quiet, extreme tension as James works to disarm various kinds of explosives—roadside devices, mines, booby-trapped vehicles, explosives strapped to living men, and one inserted into the body of a dead, adolescent male. As he does so, his comrades cover him by monitoring the activities of civilians, keeping them clear of the explosives, and watching for enemy insurgents intent on detonating the bombs. The dramatic intensity, then, is generated by the audience's concern for James's survival as, over and over, tension builds to a climax that never comes.

James's willingness to place himself in harms way while disregarding standard safety precautions creates ongoing friction with the other two members of his squad, Sgt. JT Sanborn (Anthony Mackie) and Specialist Owen Eldridge (Brian Geraghty). Indeed, in one sequence, tension has reached a point at which, fearing that James's leadership jeopardizes their lives, Sanborn and Eldridge entertain the possibility of intentionally detonating an explosive device to kill him. In the movie's final sequences, Eldridge is sent home with a leg wound that James inflicted while saving Eldridge's life. Eldridge, however, blames James for unnecessarily creating the life-threatening situation from which he saved him, and accuses James of intentionally doing so to fulfill his desire for excitement.

Upon the end of his tour of duty, James returns home to his wife and son. He stays only briefly, unable to adjust to the mundane work-a-day world of domestic life. Shopping for groceries, maintaining his home, preparing food with his wife—these activities are intolerable in their ordinariness. In the end, James returns to Iraq leaving his family life behind.

The central theme of *The Hurt Locker*, which is facilitated throughout by both composed and compiled portions of its score, revolves around Sgt. James's inability or refusal to give up the addictive exhilaration he experiences as a bomb technician and to return to the social structure of wife and family. It is worth noting that the war film genre is rife with depictions of the difficulty returning veterans face re-adjusting to civilian life. Scholarly and popular writers have discussed such re-integration challenges at length, often contextualizing them as so-called "crises of masculinity," and popular cinema has represented resolution as well as non-resolution in a number of ways. Sometimes the veterans are integrated into domesticity through a woman's love (*The Man in the Gray Flannel Suit* [1956], *The Best Years of Our Lives* [1946]); sometimes, unable to adjust, they kill themselves (*Coming Home* [1978], *Jarhead* [2005]); and sometimes they reenlist (*Stop Loss* [2008], *The Hurt Locker* [2008]). These representations offer a number of reasons for difficult adjustment. At times, the conflict is born of moving from a situation in which power over life and death, and easy, uncomplicated relationships (either heterosexual or homosocial) have been replaced with the messiness of domesticity and the expectations of "civilized" life: getting and keeping a job, acknowledging a woman's point of view, and controlling one's violent impulses. In other cases, particularly with regard to representations of Vietnam veterans, reintegration is made difficult by a society's disregard for a soldier's sacrifice. Post-traumatic stress disorder is, of course, yet another represented difficulty emerging from the soldier's inability to live with what he has done or witnessed. But among these explanations, Sgt. James's pursuit of the excitement of war as an escape from the boredom of civilian life, if not unusual in fact, is at least unusual as a popular representation.

Music for the Adrenal Gland

Thus, Sgt. James departs significantly from the "norms" of war film protagonists represented during the golden age of war movies. While he does so in different ways than, for example, Pvt. Joker in *Full Metal Jacket*, or Col. Kurtz in *Apocalypse Now*, his departure illustrates yet another direction the genre takes as if seeking an appropriate formula for heroic representation amidst a cultural atmosphere of ambivalent faith vis-à-vis United States military engagement. As a result, and congruent with Kassabian's theory, the music that helps define him also departs from Hollywood's conventional, brassy fanfare, to some extent circumventing the traditional codes of classical scoring practice, once again, by employing the more flexible device of the combination score — a score made up of both compiled and composed music.

As was true of Joker, the surface representation of Sgt. James as a fresh-faced, competent and enthusiastic soldier belies a less savory psychic current flowing beneath the narrative facade — a current revealed in large part by the music that represents him. We encounter James for the first time in his trailer listening to the song "Fear (Is Big Business)" by Ministry. As the song plays at ear-bleeding volume, we cut from a black screen to a tight close-up of Sgt. James, eyes closed and head bowed. His hands, which he clenches and unclenches, are held against his forehead, and there is a lit cigarette clinched between his fingers. The pose suggests a combination of concentration and controlled aggression. The song belongs to a particularly virulent strain of heavy metal called industrial metal, a genre with ties to thrash metal, death metal, and punk. Heavy metal music and the proliferation of sub-categories it has spawned over the last four or so decades has been attacked periodically by various right-thinking (read that as you will) groups, who have blamed a number of violent and self-destructive acts on its influence. Whether or not there is any merit at all to such charges, they have certainly contributed to cultural perceptions; and notwithstanding the discredited and naïve view of media effects that such charges bespeak, there are some pertinent observations to be made regarding Sgt. James and what his music of choice reveals about him. Frank Faulkner observes:

> [N]oting a morbid fascination with death, brutish procreative acts, World War Three and the sheer pointlessness of existence, it is nonetheless worth observing that Metal's Realist honesty in an era of nuclear-weapon inspired MAD (Mutual Assured Destruction) arguably says far more about the human condition than saccharine paens [*sic*] to teenybopper pre-sexual "lurve" and mindless, gratuitous optimism in the manner of, say, The Osmonds, Boyzone, Westlife or the Jackson Five [186].

I have argued previously that such saccharine paeans work intentionally to disrupt a coherent reading of Pvt. Joker and the "world of shit" he inhabits in *Full Metal Jacket*. Here, there seems to be an attempt to return to coherence with a more appropriate vehicle to facilitate the representation of Sgt. James. Such is the flexibility of the compiled score as theorized by Kassabian (2–3). The cultural associations that Faulkner attributes to this genre appropriately parallel James's disregard for his own well-being, and, by extension, that of his squad members. Note, for example, that in this sequence, during which James meets Sanborn for the first time, he ignores Sanborn's warning about mortar fragments and enlists his help to pry off the protective plywood nailed to his windows because "it's not gonna stop a mortar round from comin' in through the roof." Such disregard for his own preservation may or may not be read as "a morbid fascination with death," but when considered with sequences depicting his caution-to-the-wind approach to disarming bombs, and juxtaposed with the ambivalence with which he discusses his wife and family and with later sequences during which we see him profoundly bored by work-a-day domestic responsibilities at home, risk-taking is clearly a means by which he effects escape from the "pointlessness of existence." Further, regarding James's addiction to adrenaline, quoting a 1992 study by J. Arnette, Rubin, West and Mitchell note that "preferences for heavy metal music were associated with higher levels of sensation seeking" (27)— precisely the charge leveled against James by Eldridge just before Eldridge is shipped home with a leg wound, inflicted, as indicated earlier, by James himself during a dangerous situation into which he had placed Eldridge unnecessarily.

I have noted earlier that many scholars writing about the function of compiled scores argue for the explicit contribution of lyrics to perceivers' readings of the filmic message (Anderson 112, Carey and Hannan 173, Kassabian 80, Vize 32). Although the lyrics of "Fear" are not contained in the excerpt James listens to before shutting it off to greet Sanborn, "even when only a brief snatch of a popular song is heard in a film, it automatically alludes to the presence of the rest of the song as a separate entity" (Anderson 113). Too, although most of *Hurt Locker*'s audience would probably be unfamiliar with them, the lyrics are worth noting for their specific reference to (and attitude about) the setting and because they confirm the general cultural associations that have been attributed to the genre. While the first-person narrator of "Fear (Is Big Business)" speaks typically enough of alienation, paranoia and psychic disorder, he goes on to place the blame for his condition on foreign and home grown terrorists. Particularly interesting is that he minimizes his fear of Saddam Hussein, and instead, indicts the U.S. government. Similarly, Ministry's "Palestina,"— another diegetic piece that James plays in a later sequence during which the EOD squad "unwinds" by guzzling whiskey and competing to see who can punch the other hardest in the stomach — is also charged with political iconoclasm. The song is about a young girl who responds to the oppression she sees all around her by strapping explosives to her body and becoming a suicide bomber. Thus, suicidal tendencies, alienation, and thrill-seeking all become messages emerging from the diegetic score. While our visual impression of James never reaches this explicitly negative level, the musical suggestions underlying the heavy metal genre he embraces, particularly with regard to the choice of these particular songs, are indeed disturbing when considered within the context of what it takes to be a motivated, successful American hero in the 21st century. Given the anti–U.S. message in both of these songs (whether it emerges from the cultural baggage of alienation associated with the genre, from an explicit knowledge of the lyrics, or from both of these) James's motive for "defending" his country is not based upon devotion to it, but on his desire to get away from it. Unlike Pvt. Joker and other protagonists of the anti–Vietnam War films in the late 1970s and the 1980s, whose representations subverted the American soldierly myth because their behaviors and ideologies could not be reconciled to it, and unlike the heroic representations that came later, e.g., Hal Moore in *We Were Soldiers*, who tried to reclaim elements of the myth by personalizing their battles and repositioning allegiance from country to comrade, Sgt. James's heroics devolve into self-gratification. The iconoclastic messages embedded in his music of choice may indeed suggest an ultimate cynicism regarding the war: an implicit acknowledgment that the war may be ill-conceived coupled with an eagerness to participate in it because of the way it makes him feel. Such a reading makes the copy that opens the film, a quotation from Chris Hedges, particularly apposite: "The rush of battle is often a potent and lethal addiction, for war is a drug." James knows that war, like any drug, is destructive and therefore morally indefensible, yet he is willing to ignore these properties because the way it make him feel is more important to him than the moral implications of participating in it.

To recall Kassabian's theory yet again — she has pointed to popular music's ability to create "paths of identification" along which the perceiver can find common areas of identification with a protagonist through a shared response to a musical genre or to specific songs. One could argue that the opposite can also be true. I would suggest that heavy metal constructs not paths, but roadblocks to identification. The music works to subvert previous filmic representations which supported a soldierly myth that lauded a warrior's success by justifying it as being against an evil or for an ideology. Here, the aggressive, violent music works to distance the audience from Sgt. James, leading us to look askance upon his love for war instead of admiring his successful practice of it. Like the fans of the music he favors who eschew the "saccharine paeans" of mainstream pop music, James exists outside the mainstream. He disdains life's simple, domestic pleasures — those pleasures of hearth and home that the American soldierly myth suggests the military is charged with securing, those pleasures glorified, once again, in the music against which heavy metal reacts. Thus, while *The Hurt Locker* does not, on its surface, proselytize against war, it nonetheless embeds an anti-war sentiment by suggesting the psychological damage war does to those who fight it, and by dismembering claims to moral or ethical motivation for pursuing it.

Heavy metal's reaction against mainstream pop music is not only expressed in content, but also in form. While the tonal, harmonic and rhythmic patterns of most rock or pop music are consistently transparent and predictable, the same cannot be said for heavy metal. Just as metal works to subvert pop's "gratuitous optimism" by way of nihilistic or Machiavellian messages of various stripes, so too does it seek unsettling alternatives to the sometimes vapid melodic, rhythmic, and harmonic structures that provide pleasure through comfort borne of familiarity. "Fear (Is Big Business)" for example *seems* to set up a home key[1] with its repeating bass pedal,[2] but the repeating, descending chromatic line layered above it maintains no tonal relationship to the pedal note. Further, the descending line is vertically structured in perfect fifths. Thus, with no 3rd or 7th degree to spell a recognizable chord structure,[3] there is no basis for analyzing the tune within the confines of diatonic harmony.[4] While a key center could be identified based upon the repetition of the pedal note, this note is unrelated to the rest of the musical design, including the vertical structure. The tune's formal elements work against a sense of resolution — indeed, they create a musical situation in which no resolution is possible — creating the same sense of edgy discomfort that James inspires in his men.

Clearly, structures that ignore the constraints of diatonic harmony have been part of Western music for centuries. But what is remarkable here is that such boundaries are breached in the context of popular music. For better or worse, popular music is nothing if it is not formulaic and, again, predictable. Hence, just as Sgt. James chooses a musical genre that departs intentionally from the constraints that define its context, so too does James himself depart from what is expected of a combat hero.

But while Sgt. James's departure from convention, which is propelled by his motivation for putting himself in harms way, may differ from that which drives other war film protagonists, this is not to say that similarities do not exist. As I have observed a number of times, when patterns of genre change to accommodate cultural shifts in attitudes (and I should hasten to add that one example is not indicative of generic change), they do not do so all at once; thus, when one is projecting possible changes in cultural attitudes that could be reflected in changes in generic patterns, it is also important to account for similarities. While James does not assimilate because he is profoundly bored by domestic life, which offers no equivalent to the excitement of war; and while, once again, this is not the same as the difficulty represented by many other protagonists challenged by different constraints imposed by civilian life, his failure to assimilate is nonetheless, in and of itself, common to many war film protagonists. Such difficulties assimilating can emerge from a number of causes. Relationships with women that are suddenly based upon the rituals of courtship and marriage are more complicated than those enjoyed during a war, when the future seems tenuous and thus unimportant, and responsibility is not an issue. Competitors in the workplace cannot be dispatched in the same way as enemies on the battlefield, and violent confrontation — the requisite skill for which soldiers are rewarded — is now unacceptable; and there is no readily available or achievable means to effectively replace it. For these and other reasons, and notwithstanding the differences, difficulty assimilating is a common theme represented in many war films.

The main point I wish to make here is that often, and regardless of the specific reasons for it, a significant irony accompanies the protagonist's difficulty assimilating; that is, the same skills and conditions that enable a soldier to fight successfully for his country are those that the country's social order find most threatening. Significantly, it is precisely this same irony that often informs thematic generic patterns for representing the Western[5] hero. Schatz writes: "[The Westerner] is an isolated, psychologically static man of personal integrity who acts because society is too weak to do so. And it is these actions that finally enforce social order but necessitate his departure from the community he has saved. [...H]e rids society of a menace, but in so doing, he reaffirms his own basic incompatibility with the community's values" (57). General similarities between war films and Westerns have been noted by writers and have even been parodied within the films themselves. Discussing the components of war film masculinities, for example, Ralph Donald notes, "As both Carpenter (1990) and J. Smith (1975) suggest, in many ways, war films are Westerns taking place in locations other than the West" (125). And to cite a filmic example, the Lusthogs squad in Kubrick's *Full Metal Jacket* make the connection explicit by comparing themselves and the Vietnam War to movies about "cowboys and Indians." As they are being filmed for television news during the battle of Hue, they discuss ironically who will play John Wayne, who will play his horse, and who will play Ann Margaret. The Indians, they suggest, can be played by the "gooks." The implicit connection to the Western and the Western hero evident in *The Hurt Locker* is important for what it reveals about the character of Sgt. James, thus, the mechanisms within the mise-en-scène that reinforce it are noteworthy; these include the narrative structure, the visual composition, and, most apposite to the current discussion, a stylistic musical similarity in the score.

Once Upon a Time in the Middle East

In a key combat sequence, the squad is pinned down by three enemy soldiers sniping from a ruined cinderblock structure surrounded by desert.

James, Owen, and Sanborn take cover behind a dirt embankment, and Sanborn and James form a sniper team with Sanborn as the shooter and James as the spotter. The tension mounts as they await clear shots at the Iraqi soldiers. Sans mountains, the Iraqi desert landscape, complete with a dust devil, visually echoes that of the American West. An empty track waiting for an Iraqi train (or the 3:10 to Yuma) spans the horizon. Goats (rather than sheep or cattle) wander across the tracks. The ruin in which the enemy is "holed-up" could be any abandoned building on the outskirts of a dusty Western town, and the narrative device of the standoff or showdown (conducted here with automatic weapons rather than six-shooters) could be occurring between enemy soldiers or between fleeing bank robbers and the posse pursuing them.

After they have been under sniper fire for nearly ten minutes, the main theme from Marco Beltrami and Buck Sanders's original score enters for the first time as one of Sanborn's spent cartridges hits the desert floor. The cue, which combines music and sound design, begins with something reminiscent of an Arabic wind instrument called a nay, which plays an ambiguous, wavering, reverberating melody. The style — both melodically and because of the timbre's resemblance to a person whistling — is reminiscent of Ennio Morricone's scores for Sergio Leone's spaghetti Westerns, not surprising as Sanders suggests that the cue was inspired by Morricone (Koppl 2). A low bass note sets up an intermittent pulse mimetic of a heartbeat (a musical icon, if you will), a relatively common musical device indexical of tension and danger. A strummed guitar with vibrato slowly arpeggiates[6] a minor chord to accompany the cue's melody, which is played on the erhu, a bowed, two-stringed traditional Chinese instrument. The natural minor, seven-note melodic phrase descends one octave and is nearly identical in shape[7] and intervallic relationship[8] to the opening phrase in Morricone's theme for Sergio Leone's *For a Few Dollars More* (1965). The guitar is a musical staple common in many Westerns (*The Good the Bad and the Ugly* [1966], *The Wild Bunch* [1969], *McCabe and Mrs. Miller* [1971], *Pat Garrett and Billy the Kid* [1973], *3:10 to Yuma* [2007]), to name just a few), and it is worth noting that Beltrami wrote the score for the 2007 remake of *3:10 to Yuma*, which was used as a "temp track"[9] for *The Hurt Locker*. Sanders has suggested that the Western-styled score seemed appropriate "because of the setting and the fact that SSG James is like a rebellious cowboy" (Koppl 2). Thus, the musical design, in tandem with the visual and narrative references to the Western genre's mise-en-scène, work to associate Sgt. James with the characteristics of the Westerner, appropriately recalling his ironic ability to tap his violent nature to protect a social order he cannot take part in *because* of his violent nature — because he craves such violence for the excitement it provides. Functionally, then, the score works as a kind of intertextual, musical reference to the thematic patterns often found in the other genre, and through this association, it reinforces the message of the current one.

Beyond this intertextual reference to the Westerner, the juxtaposition of the Western style strummed guitar with the exotic-sounding erhu conflates cultural familiarity and cultural otherness. Throughout this and other films set in the Middle East or Africa, e.g., *Black Hawk Down* (2001), *Jarhead* (2005), *Redacted* (2007), Arabic or Arabic-flavored scores function to indicate setting. Gorbman writes:

> Strongly codified Hollywood harmonies, melodic patterns, rhythms, and habits of orchestration are employed as a matter of course in classical cinema for establishing setting. A 4/4 allegretto drumbeat (or pizzicato in bass viols), the first beat emphatically accented, with a simple minor-modal tune played by high woodwinds or strings, signifies "Indian territory." A rumba rhythm and major melody played by either trumpet or instruments in the marimba family signifies Latin America. Xylophones or woodblocks, playing simple minor melodies in 4/4, evoke Japan or China. If one hears Strauss-like waltzes in the strings, it must be turn-of-the-century Vienna. Accordions are associated with Rome and Paris; harps often introduce us to medieval, Renaissance, or heavenly settings [Gorbman 83].

But with this in mind, what is particularly significant here is that the theme's function is far broader than the Hollywood scoring practice of narrative cueing identified by Gorbman above. Here, the score not only indicates place or setting in the traditional manner, thereby creating a strong sense of otherness, but, as indicated, it also incorporates familiar intertextual reference to the Western genre, thereby transferring cultural meanings associated with that genre to the combat genre. Too, the juxtaposition of opposites, i.e., the exotic melody and instrumentation contrasted with the familiar guitar arpeggiating Western harmonies, works metaphorically to further reinforce components of Sgt. James's character congruent with the previous discussion. Thus, this simply orchestrated melody, because of its form and its cultural references, simultaneously limns three separate components of James's character: his country of origin, his country of choice, and his ironic similarity to the traditional Westerner. While he is an American male and is thus associated with all of the cultural baggage which that implies, he has nonetheless rejected the social expectations congruent with that part of his identity and is more comfortable moving within the context of the exotic Iraqi desert. The score, with its combined cultural influences, functions within the context of James's actions and his surroundings to define his character. Context, then, plays an essential role in this reading of the score. Dunbar-Hall writes:

> It would not be wrong to suggest that what gives meaning to a musical event (seen as a signifier) and its signified (either musical or extra musical meaning) is the context in which the event takes place, and in popular music context can be equated with sub-style. [...I]t is these sub-styles, through their use of specific musical events, such as rhythmic cells, harmonic motifs, types of bass lines, musical processes, or specific timbres, which in turn give meaning to the events. A popular sub-style is to be seen as a code, giving sense to the relationship between a musical event and its significance [Dunbar-Hall 229–130].

To summarize the discussion so far, Dunbar-Hall's observation works to explain both the associations that an audience makes based upon the chosen musical genre (that is, the diegetic Ministry cues analyzed above), as well as the associations created by the intertextual references made by the composed section of *The Hurt Locker*'s score to the stylistic elements common to many Westerns.

While I have not argued that *The Hurt Locker* baptizes a specific cue as a leitmotif referencing Sgt. James, I would suggest that there is a leitmotif-like function in the use of the Ministry cues as a generic group. The function is suggested by the fact that we hear "Fear" and "Palestina" diegetically when they are James's own musical selections, which he plays in his own quarters. Further indication of this intended association is indicated by the fact that "Khyber Pass," discussed below, enters when James is the central or only character in the frame. Thus the songs are associated with James specifically, and signify key components of his character through genre, form, and lyrical content.

Into the Sunset (Sort Of)

Just before the final scene, a montage sequence shows us a series of vignettes representing James at home following the end of his tour. He is living with his "wife" (we are never quite sure whether they have divorced or not) and son, performing the work-a-day tasks of domestic life. We see him wandering aimlessly through the aisles of a grocery store, ostensibly helping his wife shop. His cart is nearly empty and his wife's is full. A saccharine string arrangement of "Your Smiling Face" is piped diegetically through the store's Muzak system. Strikingly reminiscent of "Feelings," which, of course, has become synonymous with vapidity, it serves as an ironic reflection of James's unspoken response as he stares glassy-eyed down a dauntingly cavernous aisle of cereal. Following this, we see him half-heartedly cleaning the gutters of his home, preparing dinner with his wife, and finally, putting his toddler to bed. Perhaps because the child cannot understand him, he discloses the feelings that he has been unable to share with his wife. He observes aloud how eager the little boy is to embrace everything about life because it is all so new and exciting, but he warns the toddler that in time he will find that there are fewer and fewer things to love, and he says that as time has passed he has come to realize that he now loves only one thing. This final disclosure triggers a direct cut that abruptly replaces the boy's bedroom with massive, twin rotor transport helicopters hovering over an Iraqi airfield. The direct cut at this particular moment of disclosure makes it clear that the one thing James loves is not his wife, his home, or even his son; and whatever dispirited attempt at assimilation and reconciliation he has made is supplanted by his choice to return to the Iraqi desert and the exhilarating danger it provides.

The camera cuts from the exterior of the transport helicopters to a darkened interior; the huge door swings gradually open, slowly illuminating the inside; we see James waiting to disembark. He exits into the glaring Iraqi sunlight, is welcomed to Delta Company, and as the camera tilts downward from a close up of his contented face and rests on his feet, another direct cut replaces his army boots with those of his protective bomb suit. The final cut of the film places us behind James in a long shot as he walks down an Iraqi street toward, we assume, an explosive device that requires disarming. The visual construction is reminiscent of the Western hero heading off into the sunset, and just as would be true of the Western protagonist, James is intentionally leaving civilization behind because he is not emotionally equipped to accommodate the constraints it imposes.

The musical metaphor that finally and completely cements Sgt. James's expatriate status enters during this final sequence as the jump cut that indicates James has severed his domestic ties is further developed by the formal marriage of faux Islamic musical style with heavy metal rock in Ministry's "Khyber Pass." The Islamic reference is suggested by the song's title, its lyrical content as well as the vocal style. The song is named for the storied pass that cuts through the Safed Koh mountains and links Pakistan and Afghanistan. Before he was killed in Abbottabad, Pakistan on May 2, 2011, it was widely reported that Osama bin Laden had taken refuge in the pass, and the lyrics reference this possibility (as well as the incendiary suggestion that bin Laden is hiding at George W. Bush's ranch). In terms of style, underpinning the song's basic structure is a chant-like vocal by Liz Constantine, which, to untrained Western ears, could be a call to prayer issuing from a Minaret. Accompanying Constantine's vocal is the requisite heavy-handed rock drumming as well as distorted, repetitive guitar licks.

After the song enters on the cut to the transport helicopters, it continues building gradually in volume through the film's remaining minutes. Upon the first view of the helicopters we hear the opening drum part — the part of the song that is perhaps most "like" Western rock. Upon cutting to Sgt. James, however, the otherness of the cultural references emerge via the prayer- or chant-like vocal, which intensifies progressively as James gradually comes into view in the brightening interior light. Not unlike the combined elements of style identified in the composed theme analyzed above, this marriage of cultural references works to define James vis-à-vis his decision to return to Iraq, where, as indicated by the juxtaposition of the home sequence with this one, he is clearly most comfortable. Just as the song "Khyber Pass" is significantly influenced by Arabic settings, history, and musical style, so too has Sgt. James been influenced. The leitmotif-like function of the heavy metal genre, which initially suggested James's penchant for hard-edged, adrenaline-pumping activities, now confirms the finality of his decision to expatriate.

Sound Design as Narrative Cueing and Classical Hollywood Scoring Practice

Throughout this book I have referenced Gorbman's principle of narrative cueing[10] and its various applications with regard to represented masculinities in the combat film genre. As indicated by the discussion above, *The Hurt Locker's* score does indeed serve this function. But beyond this, it is important to highlight that the music in *The Hurt Locker* is often multi-purposed in its capacity to develop and explain the protagonist's personality as completely as possible — to "flesh out" his character and provide the audience a deeper understanding of what motivates his observable behavior with regard to his internal identity struggle, his thrill-seeking, his disregard for his own safety and, by extension, his disregard for the safety of his comrades. For example, I have pointed to the "Islamic" musical influences (authentic or not) as indicating not only setting, but also the setting's otherness, and that the danger encompassed by that otherness holds irresistible allure for James. I have suggested that the combining of Western elements with Arabic ones work analogically to signify James's identity ambivalence, while, at the same time, pointing to the more general issue of the uncomfortable intrusion of Western culture into an alien environment. I have also shown that the associations made to a specific musical genre function leitmotivically to indicate James's penchant for excitement regardless of possible consequences. Finally, I have shown that certain stylistic elements embodied by the score work together with other parts of the mise-en-scène as an intertextual reference, thereby transplanting thematic patterns from one genre into another. I would suggest that the multi-tasking identified here expands upon the conventional practice of narrative cueing, bringing greater dimension in the use of musical and extra-musical references than those present in the often stock or, as Eisler and Adorno were fond of charging, cliché uses standardized by classical Hollywood scoring practice (16).

Until the *3:10 to Yuma* temp track exerted its influence, Bigelow had conceived of *The Hurt Locker* as a film without a musical score (Koppl 1), and perhaps this explains why the most traditional use of narrative cueing — particularly with regard to it's illustrative function of following events and establishing mood — is effected by somewhat non-traditional means. I am referring to narrative cueing through sound design rather than through coded musical cues. Although I expect that some readers may have noticed that my discussion of certain sequences in *Full Metal Jacket* are analyses of the sound design rather than of music, as a general rule, I have not addressed sound design in this book in any methodical way, choosing instead to concentrate on the "musical" elements in the soundtrack. Indeed, the distinction between sound design, as the practice of planning, creating and organizing sonic elements, and composition, as, well, as the practice of planning creating and organizing sonic elements, seems somewhat indistinct. Nonetheless, because a widely accepted distinction is made, and because composers Marco Beltrami and Buck Sanders have said that the scoring process for *The Hurt Locker* was unique because of director Bigelow's desire to integrate their compositions with Paul Ottosson's sound design, thereby creating a soundtrack that was all of one piece (Koppl 1), it seems necessary at this point to say something about the function of Ottosson's compositions — I mean designs — with regard to their function to indicate point of view, mood and overall atmosphere.

Unlike the score, the sound designed portions of the soundtrack are singularly tasked, and in nearly all instances where the sound design exists independently of the composed score, it functions to indicate an overall sense of impending danger or sustained tension. Because the purpose is similar overall, and because there are many instances of the sound design functioning in this way, an analysis of one of these episodes will be sufficient to illustrate the point.

Many of us have experienced a sense of relief when a sound that we were not conscious of suddenly stops. A refrigerator, a dishwasher, my own dehumidifier humming away in the corner — these can drone on and on in the background somewhere beneath our consciousness. Perhaps we do not intentionally "tune out" these sounds, but tune them out we do, only to become aware of them when they suddenly stop. At that point, of course, we experience a distinct sense of relief, glad to be rid of the irritant even though we didn't realize it was irritating us in the first place. This is precisely the phenomenon that occurs in the sequence depicting Sgt. James's first mission.

The EOD squad has been summoned to investigate reports of an explosive device buried beneath rubble in the middle of a street. When they arrive, their dialog and the unsteady camera movement indicate increasing tension as they try to locate the soldiers who called in the alarm. When they discover an abandoned Humvee, a mid-pitched drone-like sound enters. The sound waxes and wanes throughout the sequence, sometimes as a mid-register drone (as when it first entered), sometimes shifting registers (although the pitch is always non-distinct) and sometimes as an airy buzz track,[11] filling sonic space and exacerbating the tension already indicated by the other filmic elements. We hear it as the squad finds and questions the men and subsequently prepares to investigate. It exits as James dons his protective suit. It re-enters as he begins walking toward the rubble. It exits when he explodes a smoke canister to obscure his progress, and is replaced by the sound of the canister, passing vehicles, honking horns, helicopters, the wind, and James's own Darth Vader-like breathing inside the bomb suit. It emerges yet again as an Iraqi taxicab speeds through the area and comes to a halt in front of James, who has leveled his hand gun at the driver. A standoff between James and the cab driver ensues as other designed sound elements are layered atop the drone. High-pitched tones, sometimes wavering and sometimes steady, exaggerate the already palpable tension until the driver slowly backs away, and James continues to walk toward the mound of rubble which may or may not conceal an IED. James reaches the site, locates the bomb, and begins working to disarm it. As he does so, the audience is unaware that the buzz track has entered yet again; it is subtle enough to be difficult to hear even if one has discerned its presence. But despite this seeming inaudibility, when James disarms the bomb by snipping the detonator's wire, we are immediately aware that the sound has stopped, and we feel a distinct sense of relief at its sudden disappearance.

The point I wish to make with this admittedly tedious account of the entrance and exit of the sound designed elements in this sequence is that in each instance, the designed cue enters as a traditional stinger[12] would, to indicate moments of increased danger, and subsequently continues, thus maintaining a sustained sense of tension. When the sound exits, it does so upon an action (as music in the classical style often does) and the tension is sustained by that which is taking place on the screen, e.g., as when the troops pull the driver from his cab, and subdue and restrain him. During the entire sequence, it is only when the ambient noise disappears entirely — when James cuts the wire — that the audience senses that the danger has passed and feels relief at the silence. What is significant, however, is that the relief is short-lived. Having believed that he had completed the mission, disarmed the bomb, and resolved the problem, the drone re-enters, James discovers another wire, the wire leads to a star-shaped cluster of six additional explosive canisters, and the process begins anew.

In a discussion earlier regarding the musical structure of the Ministry song "Fear (Is Big Business)," I pointed to the musical elements being such that they worked against traditional resolution. I drew an analogy between the lack of musical resolution and the lack of narrative resolution. The case is similar here. Just as the earlier discussion positions the compiled score as indicative of a war without end, so too do these elements of sound designed cues function to suggest the interminable nature of the conflict. In this respect, the theme represents a significant departure from combat films of the classical era which generally culminate with some kind of resolution — a battle won or a mission accomplished. Even in war films containing Alamo narratives in which all the American combatants forfeit their lives for a cause (e.g., *Bataan*), or in films in which the protagonist is killed (e.g., *The Story of G.I. Joe*, *The Sands of Iwo Jima*) we are left with a clear implication, often in the form of the final voice-over or rolling copy, that the troops will return or that the life has not been sacrificed in vain. In other words, despite an immediate defeat, the battle (and so, by extension, the war) has either been won or will be won and the "*spiritual force represented by the enemy*" (Solomon 244) has been overcome. Here, the music and the narrative that it facilitates work against such a resolution, not only with regard to winning the war, but also with regard to the protagonist finding his own kind of peace — the ability to leave the war behind and take up where he left off before the call to duty.

Assimilation Made Futile

The Hurt Locker is something more than just a tale about a soldier's struggle to assimilate following the harrowing experience of combat. As indicated previously, examples of such masculine "crises" are explored in films from Hollywood's classical period such as *The Man in the Gray Flannel Suit* and *The Best Years of Our Lives*. Such films suggest that there exist paths of redemption for the returning soldier, and that these paths eventually lead to successful assimilation. *The Hurt Locker* presents a far bleaker view — a view suggesting that the struggle to assimilate can be futile. Unlike the older movies, this one points to the inadequacy of the pleasure of domestic or civilized society to overcome an addiction to the pleasures offered by war — even a war that is ideologically unsupported by the person who fights it. It is an insidious suggestion indeed that instead of simply destroying ones ability to assimilate, war destroys one's *desire* to do so.

I suggest that this theme of unsuccessful assimilation is another instance of the ghost of Vietnam still haunting filmic soldierly representations. Such representations became prevalent in the late 1970s. Nick (Christopher Walken) and Steven (John Savage) in *The Deer Hunter* (1978), Capt. Bob Hyde (Bruce Dern) in *Coming Home* (1978) and Capt. Willard (Martin Sheen) in *Apocalypse Now* (1979), to name just a few, are all incapacitated by demons that prevent them from fitting into civilian life when they return from Vietnam. More recently, the theme of this damaged capacity continues to manifest liberally in soldierly representations in films that depict the conflicts in Iraq. Alan Troy (Peter Sarsgaard) in *Jarhead* (2005), Lawyer McCoy (Rob Devaney) in *Redacted* (2007), Steve Shriver (Channing Tatum) in *Stop Loss* (2008), Steve Penning (Wes Chatham) in *In The Valley of Elah* offer a few recent examples. Although they all fail for different reasons, and while their failure emerges within different circumstances, fail they do; and despite the fact that four or five examples may not indicate an entrenched generic pattern, it certainly can indicate the possibility of an emergent one. It seems that classical Hollywood's era of chest-thumping paeans to masculine soldierly resilience continue to be supplanted by jeremiads about the insurmountable ravages precipitated by a nation ambivalent about, or at the very least removed from, the battles it pursues. What the representations depict is a supportive environment that is inadequate to the task of assimilating men who have been taught to function in a hostile one.

VI

Re-Presenting "The Good War"

An argument put forward in preceding chapters is that popular representations of combat heroes have devolved from the picture of traditional heroism and its attendant patriotism, selflessness, acts of bravery and fierce fraternal loyalty as depicted during the age of classical Hollywood cinema, and I have shown a number of instances in which that devolution seemed to emerge from the discomfort popular opinion exhibited in the wake of Vietnam. Despite the fact that bumper stickers and public speeches give lip service to the idea of supporting our troops even in the atmosphere of ambivalent public support for specific campaigns in which those troops are engaged, the most cursory glance at current filmic representations of recent wars offers a sometimes negative, always repositioned, perspective on the myth of the American soldier.

In contrast to successful reintegration themes as depicted in 1940s, films such as *The Man in the Gray Flannel Suit* and *The Best Years of Our Lives*, we have seen that *The Hurt Locker,* with its theme of a man's damaged potential to overcome the experience of war and reintegrate into the society for which he ostensibly fights it, offers a patently negative assessment of an American soldier's motivation and behavior; and a quick inventory reveals that most other recent combat films about the Middle East are also negative in various ways.

Three Kings (1999) presents soldiers motivated by personal greed, who only redeem themselves by acting in opposition to the United States military and its disregard for the plight of Iraqi civilians. *Jarhead* (2005) offers a protagonist who joins the Marines because he "got lost on the way to college." He does not fight for his country so much as for the chance to see the "pink mist"—brain tissue exploding from a human head struck by a sniper's bullet. *The Situation* (2006) is a drama based upon rampant political and corporate corruption precipitated by the American invasion of Iraq as local politicians jockey for power, government bureaucrats do the same, and civilians caught in the middle lose their lives. *Battle for Haditha* (2007) presents soldiers who indiscriminately kill civilians for revenge, are subsequently decorated by their superiors, and are only investigated when their brutal and destructive behavior is revealed by the press. Again, civilians are caught in a lose-lose world, for if they inform on insurgents they face retribution at their hands, and if they do not, they face it at the hands of the American military. *In the Valley of Elah* (2007) offers a startlingly bleak depiction of a complete breakdown of the much-lauded fraternal bond so integral to the soldierly myth. A returned soldier kills one of his "friends" during a drunken argument, dismembers and burns the corpse with the help of his comrades, then, having worked up an appetite, heads to a local restaurant for some fried chicken. *Redacted* (2007) is a fictionalized account of the rape, murder, and immolation of an Iraqi teenager and her family by American soldiers whose superior officer is too intimidated to pursue an indictment. The military tries to minimize the incident until the press makes doing so impossible. Although the soldiers were subsequently tried, convicted and jailed, the film leaves the audience thinking that the criminals were never punished. *Stop Loss* (2008) follows the military experience of a true-blue, patriotic, good-ol'-boy from Texas who enlists to fight for his country. Having "done his duty," however, he is disillusioned by the practice of recalling troops on a technicality and as a result comes very close to fleeing the country with a manufactured identity. Although he eventually decides to obey his orders and redeploy, he does so under coercion, his loyalty replaced by anger and his patriotism replaced by cynicism. *The Men Who Stare at Goats* (2009) depicts a psychedelic drug-fueled special forces unit seeking alternatives to violent confrontation through the use of psychic powers. A farce, the film suggests that perhaps the only way contemporary audiences can feel good about U.S. combat missions is through comic purification. While the protagonist of *Green Zone* (2010) does indeed embody such classically heroic elements as loyalty, valor, and integrity; ironically, these characteristics drive him to work against his country's policies, which are in direct opposition to characteristics that define his heroic status. Because *Green Zone* depicts U.S. policy as intent upon misleading the American people to precipitate their acceptance of an unjust war waged by an unprincipled administration, traditional notions of military heroism aligning the hero with the country he represents are subverted.

The combat films abstracted above constitute the majority of recent depictions of American military involvement in the Middle East. While all may not specifically indict the American soldier (although many clearly do) it is significant that, taken together, they indict the American soldierly myth by casting aspersions upon its moorings in patriotism, integrity, and the fight for a just cause. It would seem that while support for "our troops" enjoys some popular consensus, popular culture is at a loss as to how to parse that support while representing conflicts upon which the same public looks askance. It is telling that in these examples, those protagonists who are cast in the most sympathetic light are those who, one way or another, eventually disavow either the conflict with which they are engaged or the military that is pursuing it. If, as Stanley Solomon suggests, war films take their themes from the prevailing popular attitude of the time (246), then the unavoidable implication is that that there has been a post–Vietnam seismic shift in popular attitudes about the American soldier, or at least about the wars in which he participates. "We are a hollow army, gentlemen. Vietnam has crushed our soul" opines Bill Django (Jeff Bridges) in *The Men Who Stare at Goats*.

Given the less than fervent popular support for the conflicts depicted and the sometimes startling devolution of the heroes represented, the question arises as to whether or not the tarnished soldierly myth inventoried here connects to a specific campaign, or whether there is a cultural shift toward a jaundiced attitude about soldiers in general. If such is the case, if popular culture is indeed intent upon representing the American soldier in an increasingly waning light, then we can expect his diminished stature to be common to current representations of all wars, not exclusively to those that took place in the shadow of Vietnam. The question returns the discussion to World War II, the so-called "good war" (the phrase itself comments negatively on other wars) and to the purpose of this chapter — to examine current representations of World War II protagonists and the music that facilitates them.

Unsurprisingly (as indicated in a previous chapter), the scores of 1940s combat films followed conventional Hollywood scoring practice in representing the American soldierly myth. Once again, when subject matter is conventional, so too is the form of its presentation. It is important to recall at this point that, in part, I borrowed my working description of soldierly heroism embodied by the myth from Ralph Donald's observation that these were men "performing virile, courageous, deeds designed to protect helpless civilians from some sort of aggressor" (125). Other significant characteristics informing the myth include unity of purpose and faith in a common cause — characteristics that are generally shared by classical World War II movies. Regarding such characteristics, Leo Cawley adds that there is a "moral impulse" driving American wars, that "individuals 'prove' themselves" by way of their participation in combat which "teaches truths impossible to learn elsewhere." Cawley further suggests that the "foreignness of the enemy is a sign of evil" and that by contrast Americans are better, more friendly, less selfish, and inherently better fighters than other nationalities (70). These, then, are the characteristics that will be interrogated here.

Having noted the disappearance of some or even all of these mythic qualities from current representations of wars about the Middle East — qualities that were initially coded, perpetuated, or embellished by classic World War II films — I turn now to question whether or not such heroic devolution is limited to wars waged post–Vietnam, or if representations of protagonists fighting the "good war" have also lost their luster. In other words, from the perspective of popular culture, is that war and are those who fought it less "good" than they used to be? If such is indeed the case, how is this devolution reflected in current scoring practice? Even accounting for visual and musical stylistic changes occurring naturally over time, one might reasonably assume a functionally recognizable musical connection, if not in kind at least in spirit, between the soldiers in recent World War II movies who embody the myth and their counterparts from the classical era. By the same token, one might also assume deviations in scoring practice in those representations that deviate from conventional genre patterns (such as have already been established in previous chapters). What quickly becomes evident, however, is that analysis of protagonists in either category is obscured by heterogeneous representations; i.e., the categories themselves are unclear, made so by salient thematic elements that depart from simple, conventional notions of good vs. evil, right vs. wrong, this country vs. that country, and the "Good Wife" waiting back home.

War films of the 1940s proximate to World War II had reason to espouse the war's moral imperative as well as substantial governmental support toward that end. Doing so served the national agenda of rallying the country around a common purpose, thus minimizing popular outcry at governmentally imposed sacrifice and eliciting political as well as financial support from a directly impacted populace. However, representations released well after the depicted war have generally demonstrated more varied agendas, and this is borne out by the thematic stuff of World War II films from the last two decades. Indeed, what is consistent in these current representations is inconsistency, which is to say that there are many departures from the American soldierly myth discussed above. Complicating analysis, is that these departures are not similarly patterned. The thematic material that informs them is not as coherent as, say, the post–Vietnam films discussed in Chapter III, which generally convened around the pervasive anti-war sentiment of the time; nor is it as coherent as the often repeated themes of U.S. engagements in the Middle East discussed in Chapter V, which posited the psychological toll exacted from the troops, the questionable motivation of the American military or the political machinations behind it.

Common-Man Heroism

Much has been written about film's attempt to reinstate the American myth of war in the aftermath of the 1991 Persian Gulf War and the attacks of 9/11. Prominent discussions of representations aimed at reinstating "American Triumphalism" (Auster 98) in the wake of the "dialectic disorientation" engendered by the Vietnam conflict have taken as their text Stephen Spielberg's *Saving Private Ryan* (1998). Some examples: "If the Gulf War was a military and political attempt to atone for the conflict in Vietnam, then *Saving Private Ryan* is a filmic one [...] It is no longer acceptable to simply survive a war. [...] In the new military [...] cinematically realized by Spielberg, U.S. soldiers are once again loyal heroes" (Hodgkins 77); "With a few broad strokes Spielberg touches the collective memory, evoking feelings both elegiac and patriotic" (Auster 101); "Spielberg both acknowledges and appropriates the [post–Vietnam] crisis, offering viewing audiences a "way home" to mythic America" (Owen 250). The suggestion seems to be that we have come full circle — that we can track a return to representations of the "dutiful soldier" of World War II films of the '40s and '50s.

But can we? I would argue that the circle is incomplete. We have representations of soldiers ideologically motivated, yes; however, those ideals are personal — even selfish — not uniformly patriotic. They may be congruent with the "loyal hero" of American myth, but they are not precisely motored by that myth. The grand ideals of *Bataan* (1943), in which Sgt. Bill Dane says "It don't matter where a man dies, as long as he dies for freedom," are often supplanted by personal questions, by the *search* for the kind of ideals (or a least an equivalent) that informed that narrative and others like it; and once again, we are not witnessing a return, but a search for the *way to* return. In the case of *Saving Private Ryan*, despite Sergeant Miller's (Tom Hanks) orders to bring Private Ryan (Matt Damon) home, orders inspired by the patriotic ballast packed into a letter from Abraham

Lincoln, Miller himself, never, ever, not once in this nearly three-hour film mouths one syllable sounding even remotely like patriotism or freedom. In this context such silence is deafening. Miller is not "performing virile, courageous deeds designed to protect helpless civilians from some sort of aggressor" (Donald 126). Miller is a schoolteacher who wants to go home. In what is perhaps the film's most pivotal scene of motivational disclosure, he says, "I don't know anything about Ryan. I don't care. The man means nothing to me, it's just a name. But if going to Ramelle and finding him so he can go home, if that earns me the right to get back to my wife, well then, then that's my mission."

Miller is not risking his life for the greater good, for freedom, or for poontang; he is risking it to find a way return to the personal life that is so dear to him. The question of what constitutes the greater good has collapsed into a question of how one behaves to achieve personal fulfillment. The point is not that questions of epic proportions do not exist, only that they can no longer be answered with a return to the rehearsed responses contained in the American myth of duty and patriotism. In stark contrast to Sgt. Warnicki's statement in *The Story of G.I. Joe* that "Every step forward is a step closer to home," and as the bugle-like trumpet leitmotif that has accompanied moments of introspection and extreme emotion throughout the film emerges prominently out of the wandering musical phrases that precede it, Capt. Miller says, "I just know that every man I kill the farther away from home I feel."

I do not mean to suggest, here, that *Saving Private Ryan* entirely circumvents the ideological engine that informs World War II as "the good war." In contrast to, for example, *In the Valley of Elah,* which ends with a shot of Old Glory hung upside down from a public school's flagpole as an international distress symbol, *Saving Private Ryan* opens and closes with a full-screen shot of a billowing American flag, suggesting that the film's purpose is to unpack the symbolic material it embodies. But immediately following the shot in the beginning of the film and preceding it in the end, is Ryan himself as an old man visiting Captain Miller's grave, recalling Miller's responsibility for ensuring his survival. Ryan is deeply troubled by the charge Miller placed upon him with his dying words that he must "Earn this." The point is, that as John Williams's lush orchestral cue quietly creates a sense of epic feeling and informs the viewer of the protagonist's deep emotional subjectivity, Ryan's criteria for having earned his survival is predicated upon having led a good, fair, and simple life. As he ponders his worthiness, the mise-en-scène does not display weapons or medals, Ryan does not wear a uniform, nor does the score sound the brassy bombast so common at the close of 1940s combat films as rolling copy or voice-over paeans proclaim with chest-thumping fervor the American ideals that have been upheld; instead, we see a large and adoring American family, a loving wife, and a paunchy old man wearing a striped polo shirt under a powder blue cloth jacket, who is comforted at his wife's assurance that he is a "good man." Thus, he has satisfied the criteria exemplified by Captain Miller, who did not want to save the world, but only to return to his wife. Captain Miller and Pvt. Ryan are not blood-and-guts heroes marching bravely into battle, they are ordinary guys who rise to extraordinary circumstances — not because they want to, but because they have no choice.

More recent examples of such common-man heroism are Clint Eastwood's *Flags of our Fathers* (2006) and *Letters from Iwo Jima* (2007). Released less than four months apart, these films have in common their agenda to *de-*mythologize both American *and* Japanese soldiers by debunking the hyperbolic heroism of the former and the hyperbolic demonization of the latter. In both cases, the volume of these traditionally represented characteristics is literally turned down in Eastwood's original scores, which are characterized by simple and understated melodic passages often presented by single instrumental voices — usually piano — with little or no harmonic underpinning. Gone is the brassy bombast of the forties, replaced with a smaller score to signify smaller (though not less significant) ideals. The result is a quiet reverence for pain and sacrifice made profoundly poignant because it emerges from the work-a-day concerns shared by soldiers on either side. As is true of much of Eastwood's work (e.g., *Mystic River* [2003], *Million Dollar Baby* [2004], *Gran Torino* [2008]), at the heart of the protagonists' masculinities are personal demons that inform their humanity and the viewer's identification with them. Defining personal courage, for example, that copestone of masculine myth, haunts protagonists on both sides. In *Letters from Iwo Jima,* Saigo (Kazunari Ninomiya), torn by thoughts of his wife and newborn daughter, wrestles with the cultural imperative that he give his life for a lost cause, and in *Flags of Our Fathers*, Ira Hayes (Adam Beach) is left spiritually hollow by having had undeserved and unwanted "heroism" foist upon him. Taken together, these companion pieces represent both sides as neither better nor worse than the other. They subvert the myth, but at the same time pay homage to the very soldiers that they liberate from it. As I have noted in a previous essay, *Flags of Our Fathers*

> "[R]eveals its central image (raising the U.S. flag over Iwo Jima) as a simulacrum, using it to de-mythologize the heroic myth — to point to its fabrication as a comfortable though non-existent fiction rendering the "heroes"

themselves uncomfortable. Aided by Eastwood's child-like score, the film's final sequence suggest that we remember American World War II soldiers, not as valorous fighting men, but as little boys splashing about in the ocean" [O'Brien 58].

Replacing God and Country with Self and Culture

Consistent with Cawley's observation, an individual may still engage in combat to prove one's self; but in a number of recent World War II depictions discussed here, personal success is supplanted by the metonymic reference of the individual to the ethnicity he represents, whether that ethnicity is Native American as in *Windtalkers* (2002), Japanese-American as in *Only the Brave* (2006), African-American as in *Miracle at St. Anna* (2008), or Jewish-American as in *Inglorious Basterds* (2009). In such films, the revised agenda seeks recognition for ethnic groups previously disenfranchised by the hegemonic, filmic representations of the past. In *Windtalkers*, *Only the Brave* and *Miracle at St. Anna* (to a lesser extent), music that is ethnically flavored, either by instrumentation or by genre, comprises some sections of the score, and more conventional musical material comprises other sections. These combinations work to differentiate the represented minorities while at the same time joining them to their American comrades, thus recognizing their heritage while confirming their place as American patriots.

In *Windtalkers,* the Navaho language functions as a ready-made code to radio sensitive information between allies. Native-American speakers are recruited as "code talkers." But despite their value to the war effort, the Native-American protagonists are nonetheless subject to racism, and the movie's indictment of Hollywood's and America's hegemonic structure is twofold. As are all the films in this section, *Windtalkers* is, first, a reaction to classical combat films' tendency to ignore contributions made by minorities in favor of white male protagonists. Additionally, the film positions Native Americans as technology that must be destroyed rather than be permitted to fall into enemy hands. To prevent this from happening, each code talker is assigned a "protector," who is in reality an assassin under orders to kill his charge (that is, "protect the code") should it become necessary. The Navaho soldiers, then, hold the same status as, say, an ammunition supply dump or a cache of sensitive documents.

The musical signification in *Windtalkers* is somewhat more complicated than Gorbman's prescription that "A 4/4 allegretto drumbeat (or pizzicato in bass viols), the first beat emphatically accented, with a simple minor-modal tune played by high woodwinds or strings, signifies "Indian territory" (83). Gorbman, of course, is referring to a musical cliché common to classical Hollywood Westerns meant to produce anxiety in the viewing subject by indicating that the wagon train (for example) is traveling through a hostile area. Keeping in mind that classical Hollywood never let concerns about authenticity stand in the way of creating a marketable story or a serviceable score, the point is that because the function of the culturally-coded music (authentic or not) is different dictates that the music itself will also have certain differences, at least with regard to its function to indicate ethnicity.

From the opening cue, the theme of the Native-American as patriot is effected not only by musical characteristics, but by authentic instrumentation. A layered and reverberating (as through a canyon) chant-like Native-American vocal is superimposed over a conventional orchestral cue as the camera tracks panoramic views of Monument Valley. We cut to the Native-American protagonist Private Ben Yahzee (Adam Beach) as he kisses his infant son as Old Glory waves prominently behind them. He leaves his family and friends, boards a bus filled with other Navahos, also traveling to military assignments, and recognizes his friend Charlie Whitehorse (Roger Willie) on board. At this point, the orchestral melody is briefly voiced by a wooden Indian flute. That the melody remains constant and that the culturally-coded, exotic instrument emerges seamlessly from the conventional orchestral arrangement sutures the Native-American cultural associations with those of hegemonic America. Similar constructions occur a number of times during the film. For example, as a diegetic big band cue issues from an unseen radio during a poker game below deck, and as Private Yahzee takes his turn at the table, the jazz is replaced when his friend Charlie begins playing a plaintive melody on the Indian flute. Charlie, reacting to racist comments from one of the men, hasn't joined the poker game. Instead, he answers the epithets with his music, a display of pride in his culture and his ethnicity. As the camera dollies back to reveal the table of poker players, Charlie plays in the foreground. At this point the scene dissolves to the next morning's sunrise as the flag is raised over the naval base. Thus, the Native-American music is sandwiched between American jazz and the military operation's American flag, thereby joining the Native Americans to the American war effort both musically and visually.

The Indian flute emerges significantly in a number other sequences to keep salient the theme of Native-American participation: when Ben asserts that he his fighting for his country, for his land and for his people; when, in the thick of battle, he looks at a photograph of his wife and child secured inside his helmet; during a Native-American religious ceremony; when he prays over Sgt. Joe Enders (Nicholas Cage), who has passed out from drink, tormented by flashbacks of previous battles; when Ben suggests that Joe visit him in Navaho country to ride horses, hunt and meet his son; when he prays for his dead friend Charlie, and as Joe tries to justify the fact that it was he who killed him; and finally, after Ben has returned home and prays for his friend Joe, who has fallen in battle.

I have indicated above that a significant function of combining culturally-coded instrumentation and musical style is to simultaneously merge and differentiate cultural elements; and again, the suturing of American big band jazz to Native-American flute music offers a made-to-order example. A similar strategy exploits a diegetic musical cliché common to many American war films — the soldier and his harmonica. During a period of respite on Saipan, we see a number of down-time sequences typical of the genre. In one, Charlie plays his Indian flute and Pete (Christian Slater), who plays the harmonica, asks him how he learned to play. Their conversation reveals that in one way or another their fathers were responsible, a small narrative detail that nonetheless indicates commonality despite cultural difference. Pete suggests they try a duet. He says that he knows Charlie is not about to give up playing, so they might as well try to play something together. Charlie is reluctant at first, because the thinks the instruments are not compatible.

The duet, of course, does work. The two instruments traditionally associated with ethnic folk music, one rural–American and the other Native-American, work together to create a single piece, and as they play, the film cuts to a long shot of the company preparing for, and embarking upon, their next mission. Thus, Charlie's "refusal" to give up his cultural practice, the initial reluctance to play together because of feared incompatibility, the diegetic duet accompanying the long shot of the company working together, and, of course, the ultimate success of joining the two musical voices despite their differences, provides a metaphor that encapsulates the thematic stuff of the entire film.

Miracle at St. Anna tells the story of four soldiers from the 92nd Infantry Division, Fox Company, also known as "Buffalo Soldiers"— a name generally used to designate military organizations comprised of men of color. The soldiers are cut off behind enemy lines in a small village in the Tuscany region of Italy. With them is Angelo (Matteo Sciabordi), a young boy they have rescued, a single "miraculous" survivor of a German massacre at the village of St. Anna. The massacre was staged in retaliation against the villagers for refusing to reveal the whereabouts of a notorious Partisan, Peppi "The Great Butterfly" Grotta (Pierfrancesco Favino). Eventually, Peppi and his small band of Partisans seek refuge in the Tuscany village; but among them is Rodolfo (Sergio Albelli), a traitor responsible for the massacre, who, to prevent discovery, kills Peppi and a captive German soldier who the Americans wished to interrogate but who Rodolfo feared would have exposed him. As he makes his escape, Rodolfo tries to kill Corporal Hector Negron (Laz Alonso), a black soldier from San Juan. Hector is the only American to survive a subsequent German attack on the village. The boy Angelo also survives the attack.

The film opens on events taking place many years after the war when Hector, selling stamps in a New York Post Office, recognizes Rodolfo at his window. Without hesitation, he kills the traitor with a German Lugar secreted in his drawer. Hector is acquitted of the crime thanks to the intervention of a mysterious "friend," who, in the film's final sequence, is revealed to be Angelo (Luigi Lo Cascio), now a very rich and influential man.

Like the other films considered in this section, a thematic component of *Miracle at St. Anna* is overdue recognition of contributions made by men of color serving in World War II. Nonetheless, the music signifying ethnicity is less overt, less culturally coded, than in *Windtalkers* and in *Only the Brave*. This is so for a number of reasons, not least of which is that the racial theme is made ancillary by its service to the overall context of epic feeling, which requires its own set of musical characteristics (Gorbman 81). This sense of epic feeling (one could also argue for magic realism) is created by the suggestion of divine intervention that guides the events in St. Anne, in the Tuscany village where the villagers shelter the Americans, and in the film's final moments when Hector is reunited with Angelo on a paradisiacal Caribbean beach.

The theme of marginalization is made salient in the opening sequence immediately before the generating circumstance of the killing. In 1983, Hector sits alone in his Harlem apartment watching *The Longest Day* (1962), a fictionalized account of the invasion of Normandy. Before we see Hector, we see the television screen. On it, Lt. Col. Benjamin Vandervoort (John Wayne) rides into a village to find soldiers hanging from trees and poles. Livid, Vandervoort orders that his men to "get them down." The film cuts to a profile of Hector. On the wall beside him hangs a framed World War II recruitment poster picturing Joe Louis in uniform brandishing a bayonetted rifle. A series of shots and reverse shots between the screen and Hector follow, and we hear Vandervoort say, "We're gonna hold this town till the linkup does come, whenever it is. Today, tomorrow, whenever. Till Hell freezes over. For their sake [as he gestures toward the hanging bodies] if for no other reason." The film cuts to a tight close-up of Hector's face; with obvious emotion, he says, "Pilgrim, we fought for this country, too."

The image's metaphoric reference to hate crimes against African-Americans made within the context of a combat narrative about protagonists who fight the war hoping to put an end to such hatred is, of course, significant. But particularly fascinating is the function that the score plays in associating Vandervoort's resolve to fight for the hung soldiers with the protagonists of *Miracle at St. Anna*'s resolve to fight the war hoping to end the hatred that precipitated similar treatment in their not-too-distant past. As Vandervoort gestures toward the hanging soldiers and speaks the words "for their sake," *The Longest Day*'s score issues from the television. The salient four-note musical phrase that begins the diegetic cue is of precisely the same shape — descending stepwise in precisely the same manner — as the main title that opened *Miracle at St. Anna* just moments ago, one of the film's two most prominent, recurring musical motifs. The intervallic relationship between its notes are identical, and the rhythm and tempo are nearly so. Thus, the music that accompanies Vandervoort's resolve to fight for his men becomes an intertextual reference to *Miracle*'s protagonists' resolve to fight for racial equality.

Not all of the protagonists accept the premise that their participation will lead to equal opportunity, and questions raised about the purpose of fighting the "white man's war" are often explicit in the dialog. While such questions may be accompanied by the score, they usually do not want the additional signification of culturally or ethnically specific music, as was the case in the other films discussed in this section. This is particularly (and ironically) true while the soldiers are out of the country that they are defending. The absence of culturally coded music can be seen as a reminder that the Italians mark the soldiers according to their nationality rather than according to their race. Indeed, just before the exchange between Bishop (Michael Ealy) and Stamps (Derek Luke) discussed below, Stamps remarks that he feels more at home in Italy than in America. Thus, here, it is through the absence of certain musical conventions, rather than by their presence, that the narrative is effected. It is worth recalling Meyer's apropos observation that "works of art are understood and appreciated not only in terms of what actually occurs, but in terms of *what might have happened* given the constraints of the style and the particular context in which the choice was made" (6). Note, for example, that in the sequences discussed below, the orchestral cue, which functions traditionally as a comment on the events of the narrative, is heard before the narrative cuts to America and after the it returns from America. Significantly, it is only during the flashback sequence that takes place *in* America that we hear music coded specifically as African-American.

The sequence contains a conversation that takes place in the Tuscany village immediately after Stamps has received radioed orders to capture a Nazi soldier for interrogation. Bishop is complaining about the disrespect they receive at the hands of their white officers, and Stamps is suggesting that not all white officers are unfair.

> BISHOP: The only reason white folks is thinkin' now about bein' fair in this army is because the Krauts is cuttin' their toenails too short to walk, and they're runnin' out of white folks to die.
> STAMPS: It don't matter. They said we couldn't fight. Had us float balloons, work as quartermasters, cook and clean. But the 92nd proved we can fight. This is our country too. We helped build it from the ground up. I'm here for my children and future grandchildren. This is about progress.
> BISHOP: Nigga please. Prog...? You know what? Staff Sergeant, you remember this progress?

Bishop flips a coin-sized token to Stamps. A close-up reveals the name of a Louisiana soda shop located near Camp Claiborne, the base at which the men were stationed before they deployed. The close-up of the token initiates a flashback to an incident of racial bigotry at the shop, where the owner refuses service to the black soldiers. He tells them to go around the back, and when they resist, he threatens them with a pistol. The insult is exacerbated by the presence of a group of Nazi prisoners who laugh and enjoy sundaes at one of the tables as the incident takes place. Stamps and the others are angry that the Nazis are permitted to eat in the shop, while they must go to the back door for service. Ordered back to their base by one of the MPs guarding the Nazis, they leave; but when their jeep reaches a crossing of the road and a train track (the metaphor here is obvious) they turn around, return to the shop, and demand service at gunpoint.

As the conversation between Bishop and Stamps begins, the orchestral cue enters as a single, sustained note, which soon gives way to an aimless melody with no defined key or clear direction. But as Stamps expresses hope that African-American participation in the war will usher in a brighter future for his children and grandchildren, the music's volume swells subtly and the melody becomes clearly structured as a bugle-like trumpet plays a natural minor (or Aeolian) phrase — significantly similar to the intertextual phrase discussed above — which comments positively on Stamps's hopeful dialog. But as Bishop counters Stamps's argument by flipping the token to him and thereby reminding him of the incident in the soda shop, a slightly discomforting dissonance is created by the addition of a flatted 2nd. This flatted 2nd moves the modal melody from the familiar natural minor (or Aeolian) mode into the less familiar and darker Phrygian mode.[1] Further darkening the phrase is that it is now voiced by a French horn rather than by the brighter-sounding trumpet. The darker timbre and tonality, as well as the slight dissonance created by what, at first, sounds like a departure from the diatonic natural minor scale, lends support to Bishop's incredulous response. So too does the fact that the Phrygian phrase does not resolve to the tonic note as does the natural minor phrase immediately preceding it. Instead, it ends on the unstable[2] flatted 2nd, and just as Bishop's question remains unanswered, so too does the music that accompanies it remain unresolved. At this point the flashback sequence begins.

Following a heated exchange between Stamps and the shop owner, and after one of the white MPs in charge of the Nazi prisoners orders Stamps, Bishop, Hector and Train (Omar Benson Miller) back to the base, and after the MPs lead the Nazis out of the shop, the owner brandishes his weapon again. "What you all niggers waitin' on, huh?" he says. "You all deaf nigras? Go on. Time for you to go. Want to get strung up? It's whites only in here. You tell your friends they're not welcome in here — you spread the news." As the men leave, and drive away from the shop, we hear blues figures played on a slide guitar. This is the only instance of culturally-specific African-American music to emerge during the entire film. It enters and exits at strategic places during the flashback sequence. It begins in the soda shop as the soldiers exit, and we hear it again on a shot to the owner emerging from the shop as the soldiers drive away. It enters once again on a long shot of the jeep approaching the crossroads and on a cut back to the shop where the owner holds forth about the deterioration of the country because of "the nigra in uniform and free yellow-bellied Japs running around." That the blues guitar figures sound both when the black soldiers are in the frame and when they are not, suggests that the motif is as much a signifier of place as it is of race, and while it does indeed position the soldiers culturally, it positions them geographically as well. The black soldiers' ethnicity is marked by the music *because of* their location, not apart from it — a musical reminder that is not necessary when they are simply Americans in Italy and not blacks in Louisiana.

This reading is supported by the fact that immediately upon turning the jeep around at the crossing, the guitar cue is replaced by an ascending orchestral cue, and as the black soldiers "rise up," so to speak, to claim their rights, so too does the music rise as well. Significantly, as the owner rushes to make the slops at gunpoint, the camera dollies in on a poster on the shop wall advertising war bonds. The image is of three white children on a grassy surface surrounded by a huge shadow of a swastika. The caption reads "Don't Let That Shadow Touch Them; Buy War Bonds." As the camera dollies in on the poster, the ascending brass motif previously heard as the men reversed direction at the railroad crossing enters once again. The flashback ends, and the film cuts back to an Italian street where we see Stamps, Train, Bishop and Hector staring at Nazi propaganda posters plastered to a stone wall. The posters depict African-Americans, Churchill, Roosevelt and Christ in derisive poses. Thus, as the juxtaposed posters work to associate Nazi hatred with American hatred, the music functions to universalize the fight against such hatred, and Hector's words that open the film, "Pilgrim, we fought for this country too," take on an epic cast, suggesting that the fight was not only *for* a country, but *against* the hatred that can reside in it.

Only the Brave follows the highly decorated 100th Battalion, 442nd Infantry—1400 volunteer Japanese-Americans pursuing campaigns in North Africa, Italy and France despite the U.S. Government's practice of incarcerating their friends and family in stateside internment camps. The theme here, once again, centers around a largely disenfranchised American minority that must overcome mistrust and bigotry to affirm their patriotism and fight for their country. The central combat mission depicted in the film involves the famous rescue of the 1st Battalion, 441st Infantry Regiment, a former Texas National Guard unit cut off behind enemy lines in France's Vosages Mountains.

Once again, the use of exotic instrumentation both marks and works to absorb the "otherness" of the minority soldiers; and again, the musical signification is somewhat more sophisticated than Gorbman's observation regarding classical scoring practice: "Xylophones and woodblocks, playing simple minor melodies in 4/4, evoke Japan or China" (83). Here, instead of woodblocks and xylophones, the koto and the erhu, two ancient, exotic instruments with ties to both Japan and China, emerge within the context of the orchestral cues or those cues that contain popular music. Perhaps the clearest example occurs during a flashback sequence that takes place in an internment camp when Sgt. Yukio "Yuk" Nakajo (Yuji Okumoto) is teaching his sisters to dance as his mother looks on. We hear a Japanese koto playing a solo accompanied by jazz piano. The music ends on a direct cut back to France as we see Yuk's mortally wounded, bloodied body and his comrades working to save his life in their makeshift clinic. They remove his belly band, and there is another direct cut back to the internment camp. Here, his mother and his sisters present him with the belly band and explain its significance — that it is meant to protect him when he goes into battle. They explain that the band has been stitched by women in the camp with one thousand stitches "so the spirit of a thousand loved ones will be with you." During the exchange, the koto plays a melodic line, this time accompanied by quiet strings and woodwinds. The cue continues on the cut back to the makeshift clinic where Yuk dies. The culturally coded Japanese music, then, shares sonic space with culturally-coded American jazz before it sutures the cuts between the culturally specific space of the camp where Yuk's sisters and mother give him the belly band, and the front lines of the battle. Thus, while *Only the Brave* is not scored with the same degree of visual and musical metaphor employed in *Windtalkers*, or with the intricate intertextual juxtapositions seen and heard in *Miracle at St. Anna,* the exotic instrumentation functions similarly to homogenize dedication and purpose while at the same time indicating the thematically important ethnicity.

Because the narrative it serves is, to say the least, unconventional, the score of Quentin Tarantino's *Inglorious Basterds* (2009) takes a different approach than the other films discussed in this section. The film departs in so many ways from what we might consider a "traditional" combat film, it would be difficult to score it using conventional principles. Indeed, the designation of *Inglorious Basterds* as a combat film is itself arguable; however, it is also arguable that the plot emerges from, or is made possible by, a central combat sequence. Setting that sequence apart is that it is "fictional" combat (fictional, that is, within the diegesis), presented in the form of a film produced by Joseph Goebbels (Sylvester Groth). Goebbels's film *Nation's Pride* depicts a single Nazi sniper's "heroic" victory against Allied forces. Its premier takes place in a cinema owned by a Jewish member of the French resistance Shosanna Dreyfus (Mèlanie Laurent) whose family was murdered by the Nazi "Jew Hunter" Col. Hans Landa (Christoph Waltz). The premier is attended by Joseph Goebbels, Hermann Göring, Martin Bormann and Adolph Hitler. Also present is Fredrick Zoller (Daniel Brühl), the Nazi sniper upon whose exploits *Nation's Pride* is based. Zoller, who plays himself in *Nation's Pride*, is enamored of Shosanna. The Basterds, a Jewish-American seek-and-destroy unit and Shosanna set into motion simultaneous (but unconnected) plans to destroy the theatre during the screening, thereby killing all in attendance and, by destroying the Nazi high command, ending the war in one evening. ("If you get the four, you end the war," Col. Landa rhymes with bazaar and giddy merriment as he bargains for the terms of his surrender.) Thus, *Inglorious Basterds* can be seen as a war film with a war film at its center. It sports a combat sequence that is not a combat sequence but a fictionalized representation of combat; and we look at representations of the world of war through the eyes of represented warriors who are themselves looking at representations of representations within a movie that is within the movie.

Although they are not all pertinent to the present discussion and would be too numerous to list here, it is appropriate to note, particularly in light of my intentionally convoluted, preceding observation, that *Inglorious Bastards* contains a dizzying array of intertextual references to various popular texts (particularly cinematic texts, of course). These references are made visually, dialogically and, most pertinent to this discussion, musically. Indeed, Tarantino has scored *Inglorious Basterds* with a musical stew — a pastiche comprised entirely of music borrowed from other soundtracks. The lion's share of the compiled score is made up of Ennio Morricone's compositions, and, for this reason, the film assumes the dystopian flavor of a Leone spaghetti Western (as did *Hurt Locker*), a genre with which Morricone is often associated, and from which over one-third of the score is compiled.

The Basterds identify their guerrilla tactics with the Apache resistance — thus, the scalping, and the graphic depictions of violence are congruent with the compiled score that recalls a dystopian West. The association works to indicate that the soldiers are motivated primarily by brutally exacted revenge rather than such conventional themes as patriotism and honor. With their "personal treacheries" and their comparisons to noir (Simmons 242), their "narrative obliqueness" (Simmons 292), their "comic strip violence" (Lusted 188) and their subversion of the foundation myth common to Hollywood Westerns (Lusted 191), it is not surprising that Tarantino would wish to associate his own penchant for asynchronous narrative structures peopled by good bad guys and bad good guys with a genre containing narratives and "heroes" that are similarly ambivalent. The Basterds' glee at such spectacles as watching the enemy brutally beaten with a baseball bat, their custom of scalping the enemy, their casual use of torture, and their willingness to circumvent their own word profoundly subverts the American soldierly myth in ways analogous to the Italian Western.

Other Departures

Courage and the attendant notion that Americans are better at war than everyone else is another of Cawley's heroic characteristics commonly scrutinized by current representations. Examples of such scrutiny have been explored at length with regard to representations of Vietnam and Iraq, but because these are wars that, once again, have been subject to various degrees of public disdain, and because a war film tends to "take its theme ready-made from the prevailing public view of war at the time of its production" (Solomon 246), their subversion of the American soldierly myth is not surprising. I have also discussed relatively recent films depicting World War II protagonists who are represented in positive ways, though not in ways traditionally heroic as those representations common to classical World War II films. Examples of films that fall into this category — some that have been discussed here and some that have not — include *Saving Private Ryan*, *Flags of Our Fathers*, *Saints and Soldiers* (2003), *The Great Raid* (2005) and *U-571* (2000). But perhaps more surprising, given the "good war" status of World War II, are the critical representations that emerge in post–1990s World War II films. Not all of these are specifically remarkable for their scoring practice, but are nonetheless worthy of note for their shared interrogation of the American myth. Note, for example, Sgt. Manning's ongoing reluctance to accept promotion and take command, and his deal with his commanding officer to lead a mission in return for a section-eight in *When Trumpets Fade* (1998). Note the unprecedented level of fear and reluctance to engage the enemy represented in *The Thin Red Line* (1998), and note the general representations of ineptitude attributed to the Italian Army, the German Army, and the American Army in *The Fallen* (2004), which depicts drunken commanders, troops who whimper in response to dangerous orders and try to pass them on to their comrades, and self-serving leaders willing to place their men in harm's way unnecessarily to save face.

With regard to classical Hollywood's tendency to demonize the enemy based on "foreignness," note the heartbreakingly human interaction that takes place between an American squad and a Nazi squad who stop fighting to exchange Christmas gifts and sing carols together in *A Midnight Clear* (1992). In this sequence a small band of German soldiers have decorated a tree and beckon the Americans to join them around it. They and the Americans exchange small gifts and sing simultaneously in German and English, "O Tannenbaum," "Oh Come All Ye Faithfull" and "Silent Night." Significantly, it is the enemy who initiates the quiet celebration, and the ritual singing confirms their common humanity and shared cultural beliefs and makes even more devastating the tragic miscommunication that results in the Americans having to kill the German soldiers with whom they have shared a holy, spiritual celebration of redemption the night before. The diegetic music here forces the audience to acknowledge the stark contrast between fear and trust, hate and love, war and peace.

Regarding the enemy's capacity for compassion, note also in *Everyman's War* (2009) the mercy shown to Cpl. Smith (Cole Carson) more than once by a Nazi soldier who chooses not to kill him as he runs alone and wounded through the woods behind enemy lines. Later in the film, a captured Nazi soldier relates to Smith (who cannot understand him) his hatred of what Hitler has done to his country and the loss of his children and his Jewish wife. These disclosures are immediately followed by the soldier's suicide with a found weapon, which he could have used to kill Smith but chooses to turn on himself instead. Note, too, the older German man who fled Germany to work for the U.S. government, who Smith meets at the train station as he travels home.

Everyman's War provides a good example of the thematic complexity I mentioned earlier, which separates these recent World War II representations from the "them-against-us" mentality of their forbears. For example, immediately before the German soldier chooses to show mercy by not killing Smith as he runs wounded through the countryside, there is a protracted battle sequence which, in many ways, would fit comfortably within the mise-en-scène of a 1940s combat film. But this "fit" is complicated by referential music that illustrates the sequence in an unusual way. The cue is not triumphal; it is not here to comment on American victory or superiority. Because it accompanies the sound of gunfire and artillery, (and including music in places where gunfire dominates the soundtrack is itself somewhat unusual) it works to underscore the chaotic "fog of war" and characterizes the tension of the sequence rather than the victory of the Allies.

Shortly following the battle, as Smith runs through a snow-covered field, a spiritually coded cue imbues the sequence with transcendent meaning—again, a cue that works similarly to Gorbman's category of "epic feeling." I am referring to music that "elevates the individuality of the represented characters to universal significance, makes them bigger than life, suggests transcendence, destiny" (81). As Smith runs, he is wounded, he falls, and it seems that he will not get up until flashbacks of the girl he left behind inspire him to struggle onward. The cue here works to move the specific to the general characterizing for the viewer the power of love to overcome what seems here to be an insurmountable challenge.

A singularly odd look at the war is Jeff Burr's *Straight into Darkness* (2004), which subverts a number of traditional characteristics simultaneously. The "protagonists," two AWOL soldiers in the custody of MP's, take advantage of a Nazi attack to escape but are soon recaptured by a bizarre and rag-tag group of orphaned children trained as a fighting force by the French couple who operate their orphanage. The soldiers are eventually freed to participate in a final combat sequence against an overwhelmingly large Nazi contingent. The Nazis fight not to win the war, but to plunder priceless art treasures before they lose it. The art treasures are secreted in the basement of the rural farmhouse where the paramilitary group of orphans live.

Whatever altruistic or redemptive reading one might attribute to the Americans' participation in routing the Germans is made ambivalent by their own admission that joining the fight provides their only opportunity for survival. Although there is some indication that one of the soldiers works to save his spiritual rather than his physical self, Cawley's suggestion that American soldiers are characterized by unity of purpose and faith in a common cause are born out here only if one recognizes personal survival (whether spiritual or physical) as a unifying purpose or common cause. The children prove themselves the military equals of the Americans and are certainly just as "friendly," thus contradicting two of Cawley's additional mythic components. In the end, the Germans succeed in killing the French couple, over half of the children, and one of the Americans. The others manage to flee into the cold, snow-covered countryside. The only "victory" here is the successful escape of some of the orphans and the protagonist who finds a kind of transcendent peace in the face of one of the children immediately before he dies. This peace is largely understood because of a repetitive, hypnotic musical cue based in a minor mode, which characterizes the dying soldier's tranquil, accepting subjectivity in the face of death.

Classical Hollywood Combat: A Partial Return

Saints and Soldiers (2003) departs from other post–1990s World War II films discussed in this chapter in that it is far more aligned with classical Hollywood's vision of the war. It is not explicitly intent upon debunking the heroic myth as are *Flags of Our Fathers, Saving Private Ryan,* and *Letters from Iwo Jima.* It is not driven by an agenda to revise popular cultures' previous hegemonic nearsightedness as are *Windtalkers, Miracle at St. Anna,* and *Only the Brave.* It does not explore the strange, vengeful terrain of

Inglorious Bastards. It is not peopled by dysfunctional soldierly representations as are *When Trumpets Fade, The Thin Red Line*, or *The Fallen*. And although it does contain a humanized portrait of one Nazi soldier, it does not work to mitigate demonization of the German army in general as does *A Midnight Clear*. Mostly, it just tells a story in well-crafted traditional style facilitated by a score that embodies many relatively traditional elements.

Following a brutal Nazi massacre of American POWs in Belgium, three American soldiers escape into the countryside. As they travel behind enemy lines, they encounter a downed British pilot who is in possession of vital information about a major Nazi offensive. The narrative is driven by their experiences as they work to elude Nazi patrols while they travel toward the nearest military base to deliver the flier's intelligence. With regard to the film's moorings in tradition, we have a geographically disparate group of soldiers thrown together by fate, working toward a common cause, sharing secrets, small intimacies, and stories of their wives or girlfriends. As is often the case, two of the protagonists wrestle with personal demons. They are "better" than the brutal and morally inferior enemy.

The most significant cue is a leitmotif, baptized as such during a pivotal moment of purpose and resolve. It enters as the Americans and the RAF flier Flight Sgt. Oberon Winley (Kirby Heyborne) devise a plan to deliver Winley's intelligence to a U.S. command post. As the plan takes shape, so too does the score. We hear martial snare drum figures followed by a relatively slow, legato, bugle-like brass and string cue as the soldiers agree upon the plan and subsequently move to implement it. It is important to note that the cues preceding this one are based upon minor tonalities, are comprised of joined, truncated phrases that do not form clearly delineated melodies, and function primarily to underscore the affective responses of the characters. By contrast, we now hear the first instance of melodic material constructed of wholly-formed melodic, diatonic phrases in a major key that begin and end on a tonic note. Although the affective coding of major vs. minor tonality has been framed as cliché, it nonetheless remains useful to both indicate and elicit subjective response, as it does here. The shift to a major tonality following a number of cues without clear melodic trajectory in minor modes shifts the tenor of the narrative from uncertain melancholy to, again, a sense of purpose, direction, and resolve. Thus, as the soldiers proceed with an agreed upon, common mission — a purpose beyond simply staying alive — they are defined by melodic material in a major mode and in a brass-string arrangement with clearly defined melodic phrases: not fanfare precisely, not exactly a call to arms, but with common elements of both. Because the cue is situated clearly in a single major key, and is thus self contained in contrast to the unfinished or truncated melodic phrases of the earlier cues, and because we hear it for the first time during a key sequence, it functions both metaphorically and as a leitmotif throughout the remainder of the film, entering during times of resolve, determination or epiphany.

In what is at least a partial return to classical Hollywood scoring practice, a relatively long cue that parallels the on-screen action enters as Deac (Corbin Allred), Gould (Alexander Polinsky) and Winley, disguised as German soldiers, commandeer a German jeep and drive through a German post to cross into American-held territory. As they approach the German camp, we hear low figures in brass and strings to indicate danger and a single note very high in the strings—a conventional code indicating increasing tension. A similar construction occurs again as they are questioned by a German officer. Deac manages to divert the officer's attention by requesting help to free the jeep, which has become stuck in the mud. When a group of German soldiers push the jeep, Deac speeds out of the German base toward the nearby American outpost, and we hear a rapid, repeating pulse in the strings to parallel the jeep's flight and German pursuit. The cue goes through a number of changes to illustrate the action, from pulsing string or brass figures to sustained chordal figures in the string section as the camera cuts rapidly among the fleeing jeep, Germans in pursuit, and Americans on watch, who are trying to determine which side the jeep's occupants are on. Thus, the music here parallels the onscreen events in much the same manner as we saw in my more detailed, previous analyses of illustrative cues in *The Story of G.I Joe* and in *The Green Berets*.

Heroism Reconsidered

I have suggested that the illustrative narrative cueing discussed above constitutes an uncharacteristic return to a component of classical Hollywood scoring practice because current World War II combat films, including most of those discussed here, show a marked shift away from such musical illustration, which required frequent melodic, temporal, rhythmic and harmonic changes as it sought to "catch" the events onscreen. Such wall-to-wall hyper-illustration seemed to suggest that Hollywood did not trust the viewer to appropriately perceive a character taking a fall, running away, or climbing a hill, for example, without thumping percussion, racing tempos, or ascending phrases.

If the principal function of such music was to parallel battle sequences and thereby illustrate the visual, then it follows that in more recent films the reduced instance of such music results from the fact that intensifying the action by calling attention to its every nuance has become secondary to eliciting a different kind of subjective response to characterize the fact of war as an epic struggle rather than a struggle specific to whatever war or whatever fictional or recreated battle is being depicted. Popular culture seems to have moved away from the need to base heroism upon fighting prowess and, instead, to build a different kind of hero, one that is admired for close examination of the cost in human and psychological terms.

I have characterized this as a "partial" return, because even within the traditional thematic and formal elements embodied by *Saints and Soldiers,* there are musical cues clearly aligned with the epic feeling and questioning of the soldierly myth that I have identified so often here. An example of music that signifies this subjectivity is part of a sequence that takes place in a rural house in the French countryside. The soldiers have taken shelter in the cellar. The acting leader, Staff Sgt. Gordon Gunderson (Peter Holden) follows the sound of an operatic recording, and discovers that the house is occupied by a French woman and her young daughter. Following this tense and potentially violent first meeting with the initially terrified woman, he leads her and her daughter to the basement. They introduce themselves, provide food, and, by way of greeting, kiss each soldier on his cheeks. After the child kisses Deac and the woman and her daughter leave, we cut to him sitting alone against a stone wall. As the light of the sun streams through a window and shines on his upturned face, a lush orchestral string cue, voiced, in part, to suggest choral voices, indicates his emotional response to the little girl's kiss. Deac has been haunted throughout the film by the memory of having killed a family containing many young children when he threw a grenade blindly into a building (an incident that occurred before the film's narrative began). His intense affective response to the child's kiss is made significant by the guilt and sadness he carries. The combination of the child's kiss, the lush string arrangement and its suggestion of a "heavenly" chorus, and the Madonna-like pose of Deac's upturned face bathed in light suggest a spiritual or transcendent sense of redemption.

I have visited similar points in my previous discussion of *We Were Soldiers.* It is noteworthy that that turn-of-the-century film about Vietnam, which revisits and revises previous representations, contains elements common to many turn-of-the-century films discussed here, which revise previous representations common to classical films about World War II. In my discussion of *We Were Soldiers*, I identified musically-facilitated representations of soldiers who were more inclined than earlier representations to question war in general and their "heroic" roles in it in particular. I showed how this element of having a questioning attitude was coded as a leitmotif that worked throughout the film as an indicator of soldiers' unease at the prospect of battle, their concern about their abilities to face it, and, again, about what their roles ought to be. I am suggesting here that the current trend toward emphasis on connotative narrative cueing and the attendant lack of referential (or illustrative) narrative cueing[3] works to remove the viewer from immersion in the specific *Sturm und Drang* of the onscreen action, thereby allowing more careful consideration of the affective components of war's practice.

I would posit, then, that a salient change in the current approach to scoring practice in war films common to many post–'90s World War II movies, is the attempt to reposition heroism — to mark heroism according to the protagonist's empathy and his search for meaning rather than according to his physical prowess, on personal loyalty rather than nationalism, and on common-man bravery rather than upon some larger-than-life spectacle.

VII

Comparing Classical and Current Scoring Practices

Overview of Representations

In an overarching comparison of the protagonists' characteristics in the various time frames from which the films presented here emerge, it is noteworthy that we are presented with; first, an unequivocal and unwavering ideology; second, subversion of any unambiguous ideological basis for participation in the conflict; third, a search for what ideological underpinnings may exist and their implications for redeeming (or at least explaining) soldierly activity despite the graphically depicted horror and loss resulting from that activity; fourth, an alarming devolution of the soldierly myth and the unsavory motivations for "heroic" action embodied in that devolution; and finally, in the case of films that re-present the Second World War, a variation on some of these previous themes as well others yet unexplored, most notably, the recognition of the contribution of non-hegemonic groups previously disenfranchised by Hollywood and the emergence of a relatively large group of protagonists given to questions of epic or transcendent proportion. Despite the difficulty of any study of this nature to unequivocally identify an overall trend such as a culturally-informed evolution or devolution over time, it is nonetheless safe to say that there is at least a strong suggestion that the soldierly myth has lost some of its luster, particularly in the case of representations depicting conflicts occurring following the Vietnam War; and while re-presentations of World War II seem somewhat more immune to this devolution, even these have, in many cases, seen a clear weakening of the chest-thumping patriotic fervor so common in the 1940s. It is nonetheless clear that some of what has already been written by others regarding the temporal positioning of Hollywood war films in relation to the depicted war is only partially confirmed, or, at the very least, has undergone some revision. I have mentioned elsewhere that both Stanley Solomon and Koppes and Black point to Hollywood's reluctance to negatively depict a war that is currently underway; and, according to Solomon, filmmakers are unable to stamp a combat film with their individual bias because war films tend to "take their themes from prevailing cultural attitudes" (246). When such is not the case, when a film flies in the face of such attitudes (e.g., *The Green Berets*) it risked critical and/or popular ridicule (the former was true of *The Green Berets*, though not the latter). But while it is still true that cultural attitudes are probably responsible for a genre's bias (popular culture would not remain popular otherwise), in the case of war films, the capacity of the temporal element alone to dictate that attitude is less influential. Such is clearly indicated by the patently negative representations contained in films about ongoing conflicts in the Middle East. Nonetheless, it is important to note that if the characteristics observed among the protagonists represented in most of the films discussed here reflect popular attitudes, that it is often the specific conflict represented that dictates how the protagonists will be represented. Because the representations of soldiers in recent films about World War II have not undergone the same degree of devolution as have those in conflicts following Vietnam, one can at least speculate that popular attitudes about World War II remain more positive (or at least less overtly negative) than those about the Middle East. Nonetheless, it is safe to add that post–1990s World War II protagonists are also less monochromatic than their 1940s forebears.

Keeping Score

As indicated previously, the analysis of protagonists Ernie Pyle and Bill Walker in *The Story of G.I. Joe* confirms that the principles of classical scoring practice function within combat films made during Hollywood's so-called Golden Age. This is a significant observation because in her seminal work on these principles, which informs much of the basis for comparison in this study, Claudia Gorbman focuses primarily on melodrama, and in so doing, discusses representations of women but does not specifically apply the principles to representations of masculinities. Such is also the case for a number of other writers who discuss music's role in gender construction (e.g., Kalanak, Kassabian, McClary). What is confirmed by the analyses of the cues in *The Story of G.I. Joe* (as well as other combat films from the period) is that the principles are indeed pertinent with regard to combat narratives made in the classical style. Following are examples to briefly recall the classical function of *G.I. Joe's* score. In reviewing these, as well as those that follow later, it might be useful to also review the definitions of Gorbman's principles.[1]

- The main title uses the traditional scoring practice of narrative cueing to identify the genre, point to the thematic importance of the individual soldiers, and indicate their yearning for home.
- The Artie Shaw swing/blues piece, which accompanies the he camp sequence, functions traditionally to indicate the soldiers' thoughts of home and to temporally situate the narrative.
- Also during the camp sequence, the Ann Ronell tune "Linda" functions as narrative cueing and as a signifier of emotion. It inspires thoughts of home, represents Woman as romantic "Good Object," indicates Walker's commonality with his troops, and separates Pyle with regard to his age.
- The musical collage accompanying the montage of Pyle and the men he writes about works as narrative cueing and to create continuity by indicating passing time. It underscores Pyle's role as a correspondent, represents the men's resolve, and, again, suggests their yearning for home.
- The main military theme, which is heard a number of times in the film, works as both narrative cueing and to create narrative unity. It indicates Walker's ability to successfully train his troops, thereby indicating his leadership qualities.
- The long, fragmented cues that accompany Walker's wait for Warnicki and the cue that follows it accompanying Warnicki's hearing of his son's recorded voice illustrates the slow passage of time, indicates Walker's agonizing concern, his close relationship with his troops, and Warnicki's unstable mental state. It employs a number of classical mechanisms of narrative cueing including the leitmotif, signifier of emotion, stinger, and Mickey Mousing.
- In the final sequence Pyle locates Walker's outfit; Walker is brought in dead, and the men pay final respects and offer parting words. Through narrative cueing, the stinger, and signifier of emotion, the cue illustrates the men's sadness, thus underscoring the close relationship they had with Walker.
- The end title returns to the thematic material that opened the film as the troops march toward the horizon. The return is an example of unity and the use of leitmotif, as well as a signifier of emotion.

VII. Classical and Current Scoring Practices

Once again, as indicated here, Gorbman's classical scoring principles are pertinent to representations of masculinities in classical combat films. It is also important to note, though perhaps not surprising, that they also remain vital to more current representations of the combat film protagonist when those protagonists share characteristics with, or are patterned after, traditional representations. With one interesting exception such is the case with regard to Kirby in *The Green Berets*. Following, are examples to briefly recall the classical function in the score of *The Green Berets*. The coding of the differently styled bullets will be explained later.

- The main title, "Ballad of the Green Berets," identifies the genre and positions Kirby as a "traditional" war film protagonist. It also provides credibility to both Kirby and Beckworth. It employs narrative cueing, and breaks the rule of inaudibility at the service of the narrative.
- The confrontation between Kirby and Beckworth over interrogation techniques uses narrative cueing and signifier of emotion to build tension and illustrate conflict. It also confirms Kirby's viewpoint as indicative of the film's ideological bias.
- The Montagnard child's theme is heard during sequences in which Beckworth interacts with her. It uses narrative cueing, signifier of emotion and leitmotivic function to indicate Beckworth's growing attachment. A variation on this theme enters when Beckworth sees the murdered child, and Kirby enters to discuss the murder. The same classical mechanisms indicate Beckworth's sense of loss, his inner struggle regarding American involvement, as well as Kirby's unequivocal viewpoint.
- The cue "Starlight Starbright/Ready to Fire" illustrates the main battle sequence via narrative cueing and its components, the stinger and Mickey Mousing. The cue works to increase tension, underscores Kirby's courage, and illustrates a chopper crash.
- Petersen's theme is a leitmotif which positions him as a figure of fun, and, later in the narrative, suggests his new-found credibility by its absence. The cartoon-like clarinet melody that accompanies Hamchunk's practical joke at Petersen's expense also places Petersen in a comic light.
◊ Cue accompanying Lin in the street café as she informs Kirby where and when she will deliver the Viet Cong general, and again, as she acts as a sexual trap to ensnare him. It indicates her "otherness" as foreign, female and as a narrative agent. Thus, it works to remove her from a conventionally feminine passive role. This is an example of traditional scoring practice using non-traditional signifiers.
- Hamchunk's theme is a leitmotif and a signifier of emotion, which func-

tions most significantly to indicate his sadness at discovering his friend Petersen has been killed. It also indicates Kirby's role as protector.
- The end title is a return to "The Ballad of the Green Berets," which was also the main title. It creates unity, and, in its capacity to represent Kirby's unyielding belief in the films ideology, functions as narrative cueing.

In my discussion of Walker (*The Story of G.I. Joe*) and Kirby (*The Green Berets*) I have noted that neither protagonist is assigned his own theme; however, I have also indicated how this is commiserate with Gorbman's suggestion regarding music as primarily representative of the irrational. Because hegemonic representations of masculine American heroes seek precisely the opposite — seek, that is, to position the male protagonist as in command and charged with imposing order upon a disorderly world — musical representation is more appropriate in its capacity to represent the chaotic worlds the men must tame rather than the men themselves. These different functions are reflected in formal differences. Such differences in form and function become particularly clear when one compares, for example, the illustrative function of much of the music in *The Green Berets* and the more introspective and emotional signification of the music in *We Were Soldiers*. For purposes of comparison, summaries of the cues from *We Were Soldiers* follow:

- The main title, "The Bear Went Over the Mountain" and "BINGO," which accompany Moore's family as they drive to Fort Benning and move into their house integrate Moore's military identity and his domestic identity through traditional mechanisms of narrative cueing.
- As Moore trains his troops, a martial drum cue indicates the military setting and recalls Moore's family's close tie with life in the military, thereby situating the troops as part of his extended "family." The cue functions as narrative cueing and as a leitmotif.
- "Mansions of the Lord," and "What Is War" are heard during the chapel sequence in which Geoghegan and Moore pray for guidance. The former is associated with Geoghegan and the latter with Moore. Questions regarding war and the men's roles in it are imbued with transcendence, taking the question out of the particular and situating it in the mythic. The scoring practice includes narrative cueing, leitmotif, signifier of emotion and epic feeling.
- "What Is War" enters as Moore reads to his youngest girl, and she asks what war is. The question haunts Moore later as he lays in bed. Narrative cueing, leitmotif and signifier of emotion work here to indicate the con-

cern of Moore's family and Moore's apprehension about his assignment. It also underscores Moore's questioning nature.
- "What Is War" enters as Moore is in his study reading historical accounts of the massacre of a French unit in Vietnam. Moore's wife enters and he shares his concerns with her. Narrative cueing, leitmotif function and signifier of emotion indicate Moore's apprehension and the connection he makes between the fears he has for his men and those he has for his family.
- The popular soul songs "Hold On I'm Coming" and "Hold Me, Thrill Me, Kiss Me" play diegetically at the departure party and function as narrative cueing to situate the narrative in time and place and remove the possible suggestion of anti-war bias on the part of Moore.
- "What Is War" accompanies a later study sequence during which Moore signs his will. It functions as narrative cueing, as a leitmotif and as a signifier of emotion to indicate Moore's selfless concerns and further suggests his inquiring nature.
- ◊ Theme based on the song "Sgt. MacKenzie" accompanies the flight onto Ia Drang Valley. This is an example of traditional scoring practice effected with non-traditional signifying elements. The scoring practices involved are narrative cueing, epic feeling, leitmotif, and signifier of emotion. The cue indicates Moore's concern for his men, suggests the questions that are in the soldiers' minds as they face mortal danger, and removes the question of why wars are fought from the particular and places it into the realm of myth.
- "What Is War" is connected to the previous cue and also accompanies the flight in the Ia Drang Valley. It indicates Moore's anxiety is shared by his men, underscores Moore's paternal concerns for his "boys," and expands upon the transcendent aspect of the previous "Sgt. MacKenzie" theme.
- "What Is War" accompanies Galloway as he photographs the battle. The cue further indicates the desire to understand war both for Galloway and for Moore. It indicates the transcendent nature of the question, again, moving from the particular into the realm of myth. The scoring practice includes narrative cueing, epic feeling, leitmotif function, and signifier of emotion.
- ◊ Another example of traditional scoring practice employing non-traditional signifying elements, "Sgt. MacKenzie" accompanies the final battle sequence in which the choppers come to the rescue of the American troops and summarily defeat the NVA troops. The mechanisms here are narrative cueing, epic feeling, leitmotif function, and signifier of emotion.

- "What Is War" enters on Moore's final voiceover, a reading of his condolence letter to the wife of one of his own fallen men as well as an NVA soldier's wife. It indicates Moore's sadness for his own men as well as for the enemy soldiers and moves the question of killing from the particular to the realm of myth. The traditional scoring mechanisms include narrative cueing, epic feeling, leitmotif function and signifier of emotion.

Because Kirby is a conventional filmic version of the American war hero, the score of *The Green Beret's* primary function is not to invite us into his psyche (such would be demonstrating the obvious). Instead, the music illustrates the narrative events transpiring around him. Conversely, because Moore is, by nature, far more given to introspection, and because he is represented as something of an intellectual (an "academic pussy"), the music is charged with providing far more in the way of an internal point of view. This is why much of the music (with a few notable exceptions) in *The Green Berets* would not function well alone. It requires the images it illustrates to make sense of its formal disjointedness because (to return to a point from a previous chapter) it "often sacrifices its musical coherence to effect gained in coordinating with diegetic action" (Gorbman 97). The cues in *We Were Soldiers,* however, are more individually self-contained because they work to make an overarching emotional statement and are not concerned with "catching" and thereby illustrating each event that occurs onscreen. Thus, the older score resembles, underscores, and parallels the visual, thereby immersing the audience in each specific onscreen movement, while the other seeks to comment upon it, to transcend it — to suggest, in an almost Brechtian sense, that we should consider, along with the protagonists, its larger implications.

An important consideration that has come to light in the course of this investigation has to do with the precise components of traditional scoring practice. A significant distinction exists between traditional functions of film music within the diegesis (the concepts that are signified and/or the role music plays in constructing a film's formal elements), and the specific styles of music (the material signifiers) that are generally most appropriate to any given signification. In other words, when considering, say, the bombast of a brass section accompanying the march to battle and discussing the music in terms of its illustrative or culturally-informed function according to Gorbman's principle of narrative cueing, are we to take for granted that the style of the music is a component of traditional practice, or does "narrative cueing" simply refer to what the music does rather than precisely to what kind of music does it? When, for example, the march to battle is accompanied by a style other than the brassy "tarun-ta-raa" bombast one might expect — say, for example, a plaintive or spiritual-sounding, lushly orchestrated string piece as is the case in *We Were Soldiers*— does this constitute departure from traditional scoring practice despite the fact that, functionally at least, it clearly falls under the classical category of narrative cueing (despite the fact that one is referential and the other connotative)?[2] With regard to classical scoring practice, Gorbman does address the question to some extent. She writes:

> Classical film music scores that deviate from the standard stylistic repertoire — scores using jazz or electronic music, for example — end up participating in signification just as fully as scores written in the familiar Hollywood-Wagnerian idiom. [...] In general, any musical language, other than the major nineteenth-century one, itself carried connotations simply by virtue of being unusual. Even music that attempts to subvert the principles of classical scoring will connote *something* when played with narrative images [86].

What Gorbman has not addressed specifically here is the combination or compiled score; and although compiled scores do not always function traditionally, Kalinak and others have indicated that popular songs can function in the same way as composed scores. The point is that despite Gorbman's call for a new approach to analysis based upon the use of popular music in film scores (163), simply because a portion of a given score is compiled, does not necessarily indicate that the scoring practice departs from traditional function. Such is not always the case in (for example) *We Were Soldiers, Platoon, The Boys in Company C*, or *Casualties of War*, although it clearly is the case in *Full Metal Jacket*.

With all of this in mind, I would suggest that the following three distinctions with regard to scoring practice are appropriate: (1) traditional function–traditional signifier; (2) traditional function–nontraditional signifier; and (3) nontraditional function–nontraditional signifier. These distinctions are indicated in the bulleted lists contained in this chapter with, respectively, a round bullet, an open diamond, and a solid diamond. The distinction is an important one, particularly where the representations depart from traditional stereotypes, because such departures are often signified according to traditional functional categories (e.g., narrative cueing, signifier of emotion) but at the same time call upon music that "deviate[s] from standard stylistic repertoire" (Gorbman 86).

Not surprisingly, there is no departure from traditional scoring practice in *The Story of G.I. Joe*; and, as indicated at length in Chapter II, Applebaum's score adheres both stylistically and functionally, thus confirming that the principles are pertinent to soldierly representations in combat films. Also not surprising is that the score of *The Green Berets* is, with one exception, by and large an example of traditional scoring practice. Both popular and academic criticism of *The Green Berets* have identified the film and John Wayne's portrayal of Col. Mike Kirby as a thinly disguised version of a raft of Hollywood World War II movies. Although Wayne's depiction of Sgt. Stryker in *The Sands of Iwo Jima* is not without its interesting complications, and though there are marked differences (particularly with regard to the intrusion of women and thoughts of home), Col Mike Kirby, in terms of his representation of stoic, aggressive and uncompromising masculinity, clearly resembles Stryker. This resemblance is also true of Wayne's Col. Madden in *Back to Bataan*, and Lt. Col. Vandervoort in *The Longest Day*. The similarity does not stop with roles performed by John Wayne, of course, and I could list a host of other protagonists played by a host of other actors who have portrayed the rough-talking, no-nonsense hero concealing a good heart and encumbered by some kind of baggage — either estranged women, estranged children or some other ghost to be overcome or forgotten. Thus it is, once again, no surprise that Rózsa's score is as rooted in Hollywood tradition as is the narrative it accompanies.

But despite the charge that this Vietnam combat film is simply a restatement of traditional World War II ideology, it is interesting to note the one significant example of non-traditional practice in the representation of Lin and, by extension, of Kirby via his ambivalent response to her. Because of her unique role, Kirby can neither respond to her as whore, as chattel, or as Good Romantic Object — the three basic roles Donald identifies as those most commonly afforded women by "most war films" (129). Once again, during the course of the narrative, she can be seen (either all at once or at various times) as all three of these. Interestingly enough, the deviation recalls Anahid Kassabian's remarks regarding narrative agency. What makes Lin different is that she does in fact demonstrate some degree of narrative agency (although she must use sex to do so) as opposed to more traditional and passive feminine roles. Note that in the cafe sequence, for example, it is she who steps out of the passive role to outline the plan for the men regarding how they will trap the Viet Cong general, and it is she who chooses the time and the place. Thus, she is clearly an active participant in the narrative, and, therefore, Kirby's response to her in terms of "traditional" roles of femininity becomes problematic. As noted elsewhere, Kassabian suggests the problem of musical signification for female agency is sometimes solved through the flexible signification available in popular music, particularly in the pop score's ability to create "paths of identification" (2), which allow the perceiver access to unfamiliar or unconventional representations. In *The Green Berets,* however, there is a ready solution in the form of faux–Asian music. Because Lin is marked as "other" not only by her active role in the narrative but by her ethnicity as well, she is represented on both counts by the "other" music, which is available and appropriate based upon the narrative setting. It is particularly fascinating that during the times that she is marked by this "other" music, Kirby never looks directly at her or speaks directly to her. It is only in the Da Nang nightclub sequence during which she is clearly and traditionally objectified as the object of his gaze that he regards her for any length of time.

But beyond Kirby's problematic response to Lin, *The Green Berets* offers no marked departure from classical scoring practice, and certainly the best explanation for this is the simplest: we have a traditional representation signified by way of traditional signifiers of which music is clearly a part. In keeping with the observations regarding representation and the proximity of a film's release to the war it depicts, *The Green Berets,* the only combat motion picture about Vietnam released while the war was underway, depicts its protagonist as an uncompromising and uncompromised war hero, one dedicated to the conflict and an unequivocal example of the previously discussed "traditional" heroic model identified by Ralph Donald (125), Leo Cawley (70) and Jeanine Basinger (71–72).

In stark contrast to Kirby's representation of the American soldierly myth, his unambiguous embrace of the American presence and his unwavering dedication to his cause is Joker, the protagonist of *Full Metal Jacket.* And just as the traditional hero is, for the most part, marked by traditional scoring practice, so too is the protagonist that deviates most clearly from tradition often accompanied by music that most clearly departs from it. That this is so comes as no great surprise in itself; nonetheless, what is particularly fascinating is the manner of departure and what that departure does to the music that represents — or avoids representing — him. To return to Kassabian yet again, recall that a key suggestion in *Hearing Film* is that when representations of women depart from traditionally ascribed feminine roles, the conventions of Hollywood scoring practice lose their ability to function appropriately. In other words, non-traditional roles cannot be appropriately represented with traditional signifiers (71). As mentioned earlier, one principal role departure that Kassabian identifies has to do with narrative agency. In the worlds created by classical Hollywood, men conventionally occupy the position of narrative agents while women occupy passive roles: they are the prize to be won or the poison to be counteracted. Men do things for them, to them, or about them, but it is generally the men who are doing the doing—moving the narrative forward by their action. When women assume the role of agency, then, a challenge exists for conventional signifiers—notably scoring practice—and one solution identified by Kassabian are the previously discussed "paths of identification" created by scores compiled of popular music. What is fascinating about Joker is that his representation presents an opposite situation. He is, in fact, a male war film protagonist who does not assume a strong position of narrative agency. If Joker, in the midst of his profound ambivalence and his profound ambiguity is anything at all, he is profoundly passive. He does not work to instigate the events; he works to survive them. Things happen to him, not because of him. He reacts, he does not instigate. Thus, the problem here is a reversal with respect to the one identified by Kassabian: instead of a traditionally passive role becoming active, we have a traditionally active role becoming passive. And despite Gorbman's assertion that even music attempting to subvert the principles of classical scoring practice will "connote *something*," what I have found regarding the use of the pop tunes "Goin' to the Chapel" and "Wooly Bully" in *Full Metal Jacket* is that they connote *nothing*. The cues function as non-signifiers rather than signifiers. In other words, their primary function is to indicate non-function; if you will, they are signifiers of non-signification, because of the inability to (as discussed at length in Chapter IV) reconcile in any way the song choices with the images they accompany. Because we cannot identify an ideological center in Joker's representation, so too does much of the music resist classification. Cues of this nature, then, are examples of what I suggested above could be identified as nontraditional function—nontraditional signifier. The following are the cues selected for analysis as they appeared in Chapter III:

◊ The cue accompanying the night beating of Pyle creates an ominous atmosphere, infuses the sequence with an emotionless yet organic quality suggesting the idea of dehumanization, drains the soldiers of affect (to create killing machines), and recalls Pyle's suffering during a previous training sequence. The cue functions as traditional scoring practice using non-traditional signifying elements: narrative cueing, signifier of (non)-emotion and leitmotif.
• The cue accompanying Pyle suffering on the obstacle course maintains the rhythm of the sequence thereby moving the narrative forward. It indicates the military setting and baptizes the leitmotif signifying Pyle's suffering and Harman's and Joker's role in precipitating it. It functions traditionally as narrative cueing and as a leitmotif.

VII. Classical and Current Scoring Practices 169

◊ The fire watch cue during which Pyle kills Hartman and himself creates an ominous atmosphere, infuses the sequence with emotionless yet organic quality, and suggests the idea of dehumanization. It illustrates Hartman's and Joker's lack of empathy and recalls Pyle's suffering during the training sequences and during the night beating. It contrasts Pyle's psychic anguish with Joker's desensitization. It functions traditionally with non-traditional signifying elements using narrative cueing, signifier of (non)emotion, signifier of emotion and the leitmotif.

♦ "These Boots Are Made for Walkin'" enters as a Vietnamese prostitute walks toward a street café to bargain with Joker and Rafterman. During the discussion, a Vietnamese man steals Rafterman's camera. The cue trivializes the situation, indicates a sense of displacement, and works to subvert the myth of the American soldier. There is incongruity here between the score and the image with regard to context and associations regarding the song. It is an example of nontraditional function signified with nontraditional elements.

♦ "Chapel of Love" is heard as Joker lounges in the barracks with other troops discussing boredom and battle experience. It trivializes and mocks the content of the discussion and drains the narrative of conventional meaning. There is incongruity between score and image with regard to the context and associations. The song functions nontraditionally using nontraditional signifiers.

♦ "Wooly Bully" enters when Joker reunites with Cowboy and meets the Lusthogs. It makes ambiguous the events in the sequence and drains the narrative of meaning. There is incongruity between the score and the image with regard to the context and associations with the song. It functions nontraditionally with nontraditional signifiers.

◊ "Surfin' Bird" is heard during and following the assault on Hue. It illustrates the narrative and trivializes the attack. It indicates the meaninglessness of the words used to justify killing in the sequence which follows. It functions traditionally as narrative cueing using non-traditional signifying elements.

◊ The cue accompanying Joker's execution of the sniper creates an ominous atmosphere and recalls Joker's ambivalence regarding Pyle's suffering. It illustrates rising psychic turmoil and confusion as Joker wrestles with killing the sniper. It functions traditionally using non-traditional signifiers including narrative cueing, leitmotif, and signifier of emotion.

◊ "Mickey Mouse Club Song" is sung by the troops as they march through the fire-bathed mise-en-scène of the destroyed city. It trivializes the actions of the troops, disparages their leaders and supports the ambiguity of Joker's ideology. It comments negatively on the caliber of the troops, and their mission. There is incongruity between score and image regarding the context and associations; however, stylistically, the cue contains traditional elements.

It should be noted that *Full Metal Jacket*'s "non-signification" via pre-existing music seems unique among the representations in Vietnam combat films. While there are many instances of popular music in Vietnam combat films (e.g., *Platoon, Apocalypse Now, Hamburger Hill, The Boys in Company C, Casualties of War, We Were Soldiers, The Green Berets*), in all cases, the song or songs are either diegetic, and thus, at the very least, function as a component of the setting, or they are identifiable in terms of some other classical scoring principle. The same is true of the heavy metal cues in *The Hurt Locker*. While the signifiers themselves may be somewhat non-traditional, may "deviate from standard stylistic repertoire" they are nonetheless signifying in somewhat traditional ways. In other words, the *process* of signification is recognizable even if the signifiers themselves are unconventional.

For the sequences in which Joker's representation is facilitated via traditional scoring practice but that also contain non-traditional signifiers, Gorbman's previously-quoted explanation regarding "scores that deviate from the standard stylistic repertoire" (86) holds up quite well. In many cases the non-conventional material does indeed carry connotations precisely because it is unusual. For example, I have explained that the inhuman yet organic quality of the synthesized cue in the night beating sequence emerges in part from our inability to recognize actual instruments, thereby removing association with human agency—a removal that is clearly appropriate to the narrative. At the same time, there are recognizable elements that are clearly illustrative, e.g. the "breathing tri-tone" as well as the unsettling intervallic relationships I have discussed. The same can be said of the cue that accompanies the Lusthog's search for the sniper. The sounds of tortured machinery are illustrative of the breakdown of the combat unit and the increasing dissolution of its working parts. These kinds of conventions do not require the "Hollywood-Wagnerian idiom," indeed, in this case, they function more appropriately without it. Nonetheless, they are conventional to an extent in that their metaphorical illustration of the narrative elements are situated (if not stylistically, at least functionally) within traditional principles of classical scoring. Other examples of such conventional function using non-conventional or unusual materials exist elsewhere—the river sequences of *Apocalypse Now*, for example. As Willard (Martin Sheen) moves ever nearer to the madness of Kurtz's (Marlon

Brando) bizarre compound, the synthesized score, by virtue of its unusual nature, illustrates the physical and psychological setting appropriately. One could, in fact, argue that over time, the synthesized score has itself become a stylistic convention of film music. Kalinak says as much when she writes "Synthesizers are most commonly used [...] for the unique sounds they can produce. Thus, they are often exploited in sci-fi and futuristic genres to create an other-worldly effect" (188). While not science fiction, certainly the bazaar compound as well as a number of sites along the Nung River in *Apocalypse Now* qualify as "other-worldly" as does the "world of shit" in which Pyle and Joker find themselves in *Full Metal Jacket*.

In comparing the representation of Hal Moore in *We Were Soldiers* with Mike Kirby and Joker, it is tempting, particularly in light of the apparent return to traditional scoring practice, to suggest that Moore can be read as a return to a conventional representation of the myth of the American soldier. As discussed elsewhere, such has already been suggested, at least to some extent, by other writers. This reading, however, does not hold up to close scrutiny. There are too many elements present in the representation that work to remove Moore from a purely traditional, hegemonic construction common to 1940s combat films. Despite Moore's dedication to duty and to the American ideals that that devotion suggests, his is an introspective and conflicted masculinity as compared to Kirby's unequivocal conviction. Whatever conventional American ideology may be implicit in it is overshadowed by his devotion to his family and his men. There is a notable paradox in this personal focus with regard to the extensive use of music in *We Were Soldiers* as a signifier of epic feeling, which universalizes questions and thereby distances them from their immediate reference to specific narrative events. Perhaps the best explanation for this is that Moore's representation of masculinity is itself paradoxical — a quality that is attributable to his conflicted nature.

Brenton Malin identifies a post–'80s conflicted masculinity, a model that maintains traditional elements of power and dominance but at the same time demonstrates a "new" sensitivity that departs from the stoic "hypermasculinity" that precedes it. Such an image is embodied by the representation of Hal Moore. Moore's quest for understanding, his devotion to fatherhood and his pronounced emotional response to the loss of not only the lives of his own men but also to those of the enemy mark him as precisely the kind of conflicted, masculine, heroic representation Malin identifies. Moore, of course, is a representation not of the nineties but of the noughties, and although some writers predicted a post–9/11 return to a "hard" masculinity, according to Malin, such has not been the case. He writes: "If the masculine hero of the '90s offered a conflicted blend of hypermasculine toughness and new age sensitivity, the September 11 hero is still more profoundly conflicted, eminently heroic and eminently vulnerable" (146). This combination of vulnerability and hypermasculinity is precisely what the score for *We Were Soldiers* indicates in tandem with the images of hardened and determined fighting men and the battle sequences it accompanies.

To understand how this is so despite the fact that a preponderance of the cues (outlined above) seem to indicate a significant return to the traditional scoring practice, it is necessary to look beyond even the three distinctions I have suggested (i.e., traditional function–traditional signifier; traditional function–nontraditional signifier; nontraditional function–nontraditional signifier). With regard to the traditional elements in the score, it is true that the functional categories remain largely traditional. It is also true that the composed sections of the score, while not specifically nineteenth-century Romantic style traditionally associated with Hollywood scoring practice, are nonetheless lushly scored, traditionally orchestrated and thus emotionally freighted in the manner of classical Hollywood. However, when we consider the images we would expect to see accompany the lushly scored and mellifluous string cues, and when we contrast those expectations with the images that actually do accompany the cues, we see a marked departure from the music in each of the previous films of focus. At no time is the march to battle of Moore or his men accompanied by the standard fanfare of military bombast (tarun-ta-raa music) that we hear in both *G.I. Joe* and *The Green Berets*. Instead, the contours of the musical lines are gentle; the harmonies are consonant and the overall effect is plaintive. Thus, the music works to represent precisely the kind of protagonist that Malin identifies. We *see* images of hypermasculine resolve rushing into an ultra-violent scene of carnage and conquest while we *hear* signifiers of sensitivity, sadness, even mourning—precisely the kind of irrational signification that Gorbman has indicated classical Hollywood used effectively to indicate femininity. While this is not a suggestion that Moore is to be seen as "feminized," the seemingly conflicting elements of sensitivity and aggression are clearly present and are clearly represented most effectively by the musical cues. While it would border on the ridiculous to provide images of Moore in tears as he rushes bravely into battle, or sobbing in sympathy as he watches American choppers cut down the advancing enemy soldiers, the musical cues are able to provide precisely that internal point of view—a point of view that the images cannot provide.

Thus, there emerges a fourth category for approaching the function-signifier relationship: traditional coding–nontraditional application. In this case music that has been previously coded to suggest a particular response in a particular situation is repurposed to elicit the same kind of response, but for a different kind of situation.

Transcending Beyond Immediate Questions

The films considered in this study containing particularly salient examples of music as a signifier of epic feeling that are in this category of traditional coding/nontraditional application include *We Were Soldiers* as well as most of the post–1990s World War II films discussed in Chapter VI, most particularly *A Midnight Clear*, *Windtalkers*, *Straight into Darkness*, *Saving Private Ryan*, *Miracle at St. Anna*, *Everyman's War*, and *Saints and Soldiers*. I would suggest that the thematic reasons for the nontraditional signification connect to the departure from conventional combat film protagonists as well as from anti-war film protagonists. In each of the examples listed above, the protagonists are, in one way or another, disturbed by larger questions than making sure that they effect victory for the good guys. By way of contrast, the biases of the protagonists in *The Green Berets*, *Full Metal Jacket* and *The Hurt Locker* work against such questions. *The Green Berets* is clearly meant to justify a particular action at a particular time, and although such intent may not necessarily abrogate more universal questions, the specific focus of this particular narrative lies elsewhere. Further, as has already been argued at some length, *Full Metal Jacket* makes its point by abrogating the possibility that there is a point. For obvious reasons, the meaninglessness that informs the whole thrust of *Full Metal Jacket* discounts the possibility of such questioning. Sgt. James in *The Hurt Locker* is neither patriotic nor ambiguous, and he is no more interested in justifying his penchant for placing himself into harms way than is a heroin addict.

Hal Moore, on the other hand, whether praying for guidance in a chapel or studying historic documents to illuminate the battle he is about to mount, is represented as a protagonist dedicated to such questioning, which is why the leitmotifs are often encoded with spiritual or transcendent implications, regardless of whether the material signifiers themselves are traditional (as are the "What Is War" and "Mansions of the Lord" themes) or non-traditional (as are the musical cues based on "Sgt. MacKenzie").

Conclusion: Soldiers Are *Supposed* to Be Moving Targets

To return at last to the initial question driving this study, it seems clear that war film protagonists are indeed constantly evolving and devolving and are, accordingly, often represented through different applications of the codes of Hollywood scoring practice. Nonetheless, traditional principles of scoring practice themselves remain an enduring model for identifying the function of music in combat films, significant for their ability to foreground representations of masculinities. Beyond the seemingly (and brilliantly) anomalous examples of near total departure in *Full Metal Jacket*, the musical cues by and large retain clear ties to those principles identified by a number of writers as conventional musical function in films of the 1930s and 1940s. At the same time, however, there are demonstrable instances of marked departure from the stylistic material of the signifiers themselves when the represented protagonist departs significantly from stereotypes of war-film masculinity made conventional during that initial golden age of combat films. In other words, the function of the score — its place within the mise-en-scène — is not different based upon different kinds of representations, although the material characteristics of the score do indeed demonstrate clear differences. Thus, Susanne Langer's suggestion that music is an "unconsummated" signifier of affect (240), Royal S. Brown's interpretation (27) of Langer's suggestion in terms of film music's consummating influence, and a number of semiotics scholars' (e.g., Barthes, Saussure and Lévi-Strauss) various interpretations of the signifier as arbitrary, empty, or floating (Chandler 78–79) all, despite their differences, provide satisfying explanations as to how such shifts can be possible.

In some cases, difference does not present a new problem for analysis. For example, in the case of the compiled score, popular music has at times already been coded with its own cultural — thus arguably conventional — "meaning" and therefore functions coherently according to the traditional model. This has already been touched upon by Katherine Kalinak who observes that "Like the jazz-oriented score and the theme score before it, the pop score initially challenged the classical model as a radical alternative, only to find its most iconoclastic characteristics excised in the process of fitting itself into Hollywood" (Kalinak 187). Nonetheless, the use of popular music in the film scores focused on in this study does offer many functional alternatives. We have seen that it establishes time and place as a function of the setting in which it is presented diegetically, it can function effectively as narrative cueing, it provides continuity and unity (as in the main title of *The Green Berets*), it functions as leitmotif (as do the heavy metal cues in *The Hurt Locker*) and it even subverts traditional principles of scoring practice by acting as a disrupter of meaning. Thus, while the compiled score does indeed function more flexibly than the composed score, its functions in the films explored here do a great deal more, often in a conventional sense, than just create "paths of identification" — a primary function of the compiled score according to Kassabian.

Another musical function identified in this study that seems to have "fit itself into Hollywood" is the use of musical material initially coded for one kind of representation that has been repurposed for a kind of representation quite different from that for which it was originally intended (traditional coding–non-traditional application). I am referring here to film music that falls into Gorbman's category of "Music and representation of Woman" which is communicated in "the euphony of a string orchestra" (80). I have identified at least two narrative situations in which examples of such music serve to "feminize" representations of masculinity: first, the sequences in *G.I. Joe* and *The Green Berets* in which the soldier, penetrated by a bullet, no longer controls his bleeding and is thus feminized; and second, the paradoxical representation of a conflicted masculinity which combines sensitivity with requisite aggression in *We Were Soldiers*. Both narrative situations are illustrated by a style of music Gorbman and Kalinak have identified as representative of women who are "good" or "wholesome." I am not, of course, suggesting that such music has only been used in the past for images of femininity. Nonetheless, I am pointing to an appropriate explanation for its use in the largely masculine context of the war film protagonist. That the style has been previously coded as feminine makes it appropriate in situations that have had some of their traditional characteristics altered by changes in cultural attitudes despite the fact that the cues would have been inappropriate for similar situations in the past.

I have suggested earlier that I do not believe it possible to identify a linear trend in the changing patterns of representation contained in genre films, because, like the historical and cultural construction of gender itself, there are always shifting, competing, contrasting and complementary influences that are simultaneously present. In his reading of Judith Butler's contributions to queer theory, David Gauntlett writes:

> Of course, the mass media conspicuously circulates certain kinds of male and female performance as preferable, thereby making the gender categories more 'real.' At the same time, though, the changes in gender representations in the past three or four decades [...] show that the recommended expres-

sions of gender are eminently flexible. Within particular moments, then, the media might make gendered behaviors seem more 'natural,' but when considered over time, the broad changes reveal the very constructedness of gender performances" [Gauntlett 140].

With this in mind, I believe I have pointed through a musical lens to what seem to be predominant trends of various "moments" that reflect cultural attitudes toward war and toward the men who fight it. I believe, too, that I have demonstrated the disruptive influence of Vietnam, which has thrown heroic representations into a tailspin from which they have not yet recovered. I view that difficult recovery as positive, particularly with regard to the tendency of some of the protagonists it has produced to look beyond historically inscribed ideologies inherent in glorifying the blood-and-guts heroes of the past, and toward posing overarching questions regarding the awful fact of war. Such representations can make us hope for a future in which there will be no such model to represent — a future in which soldiers' songs will become a distant memory.

Notes

Chapter I

1. I. *Invisibility:* The technical apparatus of nondiegetic music must not be visible.
   II. *"Inaudibility":* Music is not meant to be heard consciously. As such it should subordinate itself to dialogue, to visuals — i.e., to the primary vehicles of the narrative.
   III. *Signifier of emotion:* Soundtrack music may set specific moods and emphasize particular emotions suggested in the narrative, [...] but first and foremost, it is a signifier of emotion itself.
   IV. *Narrative cueing:*
      —*referential/narrative:* music gives referential and narrative cues, e.g., indicating point of view, supplying formal demarcations, and establishing setting and characters.
      —*connotative:* music "interprets" and "illustrates" narrative events.
   V. *Continuity:* music provides formal and rhythmic continuity — between shots, in transitions between scenes, by filling "gaps."
   VI. *Unity:* via repetition and variation of musical material and instrumentation, music aids in the construction of formal and narrative unity.
   VII. A given film score may violate any of the principles above, providing the violation is at the service of the other principles. (73)
2. Elliott suggests that "listening intelligently for musical works involves the knowledgeable, covert construction of at least four, and often as many as six interrelated dimensions of musical meaning, or information." The dimensions are "A performance-interpretation of a musical design that evinces: standards and traditions of practice, expressions of emotion, musical representations and cultural-ideological information" (199).
3. A stinger is one or more abrupt musical events (often a startlingly loud or dissonant chord) to indicate an emotional response such as surprise, alarm or epiphany.
4. Musical material moves by ½ step rather than within a specific key.
5. An extreme variety of musical illustration or parallelism which refers to music that follows precisely by beat and direction of movement the action taking place onscreen. The name refers to cartoon music — a good example of Mickey Mousing is the sequence in Disney's *Fantasia* called "The Sorcerer's Apprentice."
6. See note 1, this chapter.

Chapter II

1. See note 5, Chapter I
2. For more on compositional strategies as related to musical style, see Meyer, p. 20.

3. See note 1, Chapter I.

4. A motif (or motive) is a brief (sometimes just a few notes), recognizable musical figure repeated at various times throughout a composition, sometimes in different keys or registers.

5. A pentatonic scale is a 5-note scale, most commonly, the 1st, 2nd, 4th, 5th, and 6th degrees of the major scale. It is often associated with folk musics belonging to various nationalities or ethnic groups.

6. The shape of a melody refers to a graphic shape that would result from drawing a line from one melodic note to another placed upon a musical staff. Depending on the melody's characteristics, some shapes might be very smooth, some might be relatively flat, and some could be quite angular.

7. A mode might be thought of by the non-musician as a kind of scale from which melodies are constructed. Different modes and scales have, by convention, come to be associated with atmosphere or affect.

8. Because Western listeners are used to hearing the seventh degree of the major scale resolve up ½ step, it creates the "pull" I reference here, and creates an unstable feeling because the listener is left "feeling" the lack of resolution.

9. Tertian harmony refers to harmonic voicings (or chords) built on thirds, a common characteristic of much western music.

10. See note 3, Chapter I.

11. See note 1, Chapter II.

12. The term *tonic* refers to the note from which a scale is built and after which the scale is named. It is often the note from which a composition begins and where it ends. Thus, it is the tone that offers the greatest sense of rest or resolution to most listeners.

13. The end title refers to the cue that accompanies the closing credits

Chapter III

1. The tri-tone is particularly significant here, not only because it is one of the most dissonant of diatonic intervals, but because it is also the least stable, i.e., it is heard as an interval that is not meant to stand alone, but seeks immediate resolution to a place of rest. When it does not resolve, it can create discomfort because the listener's expectation is not met.

2. Parallel motion and contrapuntal motion refer to the movement of two or more musical lines. When musical lines ascend and descend at the same time and in the same direction, it is called parallel motion. Contrapuntal motion refers to opposite movement in two or more lines.

3. *Synchresis* is a term coined by Michel Chion: "the spontaneous and irresistible weld produced between a particular auditory phenomenon and visual phenomenon when they occur at the same time" (63).

4. *Pedal* or *pedal point* refer to a single, long-held or repeating tone that remains constant throughout a long portion (or an entire) composition. Other musical elements such as harmony and melody will change as the pedal remains constant.

Chapter IV

1. A cadence is a formal musical device, a recurring, patterned sequence of notes or chords that end a musical section or an entire composition. Because certain cadential sequences become familiar, they work to signal a musical piece's end or resolution. The plagal cadence is also "known as the Amen cadence because it was traditionally used for the 'Amen' at the end of hymns" (Harvard Dictionary of Music 680).

2. The Picardy 3rd refers to the major third as used for the final chord of a composition in a minor key. As indicated in the text, it is coded with religious connotation from its origin in early church music.

3. A relatively common mode or scale constructed on the 5th degree of the major scale. It can be thought of as a major scale with a minor (or flatted) 7th degree.

Chapter V

1. The basic or primary key in which a piece of music is written and in which it customarily begins. Compositions often modulate away from their home key, but then return, particularly at the end of the piece.
2. See note 4, Chapter III
3. The notes at the 3rd and 7th intervals in chords are responsible for the chord's characteristics, i.e., they determine the "quality" of the chord: whether it is a major chord, a minor chord, a major seventh chord, a minor seventh chord or a dominant seventh chord.
4. Diatonic refers to notes and harmonic structures (chords) that are taken from within a particular key. Music is called diatonic when it uses only these notes.
5. Throughout this chapter it is important for the reader to be aware of the distinction between the use of the word *Western* as a cultural reference and its use as a reference to the Western film genre. Both uses are present here, but context and awareness should help avoid confusion.
6. Arpeggiating a chord simply refers to playing its notes separately rather than all at once.
7. See note 6, Chapter II.
8. An interval refers to the number of steps (notes) between a starting note and an ending note in a given key, e.g., in the key of C major, starting on the note C, there are three steps from the starting note to reach the note E; thus, the interval from C to D is a major 3rd.
9. Temp track refers to music written for some other film or purpose that is used during the final stages of editing to accompany key sequences during screenings that take place before a final score has been completed (see Prendergast 272).
10. Music's capacity to indicate point of view, establish setting and characters, to interpret and illustrate events (Gorbman 73).
11. Buzz track refers to recorded ambient sound in a film's soundtrack.
12. See note 2, Chapter II.

Chapter VI

1. The Phrygian mode can be thought of as a scale that starts and ends on the third degree of the major scale.
2. When I refer to notes or harmonies that are unstable, I am pointing to the fact that repeated exposure to various conventional structures in Western music makes listeners accustomed to hearing (and thus makes them expect to hear) melodies and harmonies that move from a particular pitch or chord to another particular (anticipated) pitch or chord. When this does not happen, the musical elements "feel" unstable because they do not behave as it seems that they should.
3. See note 1, Chapter I.

Chapter VII

1. See note 1, Chapter I.
2. See note 1, Chapter I.

Works Cited

Adorno, Theodor, and Hanns Eisler. *Composing for the Films.* London: Athlone, 1994.
Anderson, Lauren. "Case Study 1: *Sliding Doors and Topless Women Talk About Their Lives.*" *Popular Music and Film.* Ed. Ian Inglis. London: Wallflower, 2003.
Apel, Willi. *Harvard Dictionary of Music.* 2d ed. Cambridge: Belknap Press of Harvard University Press, 1972.
Apocalypse Now. Dir. Francis Ford Coppola. Perf. Marlon Brando, Martin Sheen. Original Music Carmine Coppola, Francis Coppola. United Artists, 1979. DVD.
Auster, Albert. "Saving Private Ryan and American Triumphalism." *Journal of Popular Film and Television.* 30.2 (2002): 98–104.
Back to Bataan. Dir. Edward Dmytryk. Perf. John Wayne, Anthony Quinn. Original Music Roy Webb. RKO Radio Pictures, 1945. DVD.
Barthes, Roland. *Image Music Text.* Ed. and trans. Stephen Heath. New York: Hill and Wang, 1977.
Basinger, Jeanine. *The World War II Combat Film: Anatomy of a Genre.* New York: Columbia University Press, 1986.
Bataan. Dir. Tay Garnett. Perf. Robert Taylor. Original Music Bronislau Kaper and Eric Zeisl (uncredited). Warner Bros., 1943. DVD.
Battle for Haditha. Nick Broomfield. Original Music Nick Laird-Clowes. Image Entertainment, 2008. DVD.
Bazin, André. *What Is Cinema? Volume II.* Ed. and trans. Hugh Gray. Berkley: University of California Press, 1972.
Benjamin, Walter. "The Work of Art in the Age of Mechanical Reproduction." *Film Theory and Criticism: Introductory Readings.* Ed. Leo Braudy and Marshall Cohen. New York: Oxford University Press, 1999. 731–751.
The Best Years of Our Lives. Dir. William Wyler. MGM, 2000. DVD.
Black Hawk Down. Dir. Ridley Scott. Original Music Hans Zimmer. Sony Pictures Home Entertainment, 2002. DVD.
The Boys in Company C. Dir. Sidney J. Furie. Original Music Jamie Mendoza-Nova. Columbia, 1978. DVD.
Braudy, Leo. *From Chivalry to Terrorism: War and the Changing Nature of Masculinity.* New York: Vintage, 2003.
Brown, Royal S. *Overtones and Undertones: Reading Film Music.* Berkley: University of California Press, 1994.
Cahill, Tim. "The Rolling Stone Interview with Stanley Kubrick." *Rolling Stone,* October 28, 1987.

Carey, Melissa, and Michael Hannan. "Case Study 2: *The Big Chill.*" *Popular Music and Film.* Ed. Ian Inglis. London: Wallflower, 2003.
Casualties of War. Dir. Brian De Plama. Perf. Michael J. Fox, Sean Penn. Original Music Ennio Morricone. Columbia, 1989. DVD.
Cawley, Leo. "The War About The War: Vietnam Films and American Myth." *From Hanoi to Hollywood: The Vietnam War in American Film.* Ed. Linda Dittmar and Gene Michaud. New Brunswick, NJ: Rutgers University Press, 1990.
Chandler, Daniel. *Semiotics: The Basics.* 2d ed. London: Routledge, 2002.
Chion, Michel. *Audio-Vision: Sound on Screen.* Ed. and trans. by Claudia Gorbman. New York: Columbia University Press, 1990.
Cohen, Stephen. *Masked Men: Masculinity and the Movies in the Fifties.* Bloomington: Indiana University Press, 1997.
Collier, James Lincoln. *The Making of Jazz.* New York: Dell, 1978.
Coming Home. Dir. Greg Carson and Hal Ashby. MGM, 2002. DVD.
Connell, R.W. *Masculinities.* 2d ed. Berkley: University of California Press, 2005.
Cooper, David. *Bernard Herrmann's* The Ghost and Mrs. Muir: *A Film Score Guide.* Lanham, MO: Scarecrow, 2005.
Courage Under Fire. Dir. Edward Zwick. Perf. Denzel Washington, Meg Ryan. Original Music James Horner. Twentieth Century–Fox, 1996. DVD.
Czulinski, Winnie. *Drone On! The High History of Celtic Music.* Toronto: Sound and Vision, 2004.
The Deer Hunter. Dir. Michael Cimino. Perf. Robert De Niro. Original Music Stanley Myers. Universal, 1979. DVD.
Doherty, Tom. "The New War Movies as Moral Rearmament: *Black Hawk Down & We Were Soldiers.*" *Cineaste.* Summer 2002. 4–8.
Donald, Ralph R. "Masculinity and Machismo in Hollywood's War Films." *Men, Masculinity, and the Media.* Ed. Steve Craig. Newbury Park, CA: Sage, 1992. 124–136.
Dondis, Donis A. *A Primer of Visual Literacy.* Cambridge: MIT Press, 1973.
Dunbar-Hall, Peter. "Semiotics as a Method for the Study of Popular Music" *International Review of the Aesthetics and Sociology of Music.* 22.2 (1991): 127–132.
Easthope, Antony. *What a Man's Gotta Do.* Winchester, MA: Unwin Hyman, 1990.
Elliott, David J. *Music Matters: A New Philosophy of Music Education.* New York: Oxford University Press, 1995.
The Fallen. Dir. Ari Taub. Original Music Sergei Dreznin. The Fallen, 2004. DVD.
Fantasia. Dir. James Algar, Samuel Armstrong, et al. Walt Disney, 1940. Videocassette.
Faulkner, Frank. "Get Your Kicks on Route 666, or Why the Devil Has All the Best Tunes: Trekking Through the Darker Side of Heavy Metal Music." *Something Wicked This Way Comes: Essays on Evil and Human Wickedness.* Ed. Colette Balmain and Lois Drawmer. Amsterdam: Rodopi, 2009.
Flags of Our Fathers. Dir. Clint Eastwood. Original Music Clint Eastwood. Dreamworks Video, 2007. DVD.
Flying Tigers. Dir. David Miller. Original Music Victor Young. Republic, 2000. DVD.
For a Few Dollars More. Dir. Sergio Leone. Original Music Ennio Morricone. MGM, 1998. DVD.
Full Metal Jacket. Dir. Stanley Kubrick. Perf. Matthew Modine. Original Music Vivian Kubrick. Warner Bros., 1987. DVD.
Gauntlett, David. *Media, Gender and Identity: An Introduction.* New York: Routledge, 2002.
G.I. Jane. Dir. Ridley Scott. Perf. Demi Moore, Viggo Mortensen. Original Music Trevor Jones. Walt Disney Video, 1998. DVD.

Gorbman, Claudia. *Unheard Melodies: Narrative Film Music*. Bloomington: Indiana University Press, 1987.
The Good, The Bad and the Ugly. Dir. Sergio Leone. Original Music Ennio Morricone MGM, 1998. DVD.
Gran Torino. Dir. Clint Eastwood. Original Music Kyle Eastwood and Michael Stevens. Warner Home Video, 2010. DVD.
The Great Raid. Dir. John Dahl. Original Music Trevor Rabin. Miramax Home Entertainment, 2005. DVD.
The Green Berets. Dir. Ray Kellogg and John Wayne. Perf. John Wayne, David Janssen. Original Music Milós Rózsa. Warner Bros., 1968. DVD.
Green Zone. Dir. Paul Greengrass. Original Music John Powell. Universal Pictures, 2010. DVD.
Gung Ho. Dir. Ray Enright. Perf. Randloph Scott. Original Music Frank Skinner. Universal Pictures, 1943. DVD.
Hall, Robert A., Jr. "How Picard was the 'Picardy Third'?" *Current Musicology*. Vol. 19 (1975): 78–80.
Hamburger Hill. Dir. John Irvin. Original Music Philip Glass. Paramount, 1987. DVD.
Hanslick, Eduard. *On the Musically Beautiful*. Trans. Geoffrey Payzant. Indianapolis: Hackett, 1986.
Hodgkins, John. "In the Wake of Desert Storm: A Consideration of Modern World War II Films." *Journal of Popular Film and Television*. 30.2 (2002): 74–84.
The Hurt Locker. Dir. Kathryn Bigelow. Original Music Marco Beltrami and Buck Sanders. Summit Entertainment, 2010. DVD.
Immortal Sergeant. Dir. John M. Stahl. Original Music David Buttolph. 20th Century–Fox, 2006. DVD.
In The Valley of Elah. Dir. Paul Haggis. Original Music Mark Isham. Warner Home Video, 2008. DVD.
Inglorious Basterds. Dir. Quentin Tarantino. Universal Studios, 2011. DVD.
James, David E. "Rock and Roll in Representations of the Invasion of Vietnam." *Representations*. 0.29 (1990): 78–98.
Jarhead. Dir. Sam Mendes. Perf. Jake Gyllenhaal. Original Music Thomas Newman. Universal Studios, 2005. DVD.
Juslin, Patrick, and John A. Sloboda. "Music and Emotion: Introduction." *Music and Emotion: Theory and Research*. Ed. Patrick Juslin and John A. Sloboda. Oxford: Oxford University Press, 2002.
Kalinak, Kathryn. "The Fallen Woman and the Virtuous Wife: Musical Stereotypes in *The Informer, Gone With the Wind*, and *Laura*." *Film Reader* 5 (1982): 76–82.
_____. *Settling the Score: Music and the Classical Hollywood Film*. Madison: University of Wisconsin Press, 1992.
Kassabian, Anahid. *Hearing Film: Tracking Identifications in Contemporary Hollywood Film Music*. New York: Routledge, 2001.
Kivy, Peter. *Sound Sentiment: An Essay on the Musical Emotions Including the Complete Text of The Corded Shell*. Philadelphia: Temple University Press, 1989.
Kolker, Robert. *Film, Form, and Culture*. 2d ed. New York: McGraw Hill, 2002.
Koppes, Clayton R., and Gregory D. Black. *Hollywood Goes to War: How Politics, Profits, and Propaganda Shaped World War II Movies*. New York: Free, 1987.
Koppl, Rudy. "*The Hurt Locker*: Mainlining the War at Death's Door." *Music from the Movies*. Music from the Movies Media. 2009. Web. 18 June, 2011.
Kracauer, Siegfried. *From Caligari to Hitler: A Psychological History of German Film*. Princeton: Princeton University Press, 1947.

Langer, Susan. *Philosophy in a New Key: A Study in the Symbolism of Reason, Rite, and Art*. 3d ed. Cambridge: Harvard University Press, 1979.
Letters from Iwo Jima. Dir. Clint Eastwood. Original Music Kyle Eastwood and Michael Stevens. Warner Bros., 2006. DVD.
Linville, Susan E. "The *Mother* of all Battles": *Courage Under Fire* and the Gender-Integrated Military." *Cinema Journal*. 39.2 (2000): 100–120.
London, Justin. "Leitmotifs and Musical Reference in the Classical Film Score." *Music and Cinema*. Ed. James Buhler et al. Hanover, NH: Wesleyan University Press, 2000. 85–96.
The Longest Day. Dir. Andrew Marton, et al. Original Music Maurice Jarre. 20th Century–Fox, 2006. DVD.
Lusted, David. *The Western*. Harlow, UK: Pearson, 2003.
MacKinnon, Kenneth. *Representing Men: Maleness and Masculinity in the Media*. London: Arnold, 2003.
Malin Brenton J. *American Masculinity under Clinton: Popular Media and the Nineties Crisis of Masculinity*. New York: Peter Lang, 2005.
The Man in the Gray Flannel Suit. Dir. Nunnally Johnson. 20th Century–Fox, 2005. DVD.
MASH. Dir. Robert Altman. 20th Century–Fox Home Entertainment, 2006. DVD.
Maus, Fred Everett. "Music and Drama." *Music and Meaning*. Ed. Jenefer Robinson. Ithaca, NY: Cornell University Press, 1997. 105–130.
_____. "Narrative, Drama, and Emotion in Instrumental Music." *Journal of Aesthetics and Art Criticism* 55 (1997): 293–303.
McCabe and Mrs. Miller Dir. Robert Altman. Warner Bros. Pictures, 2002. DVD.
McClary, Susan. *Feminine Endings: Music, Gender, and Sexuality*. Minneapolis: University of Minnesota Press, 1991.
The Men Who Stare at Goats. Dir. Grant Hersolv. Overture Films/Anchor Bay Entertainment, 2010. DVD.
Meyer, Leonard. *Emotion and Meaning in Music*. Chicago: University of Chicago Press, 1956.
_____. *Style and Music: Theory, History, and Ideology*. Chicago: University of Chicago Press, 1996.
A Midnight Clear. Dir. Keith Gordon. Original Music Mark Isham. 101 Distribution, 2010. DVD
Million Dollar Baby. Dir. Clint Eastwood. Original Music Clint Eastwood. Warner Home Video, 2010. DVD.
Miracle at St. Anna. Dir. Spike Lee. Original Music Terence Blanchard. Touchstone/Disney, 2009. DVD.
Mulvey, Laura. "Visual Pleasure and Narrative Cinema." *Film Theory and Criticism: Introductory Readings*. Ed. Leo Braudy and Marshall Cohen. New York: Oxford University Press, 1999. 833–844.
Mystic River. Dir. Clint Eastwood. Original Music Clint Eastwood. Warner Home Video, 2010. DVD.
Neale, Stephen. "Prologue: Masculinity as Spectacle. *Screening the Male*. Ed. Stephen Cohen and Ina Rae Hark. London: Routledge 9–20.
Objective Burma. Dir. Raoul Walsh. Perf. Errol Flynn. Original Music Franz Waxman. Warner Bros. Pictures, 1945.
O'Brien, Wesley J. "Ghosts of Vietnam: Filmic Representations of Unconsummated American Heroism in the Beginning of the Twenty-First Century." *War and the Media: Essays on News Reporting, Propaganda and Popular Culture*. Ed. Paul M. Haridakis, Barbara S. Hugenberg and Stanley T. Wearden. Jefferson NC: McFarland, 2008.

Only The Brave. Dir. Lane Nishikawa. Original Music Philip Brophy. Indican, 2009.
Otter, Kelly. "The Role of Music in the Construction of Gender in *Gone With the Wind.*" Diss. New York University, 2002.
Owen, Susan. "Memory, War and American Identity: *Saving Private Ryan* as Cinematic Jeremiad." *Critical Studies in Media Communication.* 19.3 (2002): 249–282.
Oxford English Dictionary. 2d ed. 1989. Oxford University Press. 19 March 2004.
Pat Garrett and Billy the Kid. Dir. Sam Peckinpah. Warner Home Video, 2006. DVD.
Patton. Dir. Franklin J. Schaffner. Original Music Jerry Goldsmith. 20th Century–Fox, 2001. DVD.
Platoon. Dir. Oliver Stone. Perf. Tom Berenger, Willem Dafoe, Charlie Sheen. Original Music Georges Delerue. Orion, 1986. DVD
Prendergast, Roy M. *Film Music: A Neglected Art.* New York: W.W. Norton, 1992.
Rasmussen, Karen, and Sharon D. Downey. "Dialectical Disorientation in Vietnam War Films: Subversion of the Mythology of War." *Quarterly Journal of Speech* 77 (1991): 176–195.
Redacted. Dir. Brian De Palma. Magnolia, 2008. DVD.
Rubin, Alan M., Daniel West and Wendy S. Mitchell. "Differences in Aggression, Attitudes Toward Women, and Distrust as Reflected in Popular Music Preferences." *Media Psychology* 3 (2001): 25–42.
Sabaneev, Leonid. *Music for the Films.* Trans. S. W. Pring. New York: Arno, 1978.
Sachs, Curt. *The Rise of Music in the Ancient World East and West.* New York: W.W. Norton, 1943.
Saints and Soldiers. Dir. Ryan Little. Original Music J. Bateman and Bart Hendrickson. Excel Entertainment Group, 2005. DVD.
The Sands of Iwo Jima. Dir. Allan Dwan. Perf. John Wayne. Original Music Victor Young. Republic Pictures, 1949. DVD.
Saving Private Ryan. Dir. Stephen Spielberg. Original Music John Williams. Dreamworks 1998. DVD.
Schatz, Thomas. *Formulas, Filmmaking, and the Studio System.* Boston: McGraw-Hill, 1981.
Scott, Linda M. "Understanding Jingles and Needledrop: A Rhetorical Approach to Music in Advertising." *The Journal of Consumer Research.* 17 (1990): 223–236.
Simmons, Scott. *The Invention of the Western Film: A Cultural History of the Genre's First Half-Century.* Cambridge: Cambridge University Press, 2003.
The Situation. Dir. Philip Haas. Original Music Jeff Beal. New Video Group, 2007. DVD.
Solomon, Stanley J. *Beyond Formula: American Film Genres.* New York: Harcourt Brace Jovanovich, 1976.
Stop Loss. Dir. Kimberly Peirce. Original Music John Powell. Paramount/MTV, 2008. DVD.
The Story of G.I. Joe. Dir. William A. Wellman. Perf. Burgess Meredith, Robert Mitchum. Original Music Louis Applebaum, Ann Ronell. United Artists, 1945. DVD.
Straight Into Darkness. Dir. Jeff Burr. Original Music Michael Convertino. Screen Media, 2006. DVD.
Sturken, Marita, and Lisa Cartwright. *Practices of Looking.* New York: Oxford University Press, 2001.
Tasker, Yvonne. "Dumb Movies for Dumb People." *Screening the Male.* Ed. Stephen Cohen and Ina Rae Hark. London: Routledge 230–244.
Taylor, Timothy D. "World Music in Television Ads." *American Music* 18 (2000): 162–192.

Thelma and Louise. Dir. Ridley Scott. Perf. Susan Sarandon, Geena Davis. Original Music Joe Sample, Hans Zimmer. Metro Goldwyn-Mayer, 1991. DVD.
The Thin Red Line. Dir. Terrence Malick. Original Music Hans Zimmer. 20th Century–Fox, 2002. DVD.
Three Kings. Dir. David O. Russell. Perf. George Clooney, Mark Wahlberg. Original Music Carter Burwell, Thomas Newman, Richard Wolf. Warner Bros., 1999. DVD.
3:10 to Yuma. Dir. James Mangold. Original Music Marco Beltrami. Lions Gate, 2008. DVD.
U-571. Dir. Jonathan Mostow. Original Music Richard Marvin. Universal Studios, 2011. DVD.
Vize, Lesley. "Music and the Body in Dance Film." *Popular Music and Film.* Ed. Ian Inglis. London: Wallflower, 2003.
Wake Island. Dir. John Farrow. Perf. Brian Donlevy, Robert Preston. Original Music David Buttolph. Paramount, 1942. DVD.
Walk in the Sun, A. Dir. Lewis Milestone. Perf. Dana Andrews. Original Music Freddie Rich, Earl Robinson. Twentieth Century–Fox, 1945. DVD.
Walton, Kendal. "Listening with Imagination: Is Music Representational?" *Music and Meaning.* Ed. Jenifer Robinson. Ithaca, NY: Cornell University Press, 1977. 57–82.
We Were Soldiers. Dir. Randall Wallace. Original Music Nick Glennie-Smith. Paramount 2002. DVD.
When Trumpets Fade. Dir. John Irvin. Original Music Geoffrey Burgon. HBO Home Video 1998. DVD.
The Wild Bunch. Dir. Sam Peckinpah. Warner Home Video, 2006. DVD.
Wills, Garry. *John Wayne's America.* New York: Touchstone, 1998. Print
Windtalkers. Dir. John Woo. Original Music James Horner. MGM, 2002. DVD.
Wood, David. "In Afghanistan, Women are on the Front Lines." *ArmyTimes.com.* 11 March 2002. Web. 30 May 2004. <http://www.armytimes.com/legacy/new/0-ARMYPAPER-781455.php>.
Wrobel, Bill. "Film Score Rundown of *The Green Berets.*" Web. 10 November 2005. <http://www.filmscorerundowns.net/rozsa/greenberets.pdf>.

Index

Adorno, Theodor 32, 35, 39, 77, 130
Albelli, Sergio 144
Alien 10
Allred, Corbin 155
Alonso, Laz 144
Altman, Robert 15
Anderson, Lauren 121
Apocalypse Now 16, 17, 23, 83, 87, 113, 117, 119, 133, 170, 171
Applebaum, Louis 41, 165
Army Times 9
"As Time Goes By" 98
Askew, Luke 63
Auster, Albert 112, 138
Avatar 10

Back to Bataan 166
Baldwin, Adam 86
"Ballad of the Green Berets" 46, 47, 70, 71, 114, 161, 162
Barthes, Roland 113, 174
Basinger Jeanine 42, 46, 167
Bataan 36, 88, 95, 109, 132, 138, 166
Battle for Haditha 135
Bazin, André 13
Beach, Adam 140
Beatty, Warren 116
Beltrami, Marco 125, 130
Bendix, William 21
Benjamin, Walter 3
The Best Years of Our Lives 119, 133, 134
bin Laden, Osama 128
Black, Gregory D. 14, 159
Black Hawk Down 16, 126
bleeding wound 37, 64, 175
The Boys in Company C 165, 170
Boyzone 120
Brando, Marlon 170–171
Braudy, Leo 27
Bridges, Jeff 136

Brown, Royal S. 32, 39, 174
Brühl, Daniel 149
Bush, George W. 128
Butler, Judith 175

Cabot, Bruce 66
Cahill, Tim 73
Carey, Melissa 121
Carson, Cole 152
Carter, Mel 105
Cartwright, Lisa 10
Casablanca 98
Cascio, Luigi Lo 144
Cassell, Wally 20, 26
Casualties of War 165, 170
Cawley, Leo 42, 97, 112, 117, 136, 137, 141, 151, 153, 167
Chandler, Daniel 174
"Chapel of Love" 84–86, 169
Chatham, Steve 133
Chion, Michel 6, 22, 39, 49, 50, 110
chromaticism 35
Clan An Drumma 98, 107, 111
classical scoring practice 5, 7, 13, 19, 20, 22, 30, 31, 39, 43, 45, 48, 49, 62, 64, 119, 126, 129, 130, 132, 148, 155, 158–161, 165, 167, 168, 170, 172; *see also* Hollywood scoring practice; traditional scoring practice
cognitive dissonance 57, 82
Cohen, Stephen 64
Collier, James Lincoln 70
combination score 14–17, 74, 98
compiled score 5, 8, 9, 49, 50, 74, 83, 84, 98, 118–121, 132, 150, 165, 168, 174, 175
composed score 5, 9, 14, 46, 49, 74, 75, 77, 83, 89, 98, 118, 119, 127, 129, 130, 165, 172, 175
Connell, R. W. 12

connotative narrative cueing 40, 53, 62, 157, 165
Constantine, Liz 129
continuity 4, 19, 25, 36, 40, 41, 48, 160, 174
conventions: musical 4–7, 9, 32, 38, 39, 45, 77, 145, 167, 170
Cooper, David 39
Coppola, Francis Ford 16, 87, 113
Courage Under Fire 10, 16, 89
crisis of masculinity 81, 119, 133
Cullen, Shelly 24
cultural attitudes 6, 8, 10, 12, 43, 119–121, 123, 136, 158, 159
Czulinski, Winnie 107

Damon, Matt 138
The Deer Hunter 17, 83, 133
Dern, Bruce 133
Devaney, Rob 133
dialectical disorientation 83, 88
"Dialectical Disorientation in Vietnam War Films: Subversion of the Mythology of War" 15
Die Hard 97
Doherty, Tim 112
Donald, Ralph 9, 15, 31, 37, 46, 63, 65–67, 72, 73, 112, 124, 136, 139, 166, 167
Dondis, Donis 32, 55
Donlevy, Brian 21
D'Onofrio, Vincent 73
Downey, Sharon 15, 75, 76, 83, 112
Dunbar-Hall, Peter 127

Ealy, Michael 145
Easthope, Anthony 37, 63
Eastwood, Clint 140, 141
Eisensteinian juxtaposition 83
Eisler, Hanns 32, 35, 39, 77, 130
Elliot, David 6, 38, 40, 50
Elliott, Sam 107, 110
epic questions (or feeling) 104, 108, 111, 114, 139, 144, 148, 152, 156, 158, 162–164, 171, 173
Ermey, Lee R. 73
Everyman's War 152, 173
extra-diegetic associations 25, 103
extra-musical function 4, 29, 130

The Fallen 151, 154
Faulkner, Frank 120
Favino, Pierfrancesco 144
"Fear (Is Big Business)" 120, 121, 123
"Feelings" 127
female roles 7, 8, 10, 11, 19, 161, 166; *see also* feminine representations
feminine representations 5, 7, 9, 11, 19, 20, 37, 45, 49, 58, 64, 66, 67, 68, 161, 166, 167, 172, 175; *see also* female roles
feminization 37, 63, 64, 072, 175
Flags of our Fathers 140, 151, 153
For a Few Dollars More 125
Foxx, Jamie 117
The Flying Tigers 22
Full Metal Jacket 8, 15, 16, 17, 20, 23, 36, 72–75, 82–84, 87–89, 94, 95, 117, 119, 120, 124, 130, 165, 167, 168, 173, 174–176

Gauntlett, David 175, 176
G.I. Jane 10
genre (changing patterns of) 10, 12, 13, 17, 19, 43, 119, 123, 137, 175
Geraghty, Brian 118
Gibson, Mel 8, 98
The Good, the Bad, and the Ugly 125
Gorbman, Claudia 3–8, 14, 19, 22–25, 27, 30, 32, 35, 38–40, 42, 45, 48, 50–51, 53–54, 59–62, 64, 66–68, 73, 85–86, 94, 104–105, 108–109, 111, 126, 129, 141–142, 144, 148, 152, 159–162, 164–165, 168, 170, 172, 175
Gran Torino 140
The Great Raid 151
The Green Berets 14, 15, 20, 23, 36, 42, 43–46, 48, 58, 63, 69, 87, 97, 102, 110, 155, 159, 161, 162, 164, 166, 167, 170, 172, 173, 175
Green Zone 135
Groth, Sylvester 149
Les Guerres en Indochine 103
Gung Ho 23, 95, 103
Gyllenhaal, Jake 117

Hall, Robert A., Jr. 103
Hamburger Hill 170
Hanks, Tom 138
Hannan, Michael 121
Hanslick, Eduard 4
Hearing Film: Tracking Identifications in Contemporary Hollywood Film Music 5, 7, 8, 167
heavy metal 120–122, 128, 129, 170, 175
Hedges, Chris 122
hegemony (representations of) 51, 141, 142, 153, 162, 171
Héritier-Augé, François 64
heroism: ambivalent 72, 150; common-man 138, 140, 156, 157; conflicted 97, 98, 105, 122, 171, 172; subverted 15, 17, 43, 117, 121–123, 134–137, 158, 176; traditional 8, 38, 42, 45, 46, 48, 50–52, 107, 117, 135, 136, 138, 140, 151, 162, 164, 166, 167
Herrmann, Bernard 35

heterosexual masculinities 9, 11, 20, 11
Heyborne, Kirby 154
Hodgkins, John 138
"Hold Me, Thrill Me, Kiss Me" 105, 106, 163
"Hold On I'm Comin'" 105, 163
Holden, Peter 156
Hollywood scoring practice 5–7, 9, 13, 15, 17, 19, 22, 25, 29–31, 39, 41, 43, 45, 48, 49, 59, 105, 119, 126, 129, 130, 136, 155, 165–167, 170, 172; *see also* classical scoring practice; traditional scoring practice
Hollywood's Golden Age 5, 7, 9, 13, 42, 45, 49, 159
homosexual attraction/desire 37, 63
homosocial masculinity 9, 37, 65, 119
Howard, Arliss 74
The Hurt Locker 17, 117, 118, 119, 121, 122, 124, 125, 127, 129, 130, 133, 134, 150, 170, 173, 175
Hussein, Saddam 121
Hutton, Jim 44

Immortal Sergeant 22,
In the Valley of Elah 133, 135, 139
inaudibility 19, 39, 48, 131, 161
Inglorious Basterds 141, 149, 150
intertextual reference 126, 127, 130, 145, 147, 150
invisibility 19, 39, 48
irrational (musical signification of) 51, 162, 172
isomorphism 39

Jackson Five 120
James, David 84, 87
Janssen, David 44
Jarhead 95, 117, 119, 126, 133, 134
jazz 7, 42, 66, 142, 143, 149, 165, 174
Jecchinis, Kieron 86
Jue, Craig 44
Juslin, Patrick 50

Kalinak, Kathryn 5–7, 19, 22, 23, 38, 39, 42, 49, 64, 66, 68, 165, 171, 174, 175
Kassabian, Anahid 5, 7, 8, 15, 19, 45, 49, 50, 66, 67, 75, 85, 107, 119–122, 159, 166–168, 176
Kellogg, Ray 43
key center 35, 56, 70, 77
"Khyber Pass" 127–129
Kivy, Peter 85, 103, 112
Klein, Chris 101
Kolker, Robert 5, 12, 50, 83
Koppes, Clayton R. 14, 159
Koppl, Rudy 125, 130
Kracauer, Siegfried 12

Kubrick, Stanley 72, 78, 87
Kubrick, Vivian 78

Langer, Susanne 4, 32, 174
Laurent, Mélanie 149
leitmotif 6, 22, 33, 39, 40, 43, 47, 49, 56, 58, 61, 78–80, 82, 99, 103–105, 108, 109, 111, 127, 129, 139, 154, 155, 157, 160–164, 168, 169, 173, 175
Leone, Sergio 125, 150
Lethal Weapon 97
Letters from Iwo Jima 140, 153
Lévi-Strauss, Claude 174
"Linda" 25, 27, 160
Linville, Susan E. 10, 11, 89
London, Justin 47, 49
The Longest Day 144, 145, 166
Luke, Derek 145
Lumière, Auguste and Louis 4
Lusted, David 150

MacKenzie, Joseph Kilna 98
Mackie, Anthony 118
MacKinnon, Kenneth 51, 58
Malden, Karl 117
male gaze (or look) 37, 38, 65–67, 167
Malin, Brenton 171, 172
The Man in the Gray Flannel Suit 119, 133, 134
"Mansions of the Lord" 99, 103, 162, 173
masculine representations 8, 9, 10, 11, 20, 37, 45, 47, 63, 89, 103, 133, 162, 171, 172; *see also* masculinities
masculinities 1, 9, 11, 12, 16, 19, 37, 51, 64, 124, 129, 140, 159, 161, 174; *see also* masculine representations
"Masculinity and Machismo in Hollywood's War Films" 9
MASH 15
McCabe and Mrs. Miller 125
McClary, Susan 89, 159
Meade, Abagail 78
melodrama 4, 5, 9, 11, 14, 15, 19, 38, 39, 46, 159
The Men Who Stare at Goats 135, 136
Meredith, Burgess 20
Meyer, Leonard 3, 6, 49, 50, 112, 145
"Mickey Mouse Club Song" 84, 94, 96, 169
Mickey Mousing 35, 43, 62, 160, 161
Middle East 14, 17, 124, 126, 134, 135, 137, 138, 159
A Midnight Clear 151, 154, 173
Mildred Pierce 47
Miller, Omar Benson 147
Million Dollar Baby 140
Ministry 120, 121, 127, 128, 132
Miracle at St. Anna 141, 143–145, 149, 153, 173

Index

Mitchell, Wendy S. 121
Mitchum, Robert 8, 20, 21, 116
Modine, Matthew 8, 72, 116
Moore, Demi 10
Moore, Robin 46
Morricone, Ennio 125, 150
Mulvey, Laura 7, 8, 37, 64–66
musical ambiguity 33, 54, 55, 57, 77, 92
musical codes 6–9, 13, 42, 43, 49, 71, 119, 174
musical conventions 5–7, 9, 12, 19, 32, 38, 39, 45, 77, 145, 167, 170
musical design 6, 28, 31, 38, 77, 123
musical dissonance 57, 62, 82, 93, 147
musical metaphor 33, 39, 47, 54, 55, 70, 82, 84, 90, 126, 128, 143, 145, 149, 155, 170
Mystic River 140
myth of the American soldier 16, 17, 19, 43, 46, 47, 50, 83, 88, 91, 95, 96, 112, 116, 117, 134–140, 150, 151, 153, 156, 158, 167, 169, 171

narrative agent 11, 21, 22, 47, 52, 166–168
narrative cueing 19, 29, 39, 40, 52, 53, 85, 94, 105, 126, 129, 130, 155, 157, 160–165, 168, 169, 174
nature vs. nurture 12
Neale, Steve 8
Ninomiya, Kazunari 140
nontraditional function–nontraditional signifier 165, 168, 172
non-traditional scoring 5, 8, 9, 45, 67, 75, 130, 161, 163, 165, 166, 168–170, 172, 173, 175

Objective Burma 20
Only the Brave 141, 144, 148, 149, 153
Olds, William 44
The Osmonds 120
Otter, Kelly 5
Ottosson, Paul 130
Owen, Susan 138

"Palestina" 121, 127
Pat Garrett and Billy the Kid 125
paths of identification 5, 49, 122, 166, 168, 175
Patton 117
Pepper, Barry 98
Persian Gulf 17, 138
Pierce, Guy 118
Platoon 16, 83
Polinsky, Alexander 155
popular culture 12, 17, 43, 97, 116, 136, 137, 153, 156, 159

popular music 7, 8, 14–16, 49, 75, 83–88, 105, 121–123, 127, 148, 163, 165, 166, 168, 170, 174
Prendergast, Roy M. 4
Private Benjamin 10
Private Valentine 10
Psycho 35

queer theory 175
questioning soldier 99, 101, 103–106, 108–111, 113, 138, 157, 162, 163, 173

Rambo 21, 43, 97
Rasmussen, Karen 15, 75, 76, 83, 112
Ray, Aldo 60
Redacted 126
Reds 116
referential narrative cueing 40, 85, 152, 157, 165
Renner, Jeremy 117
"The Ride of the Valkyries" 113
"The River Seine" 67
Rolling Stone Magazine 77
Ronell, Ann 25, 160
Rózsa, Miklós 44, 52, 64, 70, 166
Ruben, Alan M. 121
Russell, Keri 114
Ryan, Meg 10

Sabaneev, Leonid 39
Sachs, Kurt 108
Sadler, Barry 46
St. Johns, Adela Rogers 116
Saints and Soldiers 151, 153, 156, 173
Sam and Dave 105
Sam the Sham and the Pharaohs 84, 86
Samudio, Domingo 86
Sanders, Buck 125, 130
Sands of Iwo Jima 22, 23, 146, 132, 166
Sarsgaard, Peter 133
Saussure, Ferdinand de 174
Savage, John 133
Saving Private Ryan 16, 17, 110, 112, 138–140, 151, 153, 173
Schatz, Thomas 46, 124
Sciabordi, Matteo 143
scopophilia 65
Scott, Linda M. 99
semiotics 6, 7, 55, 174
Shaw, Artie 24, 40, 160
Sheen, Martin 133
signifier of emotion 7, 19, 24, 30, 32, 38, 39, 40, 50, 51, 64, 75–77, 80, 81, 85, 156, 160–165, 168, 169, 172
The Situation 134
Slater, Christian 143
Sloboda, John A. 50

Solomon, Stanley 13, 14, 21–23, 36, 132, 136, 151, 159
source music 67
Spielburg, Stephen 138
star system 46, 50
Stars and Stripes 74, 86
Steele, Freddy 20, 21
Steiner, Max 30
stinger 33, 34, 38, 62, 105, 132, 160, 161
Stone, Oliver 16
Stop Loss 119, 133, 135
The Story of G. I. Joe 8, 15, 19–23, 30, 36, 39, 41, 45, 65, 87, 88, 105, 132, 139, 159, 160, 162, 165, 172, 175
Stowe, Madeleine 98
Straight into Darkness 153, 173
Stravinsky, Igor 4
Sturkin, Marita 10
Style and Music: Theory, History, and Ideology 49
"Summit Ridge Drive" 24, 40
"Surfin' Bird" 87, 88, 169
suturing mechanism 25, 38, 115
synchresis 78

tarun-ta-raa music 38, 112, 165, 172
Tatum, Channing 133
Taylor, Timothy D. 108
Tee, Brian 110
Thelma and Louise 8, 85
"These Boots Are Made for Walkin'" 83, 169
The Thin Red Line 151, 154
Three Kings 20, 134
3:10 to Yuma 125, 130
Tomb Raider 10
traditional coding–nontraditional application 173
traditional scoring practice 5, 7, 8, 8, 15, 29, 39, 45–49, 52, 67, 73, 75, 77, 78, 85, 86, 105, 119, 126, 130, 132, 146, 160–175; *see also* classical scoring practice; Hollywood scoring practice
traditional function-nontraditional signifier 165, 172
traditional function-traditional signifier 165, 172
The Trashmen 87
Tsu, Irene 44, 65

U-571 151
Unheard Melodies: Narrative Film Music 7, 39, 45
unity 19, 40, 41, 160, 162, 174

Vietnam War 14–16, 17, 42–44, 48, 53, 60, 61, 71, 73, 74, 82, 83, 89, 97, 98, 100, 101, 105, 106–108, 111, 112, 116, 119, 122, 124, 133, 134, 136–138, 151, 158, 159, 163, 166, 167, 170, 176
"Visual Pleasure and Narrative Cinema" 37
Vize, Lesley 121

Wagner, Richard 6, 49, 165, 170
Wake Island 21, 95, 109
A Walk in the Sun 23, 95
Walken, Christopher 133
Wallace, Randall 98
Walton, Kendall 54
Waltz, Christoph 149
Wayne, John 8, 16, 42–44, 46, 50, 51, 73, 80, 86, 102, 110, 116, 124, 144, 166
We Were Soldiers 8, 16, 17, 20, 36, 65, 87, 97, 98, 100, 110, 112, 115, 122, 156, 157, 162, 164, 165, 170–173, 175
Wellman, William 20
West, Daniel 121
Western film protagonists 21, 124, 126, 128,
Westerns 23, 123, 125, 127, 142, 150,
Westlife 120
What a Man's Gotta Do: The Masculine Myth in Popular Culture 37
"What Is War" 99, 103–106, 108, 111, 113–115, 162–164, 173
When Trumpets Fade 151, 154
Wiegman, Robyn 10, 89
The Wild Bunch 125
Williams, John 139
Willie, Roger 142
Wills, Garry 46, 50, 51, 53
Windtalkers 141,144, 149, 153, 173
Wood, David 9
"Wooly Bully" 84, 86, 168, 169
World War II 13, 14, 17, 18, 20, 42, 97, 136–138, 149, 141, 144, 151, 152–159, 166, 173
Wrobel, Bill 56

"Your Smiling Face" 127

www.ingramcontent.com/pod-product-compliance
Ingram Content Group UK Ltd.
Pitfield, Milton Keynes, MK11 3LW, UK
UKHW042012140426
5217IPUK00015B/1128